PRAISE FOR *GLOBAL MARKETING*

CW01496184

"An invaluable resource for academics, students and practitioners, offering insights into the opportunities and complexities of globalization. It brings key concepts and theories to life through real-world examples, making it essential for anyone looking to understand the influence and impact of marketing in a global context."
Rachel Lee, Lecturer in Marketing, Keele Business School

"An essential resource for students and professionals alike. With a comprehensive exploration of marketing strategies, globalization, cultural influences and ethical considerations, the book offers a balanced combination of theoretical insights and practical applications. Its engaging real-world examples, interactive activities and clear alignment with Sustainable Development Goals make it an vital guide for navigating today's dynamic global marketplace."
Dr Donna Towe, Lecturer in Marketing, Ulster University

"An engaging and insightful textbook that addresses contemporary issues and implications within the field. Helen Millward skillfully brings well-established marketing topics into the current era, preserving their historical significance."
Dr Matthew Hutchinson, Lecturer in Sport Business Management, Keele University

"Strikes the perfect balance between essential theory and practical application. With its clear structure, up-to-date content and engaging activities that connect theory to real-world cases, this textbook is an invaluable resource for students navigating the complexities of global marketing."
Dr Melisa Mete, Lecturer in Marketing, Henley Business School

Global Marketing

Understanding marketing in a globalized business environment

Helen Millward

Publisher's note

Every possible effort has been made to ensure that the information contained in this book is accurate at the time of going to press, and the publishers and author cannot accept responsibility for any errors or omissions, however caused. No responsibility for loss or damage occasioned to any person acting, or refraining from action, as a result of the material in this publication can be accepted by the editor, the publisher or the author.

First published in Great Britain and the United States in 2025 by Kogan Page Limited

All rights reserved. No part of this publication may be reproduced, stored or transmitted by any means without prior written permission from Kogan Page, except as permitted under applicable copyright laws.

Kogan Page

Kogan Page Ltd, 2nd Floor, 45 Gee Street, London EC1V 3RS, United Kingdom
Kogan Page Inc, 8 W 38th Street, Suite 90, New York, NY 10018, USA
www.koganpage.com

EU Representative (GPSR)

Authorised Rep Compliance Ltd, Ground Floor, 71 Lower Baggot Street, Dublin D02 P593, Ireland
www.arccompliance.com

Kogan Page books are printed on paper from sustainable forests.

© Kogan Page, 2025

The moral rights of the author have been asserted.

ISBNs

Hardback	978 1 3986 2011 7
Paperback	978 1 3986 2009 4
Ebook	978 1 3986 2010 0

British Library Cataloguing-in-Publication Data
A CIP record for this book is available from the British Library.

Library of Congress Control Number
2024055605

Typeset by Integra Software Services, Pondicherry
Print production managed by Jellyfish
Printed and bound by CPI Group (UK) Ltd, Croydon CR0 4YY

To Richard: 'Hyper-dottification'.

CONTENTS

List of figures xi
About the author xii
Acknowledgements xiii
Walkthrough of textbook features and online resources xiv

1   Introduction and background to marketing 1
Welcome to global marketing **1**
Marketing: A primer **2**
The marketing management orientations driving business **16**
Consumer behaviour **18**
Marketing research **23**
Innovation and new product development **27**
The product lifecycle **28**
Brands **29**
References **33**

2   Marketing and globalization 35
Introduction **35**
What is globalization? **36**
A brief history of globalization **40**
Does globalization really exist? **45**
The Shrinking World **46**
What drives globalization? **47**
The rise of marketing **49**
Marketing and the global arena **52**
Implications of marketing in a global world **53**
References **59**

3   Theory and practice in the global marketplace 62
Introduction **62**
Global consumerism **63**

Levitt's theory of standardization 64
The benefits of being local 68
Patterns of consumption 72
Glocalization 74
References 81

4   Culture and the global marketplace 84
Introduction 84
Defining culture 85
Theories of culture 86
Sources of culture 88
Cultural knowledge 88
Colour 94
The country-of-origin effect 95
References 100

5   Global communications 102
Introduction 102
Global communications and standardization 103
Hofstede's dimensions of culture 106
Message appeals 107
Miscommunications 109
Humour 114
Causes of offence 116
Standardization versus adaptation 120
References 122

6   Global brands 124
Introduction 124
Branding and value 125
What is branding? 126
The value chain 127
How do brands work? 131
The three key dimensions of global brands 135
Beyond branding 139
The negative side of global brands 141
References 145

7   **Cultural convergence: Consumption in the global marketplace** 148

Introduction 148
The global village 149
The three Gs: Globalization, glocalization and grobalization 150
The consequences of grobalization: 'Something' and 'nothing' 157
Convergence in practice 161
References 168

8   **Cultural divergence: Consumption in the global marketplace** 170

Introduction 170
Postmodernism 171
Increasing cultural diversity 176
Divergence or convergence? 178
Universal application 182
References 187

9   **Ethics in the global marketplace** 189

Introduction 189
Marketing and ethics 190
Ethical theories and the global marketplace 192
The ethics of ethics 193
Ethical issues and the global marketplace 196
Agents of change 202
References 211

10 **Production and the global marketplace** 214

Introduction 214
The value chain and organizational focus 215
Export processing zones 217
Exporting jobs 221
Offshoring services 227
Relevance to global consumption 230
References 237

11   Consumption at the top and bottom of the pyramid 240
Introduction 240
The bottom of the pyramid 241
Stakeholder responsibility 243
Global consumerism and the bottom of the pyramid 245
Spreading a Western conception of life 248
Is marketing to the bottom of the pyramid actually worth it? 250
References 257

Index 258

LIST OF FIGURES

Figure 1.1   Example of a direct distribution system 9

Figure 1.2   Example of a distribution system which includes an intermediary 10

Figure 1.3   Example of the product lifecycle 31

Figure 4.1   The cultural knowledge triangle 90

Figure 5.1   Old woman, young woman 105

Figure 6.1   The first three components of Kaplinsky and Morris's value chain 128

Figure 7.1   Wooden spoons 157

Figure 7.2   A visualization of the 'something'–'nothing' continuum 160

ABOUT THE AUTHOR

Dr Helen Millward is a lecturer in Marketing at Keele Business School, Keele University, UK. She is a Certified Management and Business Educator (CMBE) and an AdvanceHE Fellow. Helen is lead for the Principles of Responsible Management Education (PRME) at Keele Business School, and she teaches a range of marketing modules at both undergraduate and postgraduate level.

Her research projects surrounding education for sustainable development have previously received funding from Keele University and have been presented at Chartered Association of Business Schools and AdvanceHE conferences.

ACKNOWLEDGEMENTS

With thanks to Anne-Marie Heeney and Katherine Hartle for their valuable support during the writing of this book.

WALKTHROUGH OF TEXTBOOK FEATURES AND ONLINE RESOURCES

Learning objectives

A bulleted list at the beginning of each chapter summarizes what you can expect to learn, to help you to track your progress.

LEARNING OBJECTIVES

By the end of this chapter, you should be able to:

- understand the significance of marketing and globalization as separate concepts
- explain how globalization and marketing have developed throughout history
- articulate why it feels like the world is getting smaller through the concept of the Shrinking World

Real-world examples

A range of case studies illustrates how key ideas and theories are operating in practice to help you to place the concepts discussed in real-life context.

REAL-WORLD EXAMPLE   KFC in Japan

The American fast-food restaurant KFC specializes in fried chicken. It was founded in the US in the 1950s by Colonel Sanders (KFC, 2024), whose image is still used in the company's marketing today. The restaurant sells burgers and buckets of chicken that can be shared between family or friends.

Chapter review questions

Reflective questions encourage you to reflect critically on what you have read and reinforce what you have learnt.

CHAPTER REVIEW QUESTIONS

Product types

When was the last time that you purchased a staple product, an impulse product and an emergency product? What were these products, and why did you decide to buy them?

Activities

Questions and activities throughout the text encourage you to reflect on what you have learnt and to apply your knowledge and skills in practice.

ACTIVITY

Market segmentation

As a marketer, which type of segmentation would you suggest would be most beneficial for:

- a dental practice?
- a car dealership?
- a fast fashion brand?
- a hiking boot brand?
- a brand selling home insurance?

Explain the reasons behind your answers.

Chapter summaries

These draw together the main threads of the chapter and summarize the key learning points.

CHAPTER SUMMARY

This chapter has covered the theory of standardization as put forward by Levitt (1983) and has explored some of the many cultural differences that perhaps challenge standardization's usefulness in the global marketplace.

Key terms

These give explanations of key terms and concepts in the book to highlight them for your learning.

KEY TERMS

International poverty lines: Applied on a global scale, international poverty lines provide a way in which to measure extreme poverty across the globe.

National poverty lines: A national poverty line denotes the lowest income threshold that an individual must meet to avoid slipping into poverty in a particular country.

References

Detailed references provide quick and easy access to the research and underpinning sources behind the chapter.

Online resources

This book includes online resources for lecturers and students, comprising:

- chapter slides
- chapter introduction videos
- multiple choice questions

These resources can be accessed through the Kogan Page website:
www.koganpage.com/global-marketing

1 | Introduction and background to marketing

LEARNING OBJECTIVES

By the end of this chapter, you should be able to:

- define what is meant by 'marketing'
- explain key marketing terminology such as the marketing mix and the extended marketing mix
- discuss the differences between products and services
- explain key marketing concepts such as brands, relationship marketing, marketing research and new product development processes
- determine which marketing management orientation might be applied to a number of different products and services

Welcome to global marketing

A warm welcome to this text on global marketing. This book aims to act as a broad introduction to global marketing and its implications for a variety of stakeholders, such as organizations, customers and consumers, workers and more. The text includes a variety of marketing and globalization-related concepts and theories, providing opportunities for the critical discussion of a number of significant contemporary global marketing challenges. We will cover a range of theories throughout the text in relation to, for example, standardization, ethics, globalization, grobalization, culture and more. We will explore theories and concepts from a number of differing viewpoints throughout the text, including those of workers, global organizations, governments, host countries and so forth, often also placing emphasis on your own views of the concepts under discussion as a student, consumer, customer, employee and so on.

The book contains a number of case studies and exercise questions designed to prompt your critical consideration of the issues under discussion. In each chapter you will find intended learning outcomes, acting as indicators of what you might expect to learn in each chapter. Each chapter also features a number of key terms, written in bold throughout the text. You will find a glossary of these terms along with their meanings at the end of each chapter.

Furthermore, throughout this book, more notably perhaps in the book's latter chapters, you will find a number of discussions linked to various Sustainable Development Goals (SDGs) (United Nations, 2024). The SDGs represent a roadmap for a better and more sustainable future, covering 17 distinct progress areas. Within this book, for example, you will find links to the following SDGs:

- SDG 1 – No Poverty: Linked to discussions in Chapters 8, 10, and 11
- SDG 2 – Decent Work and Economic Growth: Linked to discussions in Chapter 10
- SDG 12 – Responsible Production and Consumption: Linked to discussions in Chapters 7, 8, and 9
- SDG 16 – Peace, Justice, and Strong Institutions: Linked to discussions in Chapters 8 and 9

As you read through the book, try to consider where you can see these links, along with any additional links to the SDGs in each of the chapters, as the above list is not intended as an exhaustive overview of the book's links to the Goals.

However, before we delve into all things related to global marketing, you may wish to read the following section, which introduces key concepts of the marketing discipline more broadly. Designed for students who may be new to studying marketing, or those who may wish to refresh their knowledge of core marketing content, this chapter provides an overview of key theories and principles associated with the marketing discipline, which may serve as a basis for this book's remaining chapters.

Marketing: A primer

As with most concepts, **marketing** might be defined in a multitude of ways. For example, the Chartered Institute of Marketing (2015) notes: 'Marketing is the management process responsible for identifying, anticipating and satisfying customer requirements profitably.' This we might see in any number of marketing activities, ranging from research and customer services through to branding and distribution. However, other definitions of marketing tend to heavily leverage the concept of **exchange**.

Holding the concept of exchange as central within marketing definitions suggests a two-way, often reciprocal activity. This might be seen in a wide range of marketing activities, for example with a customer responding to marketing stimuli by purchasing an offering, following which the customer may provide feedback about their experience with the offering to the organization or to other prospective customers. In short, however, the notion of exchange and thereby the concept of marketing, arguably, might be underpinned by the marketer having a solid understanding of customer wants and needs. After all, if customers are not willing to purchase an offering, what use is the offering to the organization?

The marketing mix

Marketing activities are traditionally viewed as being underpinned by the **marketing mix**. Introduced in the 1950s–60s, the marketing mix suggests four key elements that should be considered by marketers: product, price, place and promotion (the 4Ps). The marketing mix suggests that, in considering how an offering might be marketed, all four elements should be considered by the marketer to ensure a holistic view of how the offering should be situated in the market.

Product

The first element to be considered, that of the **product** itself, relates to the offering, but also to elements such as packaging and labels. Marketers should make efforts to keep the proposed benefits and other positive attributes of the offering in mind, to ensure that the offering meets consumer wants, needs and demands where possible.

A product can be a physical item, a service, or even an idea, a person or a place. This means that a product can be tangible (we can touch it) or intangible (we can't touch it). Importantly, a product must be something that a customer is willing to enter into an exchange for, in order to obtain it. There are three key types of product:

- **Staple products:** These are offerings that we use on a regular basis and will typically purchase often. For example, toilet roll, toothpaste or milk.
- **Impulse products:** Have you ever visited a store to purchase a specific item and gone home with something completely different? If so, this was likely an impulse product, something that you didn't intend to buy when you went to the store. For example, if you visit the supermarket to do your weekly food shop and then purchase a chocolate bar at the checkout, you are likely purchasing an impulse product.
- **Emergency products:** These are offerings that you do not intend to purchase, but must, given an arising situation. For example, if you lock yourself out of your home, you may require the emergency product of a locksmith, or if your car gets a puncture, you may need to purchase the emergency product of a new tyre or puncture repair kit.

ACTIVITY

Product types

When was the last time that you purchased a staple product, an impulse product and an emergency product? What were these products, and why did you decide to buy them?

Price

The second of our Ps, **price**, is concerned with the pricing of the item for customers, but also with ensuring that an appropriate profit might be made by the brand or organization, once any manufacturing, marketing or other costs have been considered. Kotler et al (2005) refer to price as the amount of money charged for a product/ service or the total of values that customers transfer for the benefits of the product/ service. Price is also the most flexible element in the marketing mix, as it can be easily and quickly increased or decreased as required.

Consumer satisfaction and the proposed utility of the offering are key determinants in setting an offering's price. For example, take a piano. If a consumer is unlikely to frequently use the instrument they may suggest the price is too expensive; however, if our consumer were to play every day, they may suggest that the satisfaction and use they gain from the offering are enough to justify the price. Ultimately, the broad objective of pricing is to find the right balance between what the customer is willing to pay for an offering and making the most profit possible for the organization.

However, organizations must also consider the concept of value when determining the price of their offerings. For example, consider that you want to purchase a car. In doing so, you have two options:

1 a used car for £750

2 a new car for £15,000

With the used car, the price is far lower than the alternative and financially represents good value by comparison. However, if you purchase the used car and it then breaks down, the perception of value will likely be significantly reduced. This is because cost does not just relate to the price that a customer pays for an offering. In the case of the used car, it also represents time wasted, worry, lack of warranty, lack of guarantee, cost of repairs and so on. If we now consider the new car, we can see that, even though it is significantly more expensive than the used substitute offering, it will hold its value if it is reliable. With this in mind, for the seller, the price equates to the package of benefits offered versus the price charged, while for the consumer the price typically equates to the cheapest, most worthwhile, convenient and aesthetically pleasing offering.

ACTIVITY ↗

Consumer value

As a consumer, consider whether price or value is most important to you. Explain the reasons behind your answer.

Does your answer change if you consider different types of products (e.g. a car versus a tin of baked beans), and, if so, why and how?

Do you think that your answer will change as you progress in your career? Why and how, or why and how not?

In determining the price of an offering, organizations will take several factors into consideration, such as their market position, price sensitivity of potential buyers, the wider economic environment, organizational objectives and the organization's resources, to name but a few. Regardless, it is vital that pricing decisions work in concert with other elements, such as packaging, promotion and distribution systems.

The organization will also wish to consider the **price ceiling** and **price floor** when making decisions regarding cost. A price ceiling is the highest possible price that customers might be willing to pay for an offering. If the organization chooses to price the offering above the price ceiling, there will be no demand for the offering. The price floor, on the other hand, is the lowest possible price that an organization might charge for an offering. If the organization does choose to price an offering below the price floor, they will not make any profit.

Aside from such considerations, there are a number of different pricing strategies that an organization may choose to implement. For example:

- **Cost-based pricing:** Fixed and variable costs set the price floor. This approach is product-driven, rather than value-driven, and is typically popular with customers as it is perceived as a fair way to determine the price. However, from the organizational perspective, competitors are somewhat ignored, meaning that the organization may be undercharging for their offering.

- **Competition-based pricing:** This strategy assumes that customers will judge an offering's value in comparison with prices charged by competitors selling substitute offerings.

- **Skimming strategies:** A rapid skimming strategy suggests that the organization will charge a high price for an offering and will also engage in high levels of promotion. On the other hand, a slow skimming strategy involves a high price being charged for the offering, but low levels of promotion. Here, an organization must consider whether the offering's quality and image will actually support the high price point, and whether competitors will be able to easily enter the market and undercut the price.

- **Market-penetration pricing:** An organization will set an initially low price in order to penetrate the market quickly and deeply. This strategy can be useful in attracting a large number of customers quickly to produce growth. However, organizations should be aware that markets are likely to be highly price sensitive, meaning that competitors must be kept out of the market. Costs are also likely to fall as sales volume increases.

- **Psychological pricing:** This strategy considers the psychology of pricing and not just the economics. In other words, an offering's price is used to say something about it. This is because a price can influence customer perceptions of quality and promote customer feelings towards the offering, with odd numbers often being used to communicate value. For example, would a customer feel differently about a pair of headphones priced at £74.99 compared to the same offering at £75?

- **Geographical pricing:** Geographical pricing is typically used for business-to-business markets, particularly where one organization may wish to purchase component parts from another. Considerations with this strategy may include different prices for different zones, or geographical areas, uniform or differing delivery costs due to location, and whether or not the manufacturer will cover the costs of delivery.

- **Promotional pricing:** When organizations use promotional pricing, they are typically trying to create excitement and urgency to prompt customers to make a purchase. There are several methods that organizations may use to do so, such as discounts or loss leaders, special event pricing, longer warranties, product maintenance offers and so on.

- **Discounts and allowances:** Discounts such as a lowered charge or an increase in quantity or functionality of the offering may be used to encourage customers to make a purchase. Allowances function in a similar way, such as with customers receiving benefits for trading in their old products. For example, mobile phone organizations periodically offer discounts for upgrading consumers who choose to return their old phone when purchasing a newer model. Seasonal discounts also hold relevancy in this type of pricing strategy. For example, theme parks and hotels may wish to charge a reduced price to encourage customers to visit during the winter when fewer visitors are expected, or a cinema may choose to charge half the normal price of admission on a Wednesday, as this may typically be a slower day for ticket sales.

Ultimately, price can be a useful tool in the marketing mix and can be used flexibly to react to fluid market environments and demands. While price is the most flexible element of the marketing mix, organizations do need to be wary of changing prices, particularly lowering them, too much. Price cuts may be initiated due to a number of factors, such as excess capacity, falling demand, strong competition or the product lifecycle phase, or in an attempt to capture further market share. However, if prices drop too low, organizations run the risk of customers and consumers viewing competitor offers as superior, or of creating a price war between themselves and their competitors, which can weaken brand loyalty, destroy profit margins and, ultimately, weaken organizations.

Place

The penultimate P of the marketing mix, **place**, suggests attention must be paid to the distribution channels to be used in getting the offering from the organization to the consumer, and how the locations and methods of distribution chosen will fit with customer purchasing requirements. For example, Kotler et al (2005) define place as '[a]ll the company activities that make a product or service available to target customers', while Jobber (2007) notes that it encompasses distribution channels and their management, location of outlets, transportation and inventory to ensure that the purchased product or service is available at the right quantity, time and place.

This leads us to the five 'rights' of distribution or, in other words, five factors that an organization should consider in relation to the place of their offering. These relate to the right product, place, time, quantity and price. Organizations may wish to ask themselves a number of questions during this process: for example, do customers want to purchase from somewhere nearby, or are they willing to travel? Do customers prefer to purchase online, or from a physical store? Do customers want lots of options (e.g. many locations from which they can make a purchase), or is one enough? Do customers want specialization? Do they have an expectation of service?

Unlike price, place represents some of the most complex and challenging decisions that an organization must take when considering the marketing mix. Each place chosen is likely to reach a different segment of the target audience and must be thoroughly considered. For example, consider a clothing organization. The organization may decide that they want to target consumers who are in the age range of 18 to 30 and those who are 50 to 60 years old. For consumers in the 18 to 30 age range, an online shopping option would likely be preferable. However, for those in the 50 to 60-year-old age range, online shopping may not be preferred and so a physical store may be required.

Regardless, place relies on distribution channels, which might be defined as a set of interdependent organizations which, when working together, make offerings available for customers to purchase. For example, take the soft drinks giant Coca-Cola. As customers we can purchase the offering in a variety of places, from supermarkets and convenience stores to restaurants, vending machines and airports. This provides customers with the guarantee of product availability as and when they would like to make a purchase. However, this is only made possible by the successful implementation and coordination of distribution channels.

Channel design decisions are also key when considering place. For example, organizations may wish to consider the amount of market exposure they seek and whether an intensive wide-scale approach is required if the offering is low-involvement. For high-involvement offerings, organizations may wish to consider the use of exclusive outlets or whether a restricted approach (typically via location or status) using only a small number of distributors would be more appropriate.

Channel intermediaries are also a key consideration for organizations concerned with place. Channel intermediaries act as a middle party between the manufacturer and the customer and can be split into different types:

- **Wholesalers:** Organizations which primarily sell in the business-to-business market but also sell to individual customers. Items are typically sold in bulk at a fast pace. For example, Makro or Costco.

- **Brokers/agents:** Brokers and agents do not own the goods that they sell and typically work on a commission basis. Their goal is to bring together sellers and customers. Consider, for example, an estate agent. They do not own the properties that they sell, but their job is to persuade customers to make a purchase from the seller.

- **Retailers:** Retailers sell offerings in small quantities. For example, your local corner shop.

Direct distribution, however, can also be a useful approach for both organizations and customers. For example, consider an organization producing apples based in Newcastle, a second organization producing oranges based in Stafford, and a final organization producing cheese in Nantwich. Hypothetically, let's say that we have three customers, respectively based in Burslem, Hanley and Crewe, who each want to purchase all of these offerings.

If our customers choose to visit each of the organizations to make a purchase we see a large number of journeys, duplications in storing, delivering and invoicing, wasted time, high costs and, generally, the potential for distribution inefficiency. However, if we introduce a channel intermediary such as a large supermarket chain, we see each of our organizations delivering to its stores, with our customers making only one journey to the store to purchase all three offerings. This reduces elements such as travel, delivery costs, invoicing, storage and so forth. This, however, is also good for our supermarket, as it is able to add value to the offerings via the availability of other items, through immediate availability for customers and improved accessibility.

While organizations can and frequently do work together in this way, they must also be mindful of potential pitfalls with regards to their engagement. Horizontal conflict can, for example, occur between organizations at the same level of the channel (e.g. retailer to retailer), while vertical conflict may occur between organizations at different levels of a channel (e.g. wholesaler to retailer).

From an international perspective, organizations must also be mindful that channels operating in different countries are likely to have very different distribution systems in place. This may, for example, be made up of many layers involving a number of different intermediaries. Government regulations can also impact or even restrict distribution systems, and organizations may also need to deal with scattered or even inefficient distribution systems depending on the countries in which they intend to supply their offering.

Promotion

Promotion, the final P of the marketing mix, looks at how an offering's attributes are demonstrated to prospective customers and consumers. Promotion is often discussed in terms of marketing communications (although it is also a separate entity in its own right), which we might define as a brand or organization's efforts to engage with an intended or target audience.

Marketing communications can be conveyed via a set of tools, the media and the message, for the purpose of gaining attitudinal and behavioural responses from customers, to develop brand feelings and as an effort to manage the target audience. With this in mind, the nature of marketing communications must be both creative and diverse. To accomplish this, **implicit communication** such as (for example) a person's actions, tone of voice or gestures might be used, along with **explicit communication** that relates to what a person says or writes. Regardless of the type(s) of communications used, marketers will consistently look for new ways to engage their target audience, to inform, to gain attention, to influence and to deliver a consistent message about their brand or offering.

There are a wealth of marketing communications tools at a marketer's disposal. Common examples might include billboards, posters, TV advertising, personal selling, flyers, internet pop-up adverts and radio adverts.

Figure 1.1   Example of a direct distribution system

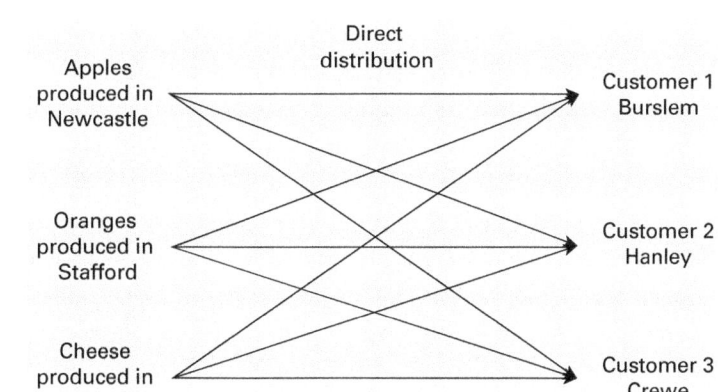

Figure 1.2   Example of a distribution system which includes an intermediary

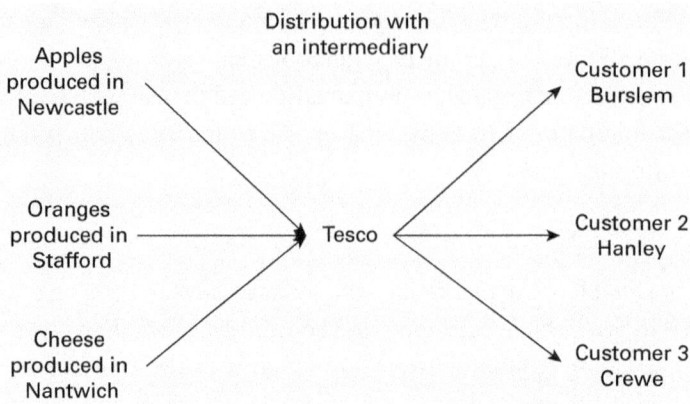

Despite the connection between marketing communications and promotion, we must remember that marketing communications are not confined to promotions. This is because elements such as the product or service itself, the price and the brand name can also be used to send messages about the offering to customers and consumers. Indeed, the **promotional mix** relates to the set of chosen and typically integrated promotional methods that an organization uses to send messages to customers. For example, consider your own thoughts about purchasing a shampoo priced at £1.99 versus purchasing a competing offering priced at £7.99. What would you expect from each product? Typically, if we see an alternative offering with a higher price point, we might expect certain benefits, such as an increased quality when comparing the two offerings, or for the more expensive item to require less product to be used each time and thus to last longer.

Within the promotional mix, marketers and organizations have a number of decisions to make. The budget must be determined as costs for various communications media will be varied (for example, a TV advert is likely to cost far more than a radio advert). Marketers must also consider the market size, along with the concentration of potential customers that they wish to reach. If the organization intends to target a niche market with a relatively small number of consumers, a 'tell and sell' approach is likely to be preferable and cheaper than using a mass media approach such as TV adverts for communications.

The target market's customer type and the information they require will also be central considerations here. If an organization intends to target the business-to-business or business-to-government markets, there will arguably be a smaller number of potential customers in comparison to a business-to-consumer target market. Again, the type of medium employed here will need to be carefully considered to ensure both that the organization reaches the desired consumers and that resources are not wasted unnecessarily in the process.

There are five key promotional tools that marketers may wish to include in their promotional mix. Advertising, personal selling and sales or trade promotions relate to information about products and brands, while direct marketing and publicity or public relations typically relate to information about the organization:

1 **Advertising:** Advertising essentially relates to a form of mass communication that is paid for by an identified party. The purpose of advertising is to inform, to raise awareness and to act as a reminder of, for example, an offering. Advertising can be useful in the introduction and growth phase of the product lifecycle, can trigger fast sales, can build attention and awareness, can build brands via repeated customer exposure and can be personalized. However, advertising is not typically well suited to the business-to-business market, in which a mass target audience does not usually exist. It can also be expensive, does not provide direct feedback and is often not as persuasive as a personal approach might be.

2 **Personal selling and exhibitions:** Personal selling is typically important for business or technical settings, to encourage repurchase during the maturity phase of the product lifecycle, and it can be characterized as interactive and adaptive. Exhibitions provide opportunities for organizational representatives to meet customers and other stakeholders; however, it is important to have the correct employees in place to project the required image and information to the target audience. Personal selling and exhibitions can be useful in reacquainting consumers with an offering's features and benefits and to help to build relations. It can, however, be expensive due to the staff costs involved.

3 **Sales/trade promotions:** Sales promotions are typically non-personal and include non-media advertising, with the goal of overcoming barriers. For example, sales promotions may include discounts, price promotions, coupons and vouchers, samples and trials or competitions and games. Trade promotions, while similar to sales promotions, focus on the sales or distribution system. For example, this may include discounts, sales competitions for sales employees, delayed invoicing and credit terms, and so on. This can result in direct and measurable effects for the organization, increased store traffic and new customers, to name just a few of the potential benefits. However, there are also a number of disadvantages associated with sales and trade promotions, such as difficulties in establishing cause and effect, and the likelihood of any consumer switch to the offering/brand being only temporary.

4 **Direct marketing:** Direct marketing includes a number of communications media such as telephone marketing, direct mail, catalogues, online shopping and internet marketing. Advantages include the ability to target consumers individually with

personalized communications, being able to build a continuous relationship while avoiding intermediaries, and the ability to convey complex messages. However, direct marketing must be effectively targeted to the right consumers at the right time in order to be successful. In addition, some consumers might find this approach too intrusive.

5 **Publicity and public relations (PR)**: Publicity and PR methods may include press releases and conferences, product publicity events, corporate communications and sponsorship. Messages not directly originating from the organization or brand in question might be seen as more trustworthy given that they are communicated by an independent source; however, there is a higher demand on human effort and other resources to effectively communicate messages. Publicity and PR are also less controllable than other methods, and are typically used in order to correct an issue with the image of an organization, brand or offering.

The extended marketing mix

As discerning readers may have noticed, the marketing mix primarily provides guidelines for marketers in dealing with a physical product. However, when we start to consider how applicable the marketing mix might be to services, it becomes apparent that further elements are required. Services, therefore, typically relate to the **extended marketing mix**.

The extended marketing mix includes an additional three Ps, in an effort to recognize that marketing is still required for offerings of an intangible nature.

The first element of the extended marketing mix, **physical evidence**, emphasizes tangible reminders of a service. This can constitute an important reminder of a service that we are yet to receive: for example, when making your decision as to which university to attend, were you offered a brochure, a branded pen or a branded tote bag? If so, the intent behind the item was likely to act as physical evidence, to provide you with a reminder of the service and what this might look like, even though you were yet to experience it first-hand.

Process, the second element of the extended marketing mix is primarily concerned with how a service is delivered to the consumer. Often, services will be standardized, meaning that each consumer should have a very similar experience, thus helping the organization to manage the expectations of its customers. If, for example, you were to visit a popular fast-food chain restaurant, you might expect to place and pay for your order on a digital screen, following which you would expect to either collect your order from the counter or to have your food brought to your table by a member of staff. Regardless of the restaurant's location, you would expect this process to be the same.

People, the final element of the extended marketing mix, asserts the importance of staff in customer service. This might be via providing expert knowledge about the offerings from their experience to help a customer to make a purchase decision, or simply by interacting with the customer during the service. Either way, from a consumer perspective, poor interactions with staff can result in negative impressions and, likely, a lack of desire to purchase the service in the future.

Services and relationship marketing

Services and relationship marketing are closely related to the extended marketing mix and as such there is an emphasis on organizations differentiating their approach in comparison to marketing a tangible product. A **service** is an intangible offering typically characterized by an action or performance. It is also key to note that, unlike with a tangible offering, the customer would not expect to take ownership of the service but rather to use it for a defined period of time or until an agreed output is achieved. While services are intangible, customers may expect to find some tangible elements that may act as a signifier of quality or as a reminder of the service. Take, for example, booking a holiday with a travel agent. The holiday itself is intangible, but you may be presented with a brochure or travel tickets, which serve to act as a tangible reminder of the service you have purchased.

As discussed earlier in this chapter, the extended marketing mix is made up of people, process and physical evidence. We might assign a number of characteristics to each element of the extended mix to help us to understand what customers may be looking for from a service. For instance:

- **People**: Polite, efficient, motivated, high standards and friendly.
- **Process**: Procedures, cleanliness, flexibility and a fast response to complaints.
- **Physical evidence**: Aesthetically pleasing environment, tangible evidence and physical clues such as layout or decoration.

When considering their approach to marketing, organizations may also consider the goods and services continuum. This suggests that most offerings will be a combination of goods and services. For example, if we take salt, this would be a pure good. It is tangible, and we can purchase the required quantity from a store and take it home with us to use as we wish. If we next consider an online mental health counselling service, this would be classed as a pure service. We have no ownership of the service and there are no tangible elements that we can purchase to take home with us.

Finally, we have a hybrid offering, which is where we see a combination of a physical good and a service. For example, if we visited a fast-food restaurant, we would expect the physical product of the meal that we ordered, but we would also expect elements of people (serving the meal), process (the way that we have ordered the meal) and physical evidence (for example, the layout and decoration in the restaurant).

Services also have four key characteristics that help to differentiate them from tangible products: intangibility, inseparability, variability and perishability.

Intangibility

Intangibility suggests that services are not tangible, but might typically take the form of a deed, performance or effort. Services do, however, use tangible clues such as testimonials, free gifts (think biscuits and coffee in a hotel room), feedback leaflets and brochures, service settings and branding clues such as logos, designs and displays. For example, if you were to plan a holiday to a destination that you had not visited previously, how would you decide where to go? Would you use a brochure to look at images and descriptions of locations, would you use the internet to check sources on the weather, food and people, or would you rely on word of mouth to inform your decision?

Inseparability

The key fundamental of **inseparability** is simultaneous production and consumption. Think about visiting a hairdressers or barbers: as your haircut is being produced by the stylist it is also being consumed by you, the customer. This makes mass production difficult if not impossible, as each service is likely to differ in some way. It also places emphasis on organizations recruiting and retaining high-quality staff to keep the service experience to a good standard. Organizations must also make sure that they are capable of delivering good quality each time the service is performed, as customers cannot pay for the service one day and exchange it for another the next if they are unhappy with the outcome.

Variability

Variability suggests that standardization is difficult (much as with inseparability) and any service faults will be difficult to control or correct. For example, if you attend your Monday morning lecture but your lecturer is tired or sick and thus does not perform to their usual standard, you may have a bad experience. As a consumer, you cannot then take this experience back and swap it for another once your lecturer is feeling better. Reliable equipment is also needed to reduce the possibility of a bad customer experience. To continue with our previous example, if the computer in the lecture room is broken, your experience as a student will be devalued as it is not possible for you to gain the promised service to the standard that might be expected.

Staff selection and training are also key in reducing variability. Organizations must hire and retain colleagues who have a good understanding of their role and the motivation to provide a high-quality experience for consumers. Organizations may also wish to put in place evaluation systems to help them to better understand the experiences of their customers and consumers. For example, you may be asked to complete an appraisal at the end of your course, to help the organization to under-stand what you liked and didn't like about your classes.

Despite efforts to standardize services, each producer and consumer interaction is likely to be unique, based on the individuals involved in the exchange or other sce-narios (like our broken lecture room computer). In this case, there may be little opportunity for quality control to maintain consistence. However, this is not all bad news for organizations and customers/consumers as, due to their nature, services are easy to adapt to specific customer needs. To conclude our lecture example, if you do not understand a theory at the end of your lecture, you can go and discuss this with your lecturer, who will adapt their service to answer your questions.

Perishability

The final differentiator, **perishability**, suggests that an excess of service supply cannot be stored. In other words, if we have more supply than demand, we lose the opportunity to sell that service forever if it is not purchased by a customer. For exam-ple, consider a flight from London to Paris. If only 10 passengers purchase a ticket for the flight, the opportunity to sell the remaining seats is lost forever once the flight leaves the airport.

The reverse is also true. If we have too much demand and too little supply, we again cannot store this consumption and lose the opportunity for sales. This might, for example, be seen in crowding at a London airport if a flight has been over-booked. As such, organizations must carefully match supply and demand, with many using part-time staff and multiskilling to help to mitigate such risks. Participation by customers themselves is also a useful tactic to manage perishability, with, for exam-ple, organizations using self-service machines. To retain our airport example, pas-sengers might print their own boarding passes at the airport, or weigh their own baggage before checking in for their flight.

Organizations can also use comfort and reservations to help to manage demand and supply. It is also possible to stimulate demand at off-peak times (consider the earlier discussion in this chapter with regard to price); however, there is still a danger of panic selling at low prices which may ultimately harm the organization's reputa-tion in the eyes of customers.

Goods-based or service-based offerings?

Aside from the four key differentiators between goods and services, we must also consider goods that act as 'self-services'. Indeed, many goods provide service-type benefits for the customers and consumers who purchase and use them. This is due to goods and services fitting this category being seen as substitutable by consumers. Take, for example, a washing machine (goods-based). We can purchase the offering and have the product in our own homes, but it also provides exactly the same service that the same washing machine would do at a launderette (service-based). The latter, of course, we don't own, but instead pay to use as a service-based offering. Equally, consider the purchase of a treadmill. You can buy this product to keep and use in your own home, or you can purchase a gym membership and use the offering as a service-based good instead.

Services and relationship marketing go hand in hand. Relationship marketing focuses on developing long-term aspects such as customer loyalty and retention. This is often achieved via an emphasis on customer service, a commitment to quality and a significant amount of contact with customers over a long period of time. In other words, organizations practising this type of marketing are seeking to build a relationship with their customers. This has a number of benefits for organizations, as they will often gain increased profitability from higher customer retention, and will spend less on marketing activities via targeting existing customers who are already aware of their offerings rather than seeking new customers.

The Customer Value Triad

A further concept of relevance in any introduction to marketing is the **Customer Value Triad**. The Customer Value Triad relates to the value, satisfaction and quality that a consumer might gain from an offering. Other key considerations might be seen with also providing a high level of service, along with the distinction between price and value. Here, particular value is placed upon the benefits gained from the offering as opposed to the cost paid. However, the Customer Value Triad is not just about exchanging money for an offering and subsequent levels of satisfaction. Value is broken down into function benefits and emotional benefits, while costs might be considered in terms of money spent to obtain the offering, time and energy costs of, for example, researching and purchasing the offerings, and psychic costs, if, for example, the offering has a strong personal meaning for the consumer.

The marketing management orientations driving business

Eagle-eyed readers may have noted that the aforementioned definition of marketing from the Chartered Institute of Marketing (2015) suggests marketing is a 'management process'. In a similar vein, we must next explore the **five management philosophies** (the production, product, selling, societal marketing and marketing concepts) driving business. However, we must also recognize that all organizations may still practise marketing functions, such as advertising and new product development, regardless of whether they are explicitly referred to in each of the orientations.

The **production concept** assumes that customers prefer availability and affordability or, in other words, that customers will purchase products that are easier to find and that are sold at a lower price than their substitute counterparts. Here, for example, we might refer to products such as salt or sugar. This requires organizations to focus on a low-cost manufacturing strategy, typically creating standardized offerings allowing focus to be placed on production volume. The production concept further assumes that customers will be price-sensitive, often choosing the cheaper substitute offering.

The **product concept** states that customers favour quality, performance and reliability. Organizations will lend focus to a strategy of innovation in their product design, in order to keep customers interested in the offering rather than allowing interest to shift to a substitute offering. Quality is a key focus, with the aim of continual improvement in levels of quality as a key goal. This is because organizations operating under the product concept assume that profit is to be made through sales volume, and that consumers want a better-quality version of the same offering if they are to remain brand loyal. For example, consider how important design innovation and quality might be to your purchase decision if you were to buy a product such as a disposable razor.

The **selling concept** holds the view that customers will not purchase an offering unless the organization undertakes a large-scale selling and promotion effort. Think about products such as double glazing for the windows in your home. Are you likely to seek out this offering on your own, or are you more likely to consider a purchase if an organization makes a strong effort to promote and sell the offering to you? The selling concept suggests that focus should simply be placed on selling what is produced, characterized by aggressive sales and promotion tactics and profit through quick turnaround of high volume. As this concept seeks to sell unsold goods, focus is often placed on a short-term transactional approach with customers, rather than making efforts to build consumer relationships and loyalty. The organizational assumption is typically that customers will be reluctant to make a purchase, but once they do they will like the offering.

The **societal concept** lends focus to the notion that organizations determine the wants, needs and interests of their target markets, and that they can deliver customer satisfaction effectively and efficiently. In other words, organizations operating under the societal concept assume that they can deliver offerings better than their competitors but, importantly, that this should be achieved in a way that improves or maintains consumer well-being and/or society as a whole. With this in mind, such organizations seek to profit through providing for society's welfare, with the assumption that customer satisfaction will be achieved through building relationships that benefit all parties.

Take, for example, a reusable shopping bag. An organization selling such a product may gain financial profit and meet the customer's requirement of being able to carry further purchases; however, this offering will also meet the goal of supporting society's long-term welfare via the reduction of single-use plastic bags.

The **marketing concept** assumes that an organization's goals might be achieved via effectively determining the wants and needs of a target market and delivering those wants and needs to customers more effectively and efficiently than its competitors. This approach relies on the organization defining customer needs prior to production, with profit being achieved through customer satisfaction and loyalty. The marketing concept further assumes that customers will not be driven by price, but rather that they are looking at the offering holistically.

ACTIVITY

Marketing in our lives: The marketing management orientations

Identify which of the marketing management concepts would be best suited to the following offerings, and explain the reasons behind your answers:

- a tin of baked beans
- a mousetrap
- a reusable water bottle
- a car
- health insurance

Consumer behaviour

As might be inferred from the above, marketers spend a great deal of time attempting to understand consumers. Here, the **stimulus response model** is of use in understanding elements that inform consumer decisions (Armstrong and Kotler, 2009). The model suggests that both external and internal stimuli will inform consumer decisions, with external stimuli being related to both marketing and other elements. For example, external marketing stimuli may include the product, price, place and promotion of the marketing mix, while other stimuli may include elements such as politics and economics, and/or socio-cultural and technological elements. The stimulus response model suggests that these external elements will be combined with internal stimuli, such as the customer's characteristics and the buyer decision process.

Internal stimuli are often referred to as residing in the 'buyer's black box'. In other words, while it might be easy for marketers to view and understand external stimuli, internal stimuli are by their nature harder to gain an understanding of, as they are personal to the customer. Once we combine both internal and external stimuli, we are presented with the customer's response to those stimuli. This might be seen via the customer's product, brand and/or dealership choices, along with the purchase timing and amount. For example, if you were to be considering the purchase of a new mobile phone, you may be influenced by external stimuli such as:

- the product itself and its attributes
- the price of the mobile phone
- if any promotions were likely to be applicable to your purchase
- the place from which you could purchase the mobile phone
- any technological advancements that may be upcoming, or that may be present in substitute offerings

Internally, however, your personal buyer characteristics, such as your age, gender or class, might also influence your ultimate response. For example, are you suspicious of marketing activities? Are you technologically aware and idealistic? Are you concerned with the number of apps and platforms that might be accessed on the device? Are you interested in the device having a high-performing camera? All of these decisions and more will influence your response as a customer.

The consumer proposition acquisition process

As we now know, the buyer decision process is perhaps more complex than it might originally seem. The **consumer proposition acquisition process** can help us to understand this further (Baines et al, 2017). This six-stage model maps out the process that consumers typically go through when making a purchase:

1 **Motive development:** At this stage, consumers decide that they want or need to make a purchase.

2 **Information gathering:** Here, consumers will consider the place from which they would typically make a purchase. Influence may also be taken from other sources, such as blogs and in relation to returns policies.

3 **Proposition evaluation:** The consumer evaluates the alternatives. This might include considerations of, for example, whether the desired offering might be cheaper elsewhere, or whether the purchase under consideration is the most fashionable.

4 **Proposition selection:** At this point, the consumer will select from which place they intend to make the purchase. However, the consumer may also source the

offering from a different location than they originally intended. If, for example, the consumer intended to make the purchase in a high-street store, but the item had sold out, they might decide to instead make the purchase online. Equally, if the item has sold out in the high-street store but the consumer sees an alternative offering that is suitable, they may decide to purchase this offering instead.

5 **Acquisition/purchase:** At this stage of the process, the consumer makes the purchase. However, there are further elements that might be considered here, such as whether the purchase is routine or of a one-off nature. This relates to the consumer's level of involvement with the offering. In other words, is the offering something that is purchased frequently (suggesting a low level of consumer involvement), or is it an offering to be purchased only once (typically meaning a higher level of consumer involvement)?

6 **Re-evaluation:** Once the purchase has been completed, consumers may spend time thinking about what they have brought. At times, feelings of regret may surface. This is called cognitive dissonance, and essentially means that the consumer may have negative feelings about their purchase. For example, a consumer may regret spending too much money on a night out, or that they purchased expensive exercise clothing when they fail to use their gym membership.

On the other hand, consumers may be influenced by many different things before they enter into the decision-making process (for example, consider the elements presented in the stimulus response model). Consumers also may not follow all steps in the six-stage consumer proposition acquisition model. For example, if you were to consider a high-involvement purchase such as a car, you may follow the stages presented. However, if you were to purchase a chocolate bar or music, your decision might relate to impulse or emotion, and as such you would be unlikely to follow all stages of the model, perhaps skipping straight from motive development to acquisition/purchase.

Market segmentation

Market segmentation can be described as the separation of the whole market into distinct groups or segments, which can each be defined and identified by characteristics and needs (Baines et al, 2019). There are many ways in which the market might be segmented; here is a non-exhaustive example:

- **Geographic segmentation:** World, region, country, town, city, population or climate.
- **Psychographic segmentation:** Social class, lifestyle, personality or motivations.
- **Behavioural segmentation:** Attitude towards offerings, readiness to purchase or brand loyalty.

- **Demographic segmentation:** Age, gender, family size, lifecycle stage, occupation, education, religion, ethnicity, generation or nationality.
- **Benefit segmentation:** The benefit(s) that consumers expect to receive from an offering.

Regardless of the type of segmentation, it is important to note that targeting different segments may require separate marketing mix approaches, to ensure appeal to consumers who may have very different characteristics, wants and needs. Broadly, however, segmentation of markets can help marketers to:

- decide which consumer segment will be the most profitable to focus on
- understand the common needs and characteristics of consumers
- understand which consumers may have similar responses to marketing actions
- create homogeneous markets

ACTIVITY

Market segmentation

As a marketer, which type of segmentation would you suggest would be most beneficial for:

- a dental practice?
- a car dealership?
- a fast fashion brand?
- a hiking boot brand?
- a brand selling home insurance?

Explain the reasons behind your answers.

Lifestyle and self-concept

The offerings that we purchase can hold benefits beyond any functional attributes which they may possess. For example, the offerings that we purchase might be used to demonstrate our individuality, or, in other words, to tell others something about ourselves. We might do so via the clothes we wear, the experiences we have and the practices of our daily lives, all of which combine to create a **lifestyle**. This can provide useful insight for marketers in terms of consumer attitudes, opinions and interests, as consumers are communicating their likes and dislikes with a multitude of signals, such as with the clothes they wear, the furniture in their homes, the car they drive and the entertainment services they may seek (Featherstone, 1991).

As marketers, if we combine this knowledge of the consumer with the **self-concept**, or, in other words, the consumer's feelings about themselves, such as with their capabilities, worth and intentions, we are often better able to target them. We might see this with the various versions of self presented by the consumer. Let's take the purchase of a new wristwatch, for example:

- **The ideal self:** If the consumer considers the ideal version of themselves, they may lend focus to a luxury offering. In this case, the consumer may decide that their ideal self would be an individual who wears a Rolex wristwatch.

- **The public self:** If the consumer wants to purchase a watch to display their public self, they may consider the image that they would like to present on a daily basis, perhaps at work or in their social life. In this instance, the consumer may opt to purchase a mid-range brand of wristwatch, or one that they view as sensible, such as a Swatch or an Omega.

- **The real self:** If the consumer decides to purchase with the real self in mind, they will be concerned with what they as an individual would really like, rather than being concerned, for example, with what their friends or their boss might think about their purchase choice. Here, the consumer may decide to purchase from a brand that they personally enjoy or consider fun, such as a Disney-branded wristwatch.

ACTIVITY ⤢

Lifestyle and the self-concept

Assuming that budget is not an issue, choose which product/brand you would purchase for your own ideal, public and real selves when considering the following offerings. Explain the reasons behind your decisions:

- a piece of art for your home
- a new car
- a movie to watch with friends
- a new coat
- a meal outside of your home

Reference groups

Aside from the version of the self for which we purchase, consumers are also influenced by other individuals and groups. **Reference groups** might be defined as 'any individual or collection of people whom the individual uses as a source of attitudes, beliefs, values or behaviours' (Foxall and Goldsmith, 1994). However, the individual does not already have to be a member of the group, or even have the desire to become a member of the group, to be influenced by it.

According to Foxall and Goldsmith, reference groups are typically seen as a source of 'comparison for personal attitudes, behaviour or performance', and typically consist of family, friends, peers, celebrities and so on. For example, if you were to explore customer reviews on Amazon or eBay, you are looking at reference group reviews to inform your purchase, with other consumers constating the group in this instance. Reference groups can be useful for consumers in determining the experiences others have already had with an offering, thus often impacting a consumer's decision whether or not to continue with the purchase.

Knowing that others have already made a purchase of the same offering can also serve to reduce the risk associated with a purchase. For example, if your friends in a reference group have already purchased clothing from a particular brand and you make a purchase from the same brand, you as the consumer are reducing the risk that others will not like the purchase you have made, and you are also reducing the risk of purchasing a poor-quality offering as you already have feedback from your reference group. Equally, reference groups can be a useful tool for organizations, as they might provide further discussion as to the positive attributes of an offering, thus placing less emphasis on the organization itself to promote the offering.

However, despite marketers' efforts to understand consumers and their behaviour, we might still question whether gaining a true understanding is possible. Consumer motivations, attitudes and values are unstable and are likely to be subject to frequent change. Customers and consumers also do not always follow linear pathways in their decision making, but instead are prone to purchasing decisions based on emotion.

Marketing research

Marketing research might be defined as 'the design, collection, analysis, and interpretation of data collected for the purpose of aiding marketing decision-making' (Baines et al, 2017). Marketing research can help marketers to understand a range of elements, such as advertising and promotion, products, distribution, the marketing environment, sales and customers.

Broadly, the **marketing research process** encourages marketers to initially define the problem to be explored, followed by a consideration of what needs to accomplished by the marketing research, how this might be achieved, and obstacles and constraints that must be navigated by the marketer during the research. When correctly applied, these steps typically lead the researcher to the heart of the problem, which can be used in helping to tackle the issues facing an organization.

During the marketing research process, marketers will need to make any decisions as to how they would like to address the issue(s) identified. Firstly, the marketer will need to decide whether primary data, secondary data or a combination of both data types would be most valuable to the organization in question in solving the identified problem(s). **Primary data** refers to new information collected by the organization itself within the scope of the marketing research process, whereas **secondary data** is information that already exists and has been collected for a different purpose. Secondary data can be **external** to the organization, meaning that it originates from outside of the organization conducting the research, or **internal**, which means that the secondary data is information that the organization itself has already compiled.

Secondary research, whether internal or external, has a number of advantages and disadvantages. It can be quick to access (imagine desk research where you might search for information online). This has additional benefits in that it is much cheaper (or sometimes free) to access this information, as opposed to the costs associated with collecting primary data. It also allows smaller organizations who may have little to nothing allocated as their marketing research budget to access information that it would be difficult or impossible for them to collect independently.

However, secondary data also has its disadvantages in that the data required may not exist, as it is yet to be collected by another party. Equally, on occasions where an organization is required to pay to access secondary data, the organization may find that they have wasted their resources as the data is not actually relevant to the problem being researched. If marketers are to use secondary marketing research, there are also potential issues in terms of dated information, accuracy, reliability and bias that must be considered.

ACTIVITY

Internal or external secondary data?

Consider the following sources of data. Decide if each source is an internal or an external example of where an organization might find secondary data:

- trade associations
- census
- government reports
- the organization's past purchase records
- the organization's past complaints records

A further central consideration of marketing research is to determine whether qualitative or quantitative research, or a combination of both types of research, is most appropriate given the problem identified. Qualitative research is primarily concerned with gathering subjective accounts from research participants, relying on generalization rather than concrete facts in terms of its results. Qualitative research might be undertaken, for example, via methods such as participant observations, focus groups or interviews. Quantitative research, on the other hand, is typically concerned with statistical accuracy, with data collection methods such as questionnaires and surveys commonly being used to gather data.

Marketing researchers will also need to determine the sampling process for their research. Here, key considerations relate to the population to be included in the study. In other words, marketers need to consider who they would like to participate in the research, and, for example, whether they are looking to include individuals from a certain age group or geographical location, current customers, competitors' customers and so on.

Once the population has been determined, the next stage is to consider how many participants are ideally required. For example, this might result in a large quantitative study being undertaken with a statistical focus, or a smaller-scale qualitative study with a focus on obtaining in-depth information from each participant. Following this, marketers must choose by which method they aim to select their participants. There are many different types of sampling, for example:

- **Random sampling:** Generating random numbers which are assigned to population elements.

- **Stratified sampling:** Using specific characteristics to design homogeneous subgroups from which a representative sample be drawn.

- **Quota sampling:** Restricting the sample by particular characteristics, with the final decision as to participant inclusion being left to the researcher's judgement.

Decisions surrounding contacting the chosen sample are also important and can play a significant role in determining the number of responses a marketer might expect to receive and how much resource is required. There are a number of available options for contacting the chosen sample, for example:

- Post:
  - Pros: Marketers are able to contact a large number of potential participants.
  - Cons: Marketing research via post typically garners a low response rate.
- Focus groups:
  - Pros: Marketers are able to gain rich insights and understanding from participants.
  - Cons: Focus groups can be difficult to organize.

- Online:
  - o Pros: Contacting potential participants via, for example, email, is a low-cost option.
  - o Cons: Emails can seem impersonal, and may not encourage potential participants to take part in the research.
- Phone:
  - o Pros: A quick and easy medium by which to reach potential participants.
  - o Cons: Phone calls can be short and impersonal.
- In person:
  - o Pros: Potential participants are typically less likely to refuse to participate or to ignore the marketing researcher.
  - o Cons: High associated costs (time and money), as a member of staff is required to undertake the research.

Once the data has been collected, the researcher will turn their attention to data analysis. Here, it is important to remember that marketing research is a *tool* to help marketers and organizations to understand the issues they face, but it cannot solve problems on its own. Analysis and interpretation from the marketing researcher are still required to make sense of the data collected. For qualitative data, content analysis is typically used, while for quantitative data statistical analysis is generally the preferred approach.

Content analysis allows for the systematic exploration of the data collected. Typically, similar themes in the data will be coded (for example, by colour) to allow for patterns and trends within the data collected to emerge. This then allows the researcher to make generalizations from the data. **Statistical analysis,** on the other hand, relates to uncovering patterns and trends in quantitative data, such as noting the similarities and differences various participants might demonstrate in indicating their liking for an offering on a Likert scale.

ACTIVITY

Is marketing research worth it?

Imagine that you are the CEO of a small organization with fewer than 50 employees. Is marketing research worth it? Critically explore the value of marketing research for the organization.

Innovation and new product development

Consider your own needs as a consumer. Do you like, want and need the same offerings as you did one year ago? Five years ago? Chances are, your current self probably likes, wants and needs very different things than you previously did. Consumer wants and needs change over time and, as such, organizations need to **innovate** in terms of their offerings in order to maintain the attention and loyalty of customers and consumers.

Let's take the example of a vacuum cleaner. Only a few short years ago, large, heavy and wired machines were the norm for most households. Now, many contemporary homes have moved away from such machines in favour of lighter hand-held or wireless vacuum cleaners, or even robot vacuum cleaners.

This is a telling example for marketers. As products reach the end of their lifecycle, innovation is required to keep up with substitute and advanced offerings from competitors, lest customers and consumers decide to jump ship and shop with the competition. If products are no longer profitable, there is a need to develop new ones. This might be accomplished in two ways: **research and development** in the organization (organic development), or via the **acquisition** of another organization.

Research and development of a new offering or brand can be both expensive and time-consuming, typically with a high failure rate. However, when organizations do get this right, they are often left with a unique product, a well-defined concept and an organization committed to the success of the new offering (Kotler et al, 2019).

In developing a new product or brand, organizations typically follow eight steps:

1 **Idea generation:** The creation of new ideas, which may originate from any number of varied stakeholders, such as employees, customers or competitors.

2 **Idea screening:** Gaining feedback from various stakeholders about the new idea, such as from directors, employees or distributors.

3 **Concept testing:** Testing a range of new ideas, to uncover the benefits and limitations of attributes.

4 **Business analysis:** At this stage, the focus is on reviewing the costs of taking the new idea further, and whether the organization has the resources to be able to do so.

5 **Product development:** The creation of a prototype, if appropriate.

6 **Test marketing:** Here, the organization will select a geographical area or specific segment with which to trial the new offering or brand.

7 **Commercialization:** The full-scale launch of the new offering or brand.

8 **Monitoring and evaluation:** Keeping track of progress (or lack thereof) made by the new offering or brand, and evaluating this progress in line with the organization's goals and expectations.

The product lifecycle

The **product lifecycle** consists of four stages through which an offering will travel from its introduction until it is removed from the market. Typically displayed in a graph format, the product lifecycle indicates likely sales and profit over time. The first stage of the product lifecycle, **introduction**, is when the offering is introduced to the market. At this stage, sales are likely to be low for a number of reasons, such as lack of consumer awareness about the product or service. Profit is typically non-existent at this stage, despite an often relatively high introductory price point, due to the high costs associated with introducing an offering to the marketplace in terms of research and development and advertising.

The second stage, **growth**, occurs when interest in the offering starts to improve, with sales and profit typically increasing during this phase. There is still likely to be a heavy cost burden for the organization at this stage, for example with marketing communications costs, to ensure that the target market is aware of the offering and its attributes. At the growth stage, competition is likely to increase, suggesting pressure for organizations to lower their prices.

At the penultimate stage of the product lifecycle, **maturity**, sales and profit have peaked and will start to level off. This is often due to consumers already having purchased the offering, and thus there are fewer 'new' consumers who may wish to make a purchase remaining in the target market. Typically, promotional costs will rise due to aggressive competition, and the organization will be required to cut prices to continue to attract customers.

The final stage, **decline**, occurs when sales and profits start to drop. This may be due to a number of reasons, such as lack of customer and consumer interest, or a new, improved competitor substitute offering entering the market. However, organizations can implement some tactics to improve their situation during the decline phase. For example, they may decide to introduce new products to replace old ones, to significantly update or differentiate their offering, or to bundle products together at lower prices to help to sell old stock.

Ultimately, the product lifecycle is a useful tool to help marketers to predict the shape of sales and profits over time, and to understand the need for different marketing activities at different points in an offering's lifecycle. However, it is also important to note that not all offerings will have the same life expectancy. For example, we might expect a fast fashion item of clothing to have a very short lifecycle, whereas with a can of branded baked beans we might expect the product to exist in the maturity phase of the lifecycle for a much longer period of time.

Figure 1.3   Example of the product lifecycle

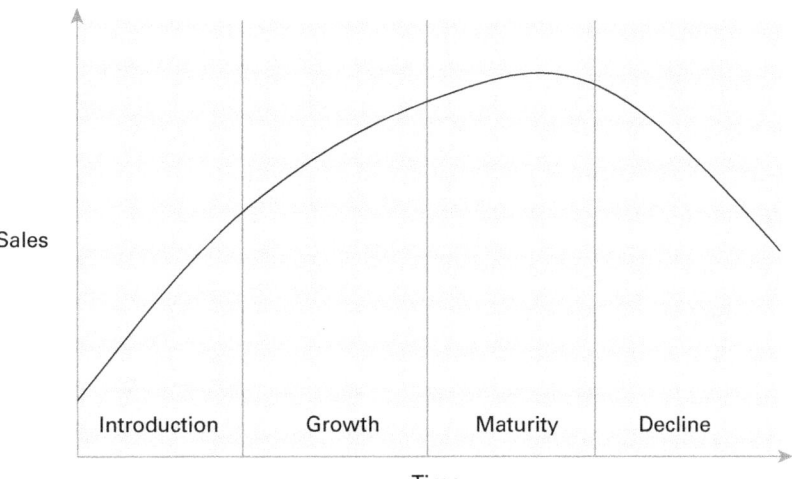

Brands

Let's now move on to discuss how we might define a **brand**. A brand is essentially an intangible element designed to differentiate an offering from those of its competitors. This might, for example, include names, symbols and/or other visuals, and more. We might also add here the definition of brands from Minsky and Geva (2020): 'what consumers, prospects and other stakeholders think, feel and say about the product, service, person or other entity'.

Brands have a rich history, rather than only being the contemporary force for differentiation that we perhaps consider them to be. The term itself hails from an ancient Scandinavian word meaning 'fire' or 'sword'. For instance, early examples of brands might be seen to include Pompeii electoral posters, branding animals in Ancient Egypt, Medieval guilds trademarking craft goods, early English bakers using identifiable symbols on their products, or even artists signing their work (Minsky and Geva, 2020).

As such, as customers and consumers, we can use brands to help us to make decisions about the offerings that we purchase and use. For example, if we consider the sports brand Adidas, we might assign characteristics like 'authentic', 'practical', 'fashionable' or 'performance-based', whereas if we thought about the car brand Volvo, we might suggest characteristics such as 'safe' and 'reliable'. This can lead to brands embodying personalities and images in the minds of consumers. For example, we might see Apple as innovative and sustainable clothing manufacturer Patagonia as ethical. The characteristics that we associate with brands can help customers to identify offerings that they may wish to purchase, to save time in considering alternatives, and also help to minimize the risk of purchasing a product that does not perform as required.

Brands will typically also have a distinctive visual identity to help customers recognize them easily. This is often in the form of a brand logo, wording or colour. If a brand holds a recognizable visual identity it can inspire trust in customers and consumers, which may inspire trust in the brand and repeat purchases, ultimately leading to profit for the brand.

Brands also add value to products. This is via **brand equity**, which essentially relates to the additional amount of money a customer is willing to pay for an offering in comparison to a generic substitute offering. For example, imagine that you are offered the choice of purchasing a branded pair of trainers priced at £100, and the same pair of trainers without the brand association priced at £50. If you ultimately choose to purchase the branded pair of trainers, you are essentially paying an additional £50 for the brand name – this is brand equity.

While brands have many benefits for organizations and customers, there are also some pitfalls of which we must be aware. A brand must be consistent with elements such as product positioning, advertising, pricing and so on, for customers to understand the message. Brands must also be wary of their associations and credibility with consumers. For example, if a brand uses celebrity endorsement and the celebrity acts badly, this can reflect poorly on the brand in the eyes of consumers. Particularly for successful brands, copy-cat products can also be an issue.

ACTIVITY

Brand characteristics

Choose three of your favourite brands. Which characteristics would you assign to them? Explain the reasons behind your answers.

ACTIVITY

Brand perceptions

Consider your perception of the following car brands:

- Ford
- Fiat

- Kia

- Volvo

Which brand would you choose to purchase a new car from? Explain the reason behind your answer.

CHAPTER SUMMARY

This chapter has sought to act as an introduction or refresher to core marketing principles and terminology. Please do revisit it as and when you need to, along with the glossary of key terms provided at the end of this chapter. The following chapter explores marketing and globalization more explicitly, both as distinct concepts and in examining the connections between the two terms. In doing so, we will cover a brief history of globalization and marketing, while also providing some critique in relation to the concept of globalization.

KEY TERMS

Brand: An intangible element used to differentiate from competitor offerings and to promote recognizability for consumers.

Brand equity: The additional amount of money that a customer is willing to pay for a branded offering in comparison to a generic offering.

Business-to-business (B2B): The sale of offerings from one organization to another, such as component parts.

Business-to-consumer (B2C): The sale of offerings from organizations to consumers.

Business-to-government (B2G): The sale of offerings from organizations to governments.

Channel intermediary: An organization which acts as a middleman between another organization and customers.

Customer vs consumer: These two terms are often used interchangeably; however, they do in fact refer to very different roles. A customer is the individual who pays for an offering, while a consumer is the person who uses the offering. For example, if you were to purchase a coffee and subsequently drink that coffee you would be both the customer and the consumer. However, if you were to purchase the same coffee, but then give it to your friend, you would be the customer while your friend would assume the role of consumer. In short, you can be the customer, the consumer, or both the customer and the consumer.

Integrated marketing communications: Brings together all communications methods to be employed for the purpose of consistency and consumer clarity. Integrated marketing communications promote a uniform approach that suggests customers should have the same impression or message from a brand each time that they come into contact with it, regardless of the medium by which this contact occurs.

Involvement: Customers and consumers typically have either high or low levels of involvement when making a purchase. Take the repeated purchase of an offering or the purchase of a low-cost offering. Involvement is typically low with this type of purchase; if we make the wrong purchasing decision, our risk is comparatively low as we can use or dispose of the offering without any major impact. Conversely, high involvement offerings often hold a higher price point and typically relate to offerings that customers would not routinely purchase: for example, a new car or laptop. Consumers are typically more involved with purchases of this nature as there is a higher element of risk involved if the right choice is not made.

Likert scale: Research participants may provide a response to a question via a Likert scale. For example, 'On a scale of 1 to 5, how likely are you to purchase this product in the next six months?'

Offerings: Products or services.

Price ceiling: The highest possible price that an organization can sell an offering for. Above this price, there will be no real demand for the offering.

Price floor: The lowest possible price that an organization can sell an offering for before the price no longer covers the costs accrued in bringing the offering to market.

Product lifecycle: The product lifecycle is typically represented by a graph demonstrating the sales and profits for a particular offering over time. The product lifecycle suggests that products will go through four key phases:

- Introduction (when the offering is introduced to the market, profit will be a negative number and sales are likely to be slow).
- Growth (the new offering is better known by the market and sales and profits rapidly increase).
- Maturity (sales and profits reach their peak as the majority of prospective consumers already have the offering).

- Decline (sales and profits start to drop as few customers are interested in purchasing the offering – this may be due to market saturation, or due to further advances being offered by a competitor's substitute offering).

The product lifecycle can be highly useful to marketers in helping them to decide where high and low levels of advertising spend are required, and when innovation might be needed. However, it is also important to note that not all offerings will have the same life expectancy. For instance, Heinz baked beans are likely to remain in the growth/maturity phase for a long period of time, while a fast fashion pair of jeans is likely to reach the decline phase quickly.

Promotional mix: The mixture of tools, techniques and strategies used to promote an offering.

Prospects: Prospective customers/consumers are individuals who are yet to purchase/use an offering, but who may be persuaded to do so in the future.

Relationship marketing: Organizational efforts to develop longer-term relationships with customers, rather than short-term transactional relationships. Emphasis is placed on elements such as customer retention and loyalty.

Standardized: Being the same, or very similar.

Substitute offering: A product or service which has very similar or the same characteristics, attributes or composition as a competing offering from a different organization or brand.

References

Armstrong, G and Kotler, P (2009) *Marketing: An Introduction*, Pearson

Baines, P, Fill, C and Rosengren, S (2017) *Marketing* (4th ed), Oxford University Press

Baines, P, Fill, C, Rosengren, S and Antonetti, P (2019) *Marketing* (5th ed), Oxford University Press

Chartered Institute of Marketing (2015) *7Ps: A brief summary of marketing and how it works*, www.cim.co.uk/media/4772/7ps.pdf (archived at https://perma.cc/GR6W-NF25)

Featherstone, G (1991) *Consumer Culture and Postmodernism*, Sage Publications

Foxall, G R and Goldsmith, R E (1994) *Consumer Psychology for Marketing*, Routledge

Jobber, D (2007) *Principles and Practice of Marketing*, McGraw-Hill Education

Kotler, P, Keller, K L, Goodman, M and Hansen, T (2019) *Marketing Management* (4th ed), Pearson

Kotler, P, Wong, V, Sauders, J and Armstrong, G (2005) *Principles of Marketing* (4th ed), Pearson

McCarthy, J E (1968) *Basic Marketing: A managerial approach* (3rd ed), Richard D Irwin, Inc.

Minsky, L and Geva, I (2020) *Global Brand Management: A guide to developing, building and managing an international brand*, Kogan Page

United Nations (2024) The 17 Goals, https://sdgs.un.org/goals (archived at https://perma.cc/5G6V-6AXR)

Answers for activities

Marketing in our lives: The marketing management orientations

- A tin of baked beans – production
- A mousetrap – product
- A reusable water bottle – societal
- A car – marketing
- Health insurance – selling

Market segmentation

- A dental practice – benefit
- A car dealership – behavioural / psychographic
- A fast fashion brand – psychographic
- A hiking boot brand – geographic
- A brand selling home insurance – demographic

Internal or external secondary data?

The first three are external. The last two are internal.

2 | Marketing and globalization

LEARNING OBJECTIVES

By the end of this chapter, you should be able to:

- understand the significance of marketing and globalization as separate concepts
- explain how globalization and marketing have developed throughout history
- articulate why it feels like the world is getting smaller through the concept of the Shrinking World
- explain how marketing practice has shifted over time from persuading people to buy what you can produce to discovering what they need and fulfilling that need
- explain the concept of Westernization through the spread of brands from the West to the rest of the world
- describe the benefits and downsides of globalization and globalized markets

Introduction

This chapter introduces the two underlying themes of this book: globalization and marketing, and focuses on the rise and interlinked nature of these key concepts. First, we look at globalization. What is it? How can it be defined, and (perhaps surprisingly) does it definitely exist? We look at how globalization has developed, the key things driving it and some of its many implications.

As part of this, we consider a concept called the Shrinking World (Dicken, 2015). This helps us visualize how technological and travel advances change how we think about and operate in the world. You are likely to have ideas about what globalization means to you. This chapter aims to build on those and perhaps challenge your preconceptions. We look at a range of opinions about globalization and help you to consider the twists and turns of its many benefits and downsides.

In the second part of the chapter, we bring in marketing and look at its development and role in a globalized world. We look at how marketing works in today's global business landscape, considering the important shift away from standardization in the early 1900s towards understanding customer needs. As such, we look at marketing's role in empowering the consumer on a global scale. We also consider how marketing logic perhaps drove (or at least legitimized) the concept of customer service more generally between stakeholders and consumers. Did it shift expectations between government and citizens, or doctors and patients?

Throughout, we will start to explore some key topics that we will return to in the rest of this book: for example, global consumerism and production, communications and ethics. While Chapter 1 provided a brief overview of some central marketing concepts such as the marketing mix, market segmentation and marketing research, Chapter 2 begins to look at marketing in a global context.

The chapter concludes with a case study exploring a potential downside of globalization – the loss of the local. We look at the spread of Western fast food to Japan and the culture of KFC at Christmas.

What is globalization?

Globalization as a concept might not be as straightforward as you first think. Many of us have grown up in a global world. It's easy to accept globalization unthinkingly and expect it as part of our everyday lives. But how often do we stop to think about what it means, for both the world and us as individuals?

Below are some aspects of globalization that might spring to our minds when we hear the term:

- **Global business:** We think nothing of companies like Nokia, Samsung, Citi, Microsoft, HP and Coca-Cola having a presence in all corners of the globe. Global financial infrastructure and supply chains mean that organizations can do business across national borders and cultures.

- **Trade:** Linked to the above, developments in infrastructure and technology mean that nations can trade freely with each other and there is increasing economic interdependence between nations. Free trade agreements reduce import and export barriers. As we'll see later in the chapter, this is very far from what life was like before globalization.

- **Technology:** Technological developments mean that we can communicate quickly and easily with people around the world in various ways. Emails, texts, video conferencing calls and social media allow us to communicate instantly with one another.

- **Transport:** As individuals, we can fly to far-flung destinations with relative ease. This opens up opportunities for holidays, seeing our friends and family on the other side of the world or even choosing to live in a different country. Global transport links also mean that organizations can move products or their component parts around the world.

- **Production and consumption:** Products can be created or manufactured in one country and sold in any market around the globe. Global consumerism is a key theme running throughout this book. Choices made by individuals and businesses drive the production and consumption of globally traded goods and brands. As we will touch on later in this chapter (and explore in depth in Chapters 3 and 10), while this may benefit the organizations by reducing costs, there are significant downsides to consider such as the quality of life for those producing the products as well as implications for the environment.

- **Fairtrade:** This concept is very much linked to global consumerism and might be something you associate with globalization. Those who produce the products we buy in the West can work in appalling environments for low wages. You may be familiar with the concept of sweatshops – factories or workplaces in places like Asia (such as Bangladesh, Cambodia, Pakistan or China) or Central America (such as Honduras or Haiti) that employ local people to work in industries like textiles, electronics or agriculture. These sweatshops treat workers unfairly, expecting them to work very long hours in poor conditions and paying them little for what they do. Throughout this book, we will consider how we, as consumers, can help to influence this global problem. How can we ensure we don't buy products manufactured in this way? What can we do as consumers to fight against it?

Globalization has many different facets and associations. Many of the things in the above list might initially appear to be benefits. It's hard to imagine a world without global business, fast and seamless communication, or the fact that we can travel to all corners of the globe with relative ease. These things all undoubtedly benefit the world and us as individuals. But how often do we consider the other side of globalization? How often do we think about the background processes which enable these apparent benefits, such as the harsh working conditions for those who produce goods sold in the West?

This chapter should help you to challenge some of your preconceptions about globalization, and whether it is fair and equal. It will help you to think about how perspectives of globalization might differ around the world. Is a student from the UK likely to think about globalization in the same way as a worker in a Chinese factory? This chapter will help to develop your understanding further.

ACTIVITY

What does globalization mean to you?

Before we begin, take a moment to consider what springs to your mind when you hear the term 'globalization'. How many of the points in the above list did you think of? What do you see as the benefits and downsides?

In Chapter 1, we saw that marketing can be defined in many different ways. The same is true for globalization. Like most concepts, finding a single, all-encompassing definition can be challenging. Two of the most helpful definitions come from Steger (2003) and Daniels et al (2015). While both were written some years ago, they are still highly relevant today. Importantly, both see the notions of interdependency and connectedness as central to the concept.

Steger emphasizes the importance of globalization as 'a multidimensional set of social processes that create, multiply, stretch and intensify worldwide social inter-dependencies and exchanges'. (Eagle-eyed readers will remember that the notion of 'exchange' is central to many marketing definitions too – refer to Chapter 1.) For Steger, globalization also fosters 'a growing awareness of deepening connections be-tween the local and the distant'.

Daniels et al's (2015) definition is similar. They consider globalization as a set of 'interdependent relationships among people from different parts of the world'. They also add a different angle – 'the reduction of barriers to the movement of trade, capital, technology and people'. In this way, globalization can be thought of not only in terms of what it gives us – trade, travel, etc. – but also in terms of what it removes. It reduces barriers that existed in the past. This element of the definition can be help-ful, as reminding ourselves of what the world was like before globalization occurred on its current scale helps us to understand its full impact and continuing role in our changing world.

Bringing it all together – what does globalization mean?

How can we use these definitions to formulate our own understanding of globaliza-tion? What's clear is that there are many different angles to consider. Theorists view the concept through different lenses and there is much debate about the term.

Bearing in mind Steger's and Daniels et al's definitions, we can boil globalization down to six key, interrelated aspects. This is by no means an exhaustive list, but these points underlie much of what you will learn about in this book:

1 **Connectedness:** Individuals and organizations across the globe are more connected than ever before. Developments in transportation and communication mean that we can send information around the world easily and choose to visit or live in different nations.

2 **Collective global 'identity' and thinking:** Does this greater level of connection point to a shift away from national to global citizenship? Does globalization mean that organizations and individuals around the world are becoming more homogeneous? Do you see yourself as belonging to one nation, or do you feel connected with a broader global community? So long as we have the financial means, we can do what we want to do and buy what we want to buy no matter

where we live. This is particularly true in the West, where people tend to have more disposable income than in the rest of the world. We can construct our identity through the things that we buy.

3 **Broadening awareness:** Steger talks about our 'growing awareness of deepening connections'. The increasing connectivity of all people, nations and cultures around the world expands our awareness and makes us think on a more global scale. Before globalization, people only thought about their local area. As we will see later in the chapter, most people had no way of knowing what was happening beyond a few miles of their homes. We now think nationally and globally.

4 **Changing social relations:** This is another connected point that relates to Steger's 'social interdependencies and exchanges' and Daniels et al's 'interdependent relationships among people from different parts of the world'. Greater connectedness and broadening awareness allow us to interact with people with culturally different backgrounds. A potential benefit of this is that it makes us more culturally in tune with people from around the world. As we later discuss, a potential downside is that changing social relations merge cultures in a way that erodes nations' identities.

5 **Changing dynamic between the local and distant:** Steger talks about our 'deepening connections between the local and the distant'. In the past, the focus was on who you could interact or trade with locally. Our broadening awareness and greater connectivity with the rest of the world means that distance is no longer a barrier. Faraway nations are no longer an unknown.

6 **Lost significance of the local:** The above five points could all be largely considered positives of globalization. It's worth mentioning this downside here as a key aspect of globalization. Many theorists discuss how globalization has removed cultural indicators in different cultures and countries. The erosion of local cultures and practices could be considered a significant negative effect. We illustrate this in part with a case study demonstrating an example of the adoption of Western culture using the Japanese Christmas tradition of KFC buckets at Christmas.

ACTIVITY

Defining globalization

Bearing in mind Steger's (2003) and Daniels et al's (2015) definitions, as well as the aspects of globalization we discussed earlier in the chapter, write your own definition of globalization. Try to make it no longer than 50 words. Note that you might want to revisit this definition once we have considered the history, drivers and some of the positive and negative implications of the concept later in the chapter.

A brief history of globalization

It can be hard to imagine life before we had easy access to all corners of the globe. We take globalization so much for granted that we rarely think back to a time when people's awareness of the world would have been limited to their immediate locality. What follows is a whistlestop tour of the history of globalization. The starting point of globalization is very much up for debate. Many scholars position its beginnings around 1800, while others believe it dates back far further. What's clear is that it evolved slowly over hundreds of years.

Before the 18th century

Before the 18th century there was some notion of the 'earth' as a single place, but trade on a global scale was by no means a central concern. Religion was the primary unifying force and divided people into communities around the world. The vast majority of trade took place in the same territory. There were, however, some early indicators of globalization in this period. The very earliest trade in coffee took place in the 15th century when coffee beans were exported from Ethiopia to Yemen (Nescafé, 2024). Coffee trade was followed by trade in spices, tobacco, furs and sugar.

In the 16th century, the ship *Victoria* became the first to circumnavigate the globe. It left Ondarroa in Biscay, Spain in 1519 as part of a fleet of five vessels and was the only one to return three years later in 1522. The expedition's purpose was to travel west across the Atlantic in search of the East Indies and the spices that grew there (Royal Museum Greenwich, 2024). The entire objective was to open up the trade route.

So, while global trade might not have become a primary concern until the 18th century, it was by no means completely off the agenda until this time. The importance of this first trip around the world on the development of globalization cannot be overestimated. In fact, could it give us enough evidence to say that globalization began as early as the 1500s?

The mid-19th to mid-20th centuries

During the mid-19th to mid-20th centuries, globalization started to become much more of a prominent force. The key advancements can be grouped into four main themes:

1 **Communication and connection between nations:** The introduction of telegraph lines in the 1850s opened up communication channels between people in different countries. In the 1890s, radio communications were introduced which further enabled people to understand what was happening in countries other than their

own (Britannica, 2024a). Physically travelling to other countries became a reality for some in 1919, when the first international passenger flight happened between London and Paris (British Airways, nd). It was a first step towards facilitating cost- and time-effective face-to-face connections between people in different nations – something most of us associate with globalization today. It's worth noting, however, that this mode of transport was only available to the select few who could afford it. This was also true for the new communications technology. Still in its infancy, it was expensive, slow and unreliable.

2 **Global products:** This period also saw the rise of global products. Campbell's Soup and Heinz were founded in the late 19th century. Similarly, Coca-Cola was founded in 1886 in Atlanta in the USA. Coca-Cola is one of the best examples of how a product can gain traction in the global arena: 20 years after its launch, in 1906, it was being sold in Britain, Canada, Cuba and Mexico. And by 1929, just 43 years after its launch, it was being sold in 78 countries (The Coca-Cola Company, 2024). While this might not seem too remarkable by today's standards, for a product to achieve this in the early 1900s was impressive, given the barriers to globalization that existed at that time. We will consider Coca-Cola as a global marketing phenomenon in some depth throughout this book.

3 **International banking:** While financial transactions were not yet happening between a global network of banks during this period, international transactions could occur between two countries. This was a significant leap forward. Community branches of banks were still going strong.

4 **Wider global thinking:** The first modern Olympic Games was held in Athens in 1896. It reflected a burgeoning interest in uniting nations through shared cultural experiences. Around 280 athletes from 12 countries competed in front of an estimated 60,000-strong crowd (Britannica, 2024b). A further example of the rise of global thinking was the introduction of the package holiday, which lowered the cost of travel and made it more achievable from a practical point of view. It came in 1949, when an entrepreneur named Vladimir Raitz founded Horizon Holidays, providing all-in trips to Corsica relatively cheaply (Bray, 2010). It heralded an increasing availability of travel and connection across the world. It is worth noting, however, that while both these events could be taken as evidence of wider global thinking during this period, it is still likely that the vast majority of people wouldn't have known about them. So at this point, there is still some way to go with the evolution of globalization, on an individual level at least.

The 1960s to the present day

Arguably, the period between the 1960s and the present has seen the most advances in globalization. Global markets and supply chains have taken hold. Rapid advances in communication technology mean we are more connected than ever. This greater connectivity has given way to equally rapid advancements in the financial markets. Trading 24 hours a day, seven days a week is now possible. Financial organizations such as Mastercard have seen huge growth and can operate in more countries than ever.

Global markets

The introduction of global markets saw the establishment of highly coordinated global frameworks. Logistics and supply chains became more sophisticated and global trade began to occur seamlessly with greater efficiencies. The rise of the internet led to the rise of online ordering. As consumers, we can get whatever we want if we have the financial means. Many businesses we are familiar with today came about in the 1960s. Examples include Walmart, Best Buy, Ralph Lauren, Calvin Klein and The North Face. Global markets and supply chains allowed these businesses to flourish and become what they are today.

These global markets also presented significant opportunities for the advertising industry, which further enabled organizations to move into the global arena. Take Mastercard's infamous Priceless campaign. Conceived in 1997, its adverts gave glimpses into special experiences – unifying moments filled with love between friends and family. The message? 'There are some things money can't buy. For everything else, there's Mastercard.' It positioned Mastercard as a credit card company with a big heart, concerned about facilitating special moments between people. Its global appeal saw the campaign expand to 210 countries with the only change being the language of the tagline (Stalzer, 2019). The campaign enabled a cost-effective global marketing strategy for the brand. We delve into Mastercard's Priceless campaign further in Chapter 5.

Electronic communications

As we will learn later in the chapter, this was facilitated (but not driven) by the significant technological advances during this time, particularly in electronic communications. Developments in space-based communication were particularly rapid in the early 1960s. In 1963, Syncom 2 became the first satellite to enable direct dialling between nations. The potential for satellite communications was demonstrated to the public by President John F Kennedy when he used it to call Nigerian Prime Minister Abubakar Balewa. It was the first two-way call between heads of state via satellite (NASA, 2024).

Exciting developments were not only happening with satellite communication. Optical fibre communication (communication that relies on light as the transmission medium) was gathering pace around the same time. It was this revolutionary technology that eventually enabled the World Wide Web, invented by Tim Berners-Lee at CERN in 1989, and made available to the public in 1991 (CERN, 2024).

Advancements in electronic communications have continued apace until the present day. By 1965 approximately 150 million fixed telephone lines connected people around the globe (World Bank Group, 2024). And then came mobiles. The first ever mobile phone call was made in 1973 by a Motorola engineer to a rival at Bell Laboratories working on a car-based mobile phone. The call informed him that he'd lost the race to invent the first handheld, portable cell phone (Lu, 2023). It's now hard to imagine life without our mobiles. In 2021, there were an estimated 15 billion of them in operation worldwide. This number is expected to reach 18.22 billion by 2025 (Statista, 2024a).

Financial markets

This period has also seen the evolution of better integrated and more efficient financial markets. The fact that you could instantly deal with anyone anywhere in the world gave organizations access to huge markets and around-the-clock trading. For instance, 'In the 1990s, the Dow Jones industrial average posted its biggest gains of any decade in its history' (Bebar, 1999). There are clearly huge benefits associated with this element of globalization, but there are also potential downsides to consider. Do these changes to our global financial market impact financial security? Do they push us towards debt? Do they devalue our economy?

The introduction of the euro in 1999 was intended to create economic integration in Europe and a common currency that had a similar standing in the world economy to the US dollar. It has helped to make the eurozone a more attractive trade prospect for non-EU countries, promoting EU trade with the rest of the world.

Financial organizations began to enjoy a worldwide presence. We've already seen how Mastercard's global advertising campaign played a part in the credit card becoming one of the largest card brands in the world. It's been a similar story for American Express. Founded in the US in 1850, American Express opened its first European office in Paris in 1895. By the early 1900s, the company had started to operate internationally, processing transactions in England, Germany, Argentina, Brazil, China, Japan, Egypt and India. By the early 21st century, this number had increased to more than 40 countries (Britannica, 2024c). Today, merchants accept American Express in 192 countries across the world (Statista, 2024b).

Environmental awareness

As we will learn later in the chapter, the connections between globalization and the environment can be viewed positively and negatively. While advancements in production and consumption have arguably contributed significantly to global warming and environmental degradation, globalization has also united the world over environmental issues. Many, if not most, consumers and stakeholders who contribute to global warming also care deeply about how they can help to halt the change.

Our increasing global identity has united governments to tackle issues such as global warming, the depletion of the ozone layer and biological diversity. In the case of the ozone layer, this has resulted in an achievement many didn't believe was possible. In the mid-1970s, scientists discovered that man-made chemicals such as those found in aerosols could harm the ozone layer (the layer protects Earth's inhabitants, crops and ecosystems from the sun's harmful rays). In 1985, scientists' worst fears were confirmed when a hole was found over Antarctica. It was a devastating discovery. Governments jumped into action and adopted the Vienna Convention for the Protection of the Ozone Layer. By 2008, it was the first and only UN agreement to be ratified by every country worldwide.

Today, the hole is expected to close by the 2060s. The world united over the issue and fixed it on a global scale (UNEP, 2021). Many hope that the same will be true for biodiversity goals. In December 2022, the world agreed to adopt the Kunming–Montreal Global Biodiversity Framework to stop and reverse the loss of nature by 2050 (UN, 2024). The framework supports the Sustainable Development Goals and sets out a global vision for achieving harmony with nature by 2050.

Global consciousness

As we noted earlier, collective global identity and thinking are perhaps key elements of globalization as we understand it today. We take many of the elements we've discussed for granted, such as electronic communications, global markets, financial markets and the environment. Our level of acceptance is a key indicator of our increasing global consciousness. We don't often stop to think about these things as points of progress, yet when you consider the history of globalization and where we've come from, it's remarkable what we can achieve today. We've gone from the days of *Victoria*'s feat of circumnavigating the world to accepting the world as a single place that we can communicate and trade with.

Globalization is now so deeply embedded in our consciousness that it affects our behaviour, thinking and identity without us realizing it. The opportunities we have available to us have broadened our thinking. We take our almost limitless lack of boundaries for granted. We can now go to live and work almost anywhere in the world. We can take time out to travel and live a much more varied life than our predecessors. We can construct our identity in any way that we choose, whether that's what we buy, who we connect with, the activities we get involved with or the causes we support. Our deepening awareness of the world as a single place might suggest that we have more of an understanding of how our actions impact others. Our global consciousness affects everything. It is truly part of our daily lives.

Benyon and Dunkerley (2000) agree with this view of global consciousness. Back in 2000, they suggested that globalization, in whichever form we might view it, has huge impacts for everyone in the world. These theorists agree that no matter how we think about globalization and what it represents, the opportunities it gives us affect us all (as do the downsides – see later in the chapter). They boldly state that 'globalization might justifiably be claimed to be the defining feature of human activity at the start of the twenty-first century'. Based on what you have read so far, would you agree with this statement?

Does globalization really exist?

The title of this section might surprise you. You've just been asked to consider whether globalization could be a defining feature of human activity at the start of the 21st century, and now we're asking whether or not it really exists.

Given that you are likely to be studying a module in which globalization plays a key part, it might interest you to learn that some theorists believe it doesn't exist as a significant phenomenon. Not everyone shares Benyon and Dunkerley's view that it is a powerful, defining force. On the contrary, they believe it is unnoteworthy and exaggerated.

There are various counterarguments to the significance of globalization as a concept, most of which centre around the claim that it is not distinctive enough to be labelled a trend. Some theorists have questioned whether it is all, in fact, a myth. Some argue that the West pushing products and opinions towards the rest of the world is nothing more than a continuation of colonization, interrupted by the two World Wars and the Cold War. Others take the view that while global relations might be seen as a good thing, the world as a globalized whole is not a reality.

For example, Hirst (2000) suggests that while there is evidence of international trading, most capital remains within national boundaries. Hirst believes that this leads to unequal distribution of wealth as organizations' production and sales efforts are focused on those geographical areas where the most money can be made, rather than offerings being truly global and equally available to all. Similarly, Latif (2010) questions whether it is a myth or reality, and talks about how sceptics view globalization as an exaggerated concept, or a 'buzzword… rarely heard before the mid-1980s'. For these sceptics, 'the historical evidence of globalization confirms nothing but the heightening level of internationalization, that is, interaction of the predominantly national economies'.

ACTIVITY ⬏

Does globalization exist?

What do you think? Does globalization exist as a definable concept?

The Shrinking World

Most theorists do accept that globalization exists as a definable concept. One such theorist is Dicken, who has used globalization to explain the Shrinking World phenomenon (Dicken, 2015). This idea is used by many to explain how advancements in transport and technology over time can make it feel like the world we're living in is getting smaller. While the physical distance between places remains the same, the reduced time it takes to transport people or products or communicate information can make it feel like the world is shrinking. This concept is known as **time–space compression**. Dicken uses developments in transportation from the 1500s to the present day to illustrate how our perception of the size of the world has changed over time.

The world felt at its biggest between 1500 and 1840. Humans could only travel at a maximum speed of 10 mph (this was the best average speed of horse-drawn carriages and sailing ships). Consequently, the world was seen as an enormous space that was near-impossible to traverse and communicate across. Between 1850 and 1930, steam locomotives were introduced. These could travel at an average speed of 65 mph. Steamships were introduced during the same period, and could manage 36 mph. While these speeds might feel leisurely to us today, they represented a significant step forward at the time. The world felt a more manageable size. Global travel was more within reach, even if it may have been too expensive and time-consuming for most people. The reduced time it took to travel over distances made the world feel smaller.

The 1940s saw the introduction of propeller aircraft which could travel at 200 to 300 mph. These were huge speeds compared to what people had experienced previously. Once again, the world felt like it shrank. Then came the 1960s. Jet passenger aircraft were introduced capable of travelling between 500 and 600 mph. These speeds remain fairly unchanged today, and mean that we can get almost anywhere in the globe in a couple of days. The world is no longer incomprehensibly large. Every corner of the globe is within our reach.

Interestingly, we might also conceptualize Dicken's figure of the Shrinking World in a different way. The bottom of the image, in its original form, shows the world as a large place, with communication, travel and the like being slow or difficult to achieve. As time passes and new developments and innovations take place, the other conceptions of the size of the world as shown by Dicken become smaller and, by the same logic, communications, travel and so forth become much easier and quicker.

If, however, we then decide to turn Dicken's original image upside down, we are presented with a different view, arguably, of how we see the world. In this case, our bottom image will be the smallest view of the world; in other words, over time we have begun to think of the world as a smaller place, with many of the mysteries about the world as a whole as we might have conceptualized them in the past being replaced with knowledge and speed.

It's interesting to think about whether we have reached the limits of time–space compression from a transportation point of view. Will we ever feel the world is smaller than we do now? We may have done this briefly with the introduction of Concorde in 1969. Concorde was a supersonic airliner with a top speed of 1,354 mph. It allowed people to travel from London Heathrow to JFK Airport in New York in around three and a half to four hours. The lucky few who got to travel on it may have felt the world was that much smaller because of it. After the fleet of Concorde airliners was retired in 2003, our top speed reduced to 600 mph once again (Britannica, 2024d).

ACTIVITY

Further time–space compression

Dickens applied the theory of time–space compression to travel, but there are many different ways to think about our perception of the size of the world, e.g. communication and trade. Make a short list of what else might have contributed to time–space compression since the 1960s.

What drives globalization?

A huge number of factors drive globalization – too many to cover in one chapter of a textbook. Five drivers are arguably more significant than others: market, competitive, cost, government and technological.

Market drivers

Market drivers can primarily be thought about in terms of customer behaviour and fulfilling customer needs and preferences on a global scale. As we will discuss further in Chapter 7, customer needs around the globe are gradually converging, with people wanting access to similar products no matter where they live. This gives businesses opportunities to break into new markets and scale standardized (or at least similar) offerings, adapting to local tastes and preferences where necessary.

Market drivers are also determined by customer behaviour. Online ordering and global distribution channels allow customers to acquire goods from anywhere in the world. This is far removed from our predecessors who only had a mile or two in which to procure their products. As we will see in this book, the more customer behaviour develops in this direction and global customer needs converge, the more important global marketing becomes.

Competitive drivers

Globalization presents a huge opportunity for businesses to operate across borders. Certain industries, such as the automotive industry (which has high levels of imports and exports), are particularly ripe for global expansion. Businesses operating in these industries no longer compete for market share in national or even continental boundaries, but on a global scale. If one organization is taking opportunities presented by globalization, a similar organization would likely need to do the same to compete at the same level.

Cost drivers

Globalization causes shifts in the cost of activities. From a business point of view, as competition intensifies, businesses continuously look for ways to cut costs. This might be the cost of trade but also the cost of production. Companies can choose to source parts in less expensive countries or manufacture products where labour is cheaper (we will explore this concept further throughout this book and particularly in Chapter 10).

From a consumer point of view, globalization has reduced the cost of products and activities in daily life. For example, as we've seen, it's now possible to fly around the world for relatively little expense.

Government drivers

Government policies can influence how a nation operates and is viewed by the global community. Trade agreements can encourage buying and selling between certain countries. Privatization (when government-owned businesses are sold to private-sector bodies) can encourage **foreign direct investment (FDI)** and accelerate globalization. Subsidies can be set up which also encourage FDI. The deregulation of certain industries such as the financial industry can make it easier for transactions to take place around the world.

Technological drivers

While we don't consider technological advancements in a great deal of depth in this book, they have undeniably facilitated globalization and the world as we know it today. Technological advances are at the root of the Shrinking World phenomenon. While such things as digitization, big data and AI haven't determined why and how globalization has developed, they have provided the tools to help us reach where we are today.

For example, technology is at the root of Amazon's success. Once a small online bookstore operating out of a garage, the company has been transformed through technology into the massive conglomerate we know today. The organization has consistently pioneered new technologies, such as warehouse robots, to streamline operations. Amazon was also one of the first businesses to use artificial intelligence and machine learning to drive customer recommendations using their global sales data. It's remarkable how companies like Amazon can now process, store, use and transmit data on a global scale.

ACTIVITY

Further drivers of globalization

We've just learnt about five key drivers of globalization. Can you think of any others?

The rise of marketing

We'll now consider the rise of marketing and how it relates to globalization. The concept of marketing, as we know it today, has developed slowly over time. Some argue that it started at the time of the Industrial Revolution, which began in Britain in the 18th century and spread to other parts of the world such as the United States and Western Europe in the 19th century. This period of huge change affected almost every aspect of everyday life, and the ability to mass-produce goods saw the beginnings of a consumer marketplace.

As the business arena became increasingly competitive in the early 20th century, the need for marketing grew. Businesses had to find ways to persuade consumers to buy from them instead of somebody else. Ford's Model T, introduced in 1908 (History.com, 2024), is an interesting example of a business model and marketing strategy at that time. The car was mass-produced to a standard specification that made it affordable for the average American family. All other available automobiles were custom-made and expensive, far beyond the means of most Americans.

Henry Ford dreamt of launching an affordable and durable car that was easy for the average person to operate. However, the company did not achieve this by giving the customer a choice about the type of Model T they bought. For some time, every Model T produced was exactly the same. Henry Ford is famously purported to have said: 'Any customer can have a car painted any colour that he wants, so long as it is black.'

Between 1914 and 1925, Ford prioritized production efficiency and standardization (and therefore affordability) over giving their customers a choice. The slogan in a 1909 sales brochure read 'Watch the Ford Go By, High Priced Quality in a Low Priced Car' (Blue Ocean Strategy, 2024). Interestingly, according to Ford's corporate website, this policy was only in place between 1914 and 1925. The car was available in various colours including blue, red, grey and green before and after this time (Ford, 2024).

Ford's Model T is an early example of successful standardization. We return to the concept of standardization throughout this book and particularly in Chapter 3.

Earlier in the chapter we discussed how many businesses we are familiar with today, such as Walmart, Best Buy, Ralph Lauren, Calvin Klein and The North Face, came about in the 1960s. During this period, competition intensified in many industries. People had a far greater choice about where to buy their products, and businesses needed to be persuasive to acquire and retain customers. The importance of marketing therefore began to build. Businesses started to set up marketing departments. There was an increasing amount of attention on marketing strategy, which was perhaps driven in part by the rise of management education in America.

Harvard Business School introduced the world's first MBA programme in 1908, but it was in the 1960s that American business schools started to gain influence and to train managers at scale (Harvard Business School, 2008). With this, the idea that marketing was central to business success began to take hold, and ideas about how to 'do' marketing began to evolve. These included the marketing mix, or the 4Ps of marketing: product, price, place and promotion (refer back to Chapter 1 for a detailed explanation of this concept). This marked the beginning of more customer-centric marketing, with marketers realizing the importance of considering their customers' wants and needs.

The 1990s is often considered the 'decade of marketing', as developments during that time represented a fundamental shift in marketing's role and function. For example, companies began to recognize the importance of building a brand and to take advantage of the opportunities presented by the internet. They also began to truly focus on understanding their customers' needs and producing offerings to fulfil them. Increasing amounts of time and resources were spent discovering what people wanted and delivering it. Marketing campaigns began to demonstrate the extent to which companies understood and wanted to cater for their customers' desires, concerns and requirements. Rather than focusing on shaping people's views to fit what they could produce (as in Ford's 'any colour so long as it's black' school of thought), companies increasingly shaped their offerings to fit what their customers wanted.

This customer-centric focus also began to be adopted elsewhere, outside the domain of the business–customer relationship. Marketing logic began to be applied to public sector services and politics. Stakeholders such as government officials, doctors and teachers began to think more carefully about what people wanted. A shift started to emerge. Services became less about what stakeholders *thought* was needed, and more about what people *actually* wanted and needed. Marketing effectively legitimized a focus on the consumer and customer service. The government began to think more about citizen needs and desires. Doctors began to think about their patients as consumers of a service that they should be able to influence and teachers also applied the logic to students. For the consumers of these services, this was a seductive idea. They were no longer simply dished out offerings, but found that they had the freedom and power to choose what they wanted.

This trend has continued until the present day. It is generally accepted that keeping customer needs at the forefront of decision making will lead to higher profits. In 2016, Coca-Cola launched a global marketing campaign in response to growing consumer concerns about the high sugar content in many carbonated drinks (The Coca-Cola Company, 2016). The boxed case study explains how the organization went about it.

ACTIVITY

Coca-Cola launches a global marketing campaign to respond to customer health concerns

In 2016, Coca-Cola launched its first global marketing strategy for over a decade. Sales of fizzy, sugary drinks were in decline and the company realized it needed to do something to respond to consumer health concerns surrounding excessive sugar consumption.

At that time, Coca-Cola's products included Coca-Cola, Diet Coca-Cola, Coca-Cola Zero and Coca-Cola Life (a reduced-calorie version of Coca-Cola discontinued in all markets by 2020). Until 2016, these had been marketed as separate products – sub-brands under the main brand – until the 'one brand' strategy united them under a single strapline: 'Taste the Feeling'.

The message was clear. No matter what your preferences were, your lifestyle or diet, drinking any Coca-Cola variant made the moment special. The campaign used emotion as a connecting force, with adverts depicting moments designed to 'connect with consumers around the world'. In the words of Marcos de Quinto, The Coca-Cola Company's former Chief Marketing Officer, the investment showed 'how everyone can enjoy the specialness of an ice-cold Coca-Cola, with or without calories, with or without sugar' (The Coca-Cola Company, 2016). The sugar content didn't matter anywhere near as much as Coca-Cola's central role in the stories being told.

This is a clear example of a company taking on board what consumers want and adapting (or at least giving the perception of adapting) to meet their needs.

Questions:

- Why would Coca-Cola, as a soft drinks brand, decide to tackle customer concerns related to health?

- Given that a number of Coca-Cola's product lines have been discontinued since the campaign, how successful was the 'Taste the Feeling' campaign?

- Is it important for organizations to actually meet the needs of their customers and consumers, or is the perception of adapting in order to meet these needs enough? Explain the reasons behind your answer.

Marketing and the global arena

When you hear the brand name Nike, what's the first thing that springs to mind? There's a good chance you'd immediately visualize the Nike swoosh. Similarly, if you heard the name McDonald's you might think of its golden arches. Apple, you might think of its apple, and Amazon, you might think of its smile. Some Western logos have become so well-known that the shape of their logo is all that is needed in their advertising – the brand name is not necessary. Think also of Facebook, Volkswagen or X (formerly known as Twitter). Most of us can probably bring these logos to mind fairly easily.

But what if I said Huawei, Inca Kola or Tencent QQ? Are they as familiar to you? And if you have heard of them, can you visualize their logos? Inca Kola is a Peruvian golden cola which is not widely sold outside Peru (although it is sold in parts of South America, North America and Europe). It is unfamiliar to many people in the West. Huawei and Tencent QQ are both Chinese brands. Tencent QQ, also little-known in the West, is an instant messaging software service.

Huawei, on the other hand, while not as ubiquitous as the likes of Facebook and McDonald's, is perhaps China's most well-known brand in the West. It is one of the world's biggest and most innovative telecommunications companies. It makes smart-phones as well as the networks that power the internet and mobile phones. In 2014, it became the first Chinese brand to break into Interbrand's top 100 best global brands (Yueh, 2014). Due to its success, you might be able to recall the brand's logo, but is it as familiar as McDonald's' or Apple's?

As a general rule, Western brands are far more well-known and sought-after around the world than brands which originate in the rest of the world. Brands tend to spread from the West to elsewhere, not the other way around. China is one of the most populated countries in the world. It has high levels of manufacturing and consumption, but it is not well-known for its brands. In fact, products are frequently manufactured in China under Western brand names. The Chinese market is the biggest buyer of luxury goods in the world. Western jewellery brands such as Chanel, Bulgari and Van Cleef & Arpels launch big campaigns in China as they look to appeal to Chinese customers to drive sales (Li, 2022).

But Chinese companies are starting to compete by creating their own luxury brands for customers in their home market and elsewhere. These designs offer something new and unique and are particularly favoured by younger clientele who 'do not want to wear what their parents wear' (Abrams, 2019). Could this spell the beginning of a shift in Chinese consumer jewellery preferences? Could it be possible that Western brands will face increasing competition from their Chinese counterparts?

Implications of marketing in a global world

We'll end this chapter by drawing together some of the main implications of marketing in a global world, concluding with a case study which could suggest a potential downside of globalization – the loss of local culture in Japan. Much of what we look at below is covered in greater depth in the remaining chapters of this book. This is intended as a broad introduction to the implications of globalized marketing; to get you thinking before we delve into these topics in greater depth.

We've touched on the fact that the benefits and disadvantages of globalization are often not as straightforward as they seem. While many of the things we have discussed in this chapter point towards the success of globalization, there are potential downsides. Economic growth and development come with a price.

Many of the implications are multilayered and can be viewed from different perspectives. For example, an issue may have obvious benefits and less obvious disadvantages, but then further benefits related to those disadvantages. Remember that globalization is an unevenly spread force. It's easy to view globalization as nothing more than the spread of Westernization and capitalism. In some locations, such as developing countries, we see little in terms of the benefits from globalization, whereas Western countries see the benefits daily. As you read, try to develop your own ideas to consider where you sit on the continuum of benefits and disadvantages of globalization and marketing.

Global consumerism and increased production

As we've covered, the global marketplace means that, as consumers, we can get what we want, when we want it, provided we have the financial means. As we will go on to consider further in Chapter 3, this desire for material possessions is known as global consumerism. Global marketing can be seen to promote global consumerism and therefore the increased production of goods.

The fact that we can get what we want when we want it has its obvious benefits, but there are also significant downsides. As we've discussed, many Western businesses have outsourced the production of goods to countries like China, where it can be done at a fraction of the cost. Those producing our goods can often work in terrible conditions on low wages and can't afford to buy them themselves. A lack of unionization makes it difficult for workers to fight for change. Outsourcing production can also harm the business's home country, as jobs are lost and the local economy suffers. Investment from a global organization can be attractive for the governments of nations such as China. However, there is often little consideration from those governments of the benefits and limitations of such organizations for local working people.

Global markets have also resulted in a 24/7 mentality. Greater connectivity with different parts of the world can mean that, as consumers, we never switch off. While this can have its obvious benefits in terms of greater flexibility, research increasingly highlights the negative effects on our mental health of never allowing ourselves to disconnect. The same is true for workers. As globalization predominantly signifies a spread of Westernization, workers on the other side of the globe can find themselves working through the night to fall in line with Western time zones.

Increasing production also comes with significant environmental and sustainability challenges. The pervasive nature of global consumerism and the fact that we all have an insatiable desire to consume goods have a significant environmental impact. We discussed global warming and biodiversity challenges earlier in the chapter. The 12th global Sustainable Development Goal is 'Ensure sustainable consumption and production patterns'. The United Nations recognizes that '[w]orldwide consumption and production – a driving force of the global economy – rest on the use of the natural environment and resources in a way that continues to have destructive impacts on the planet' (UNRIC, 2024). The world has finite resources, and the companies that produce our goods must find ways to do more with less. They must minimize their use of raw materials and employ careful strategies to manage waste.

The world of fast fashion, for instance, has a particularly concerning business model. In 2024, authorities in South Korea found high levels of toxic chemicals in Shein clothing (Le Monde, 2024). Not only does this present a health concern for those producing and wearing the clothes, but the environment suffers too as these pollutants end up in our water supplies.

It's very easy to argue that globalization has harmed our environment. Increasing global trade and migration have led to increased energy consumption, which is problematic as so much of the world's energy production is still reliant on fossil fuels. However, as we learnt earlier in the chapter, these challenges have also served to unite the world and increase our understanding of the problems, as well as how to address them.

Challenges to individualism

As consumers, we construct our identity through the things that we buy. We use products and brands to create a sense of self and communicate and showcase this sense to others. Our ability to buy our goods from all over the globe means that we have a huge pool of products and brands to draw from as we craft the identity that we wish to project. We could therefore argue that globalization enables individualism by giving us access to a greater range of products than if we could only buy from within national or continental boundaries.

However, are we as empowered as we think? We can only construct our identities from the products that marketers from around the globe give us access to. Brands market the products that they want us to buy. So, does that mean that the brands are in control, and not us as consumers? Perhaps. But then you could twist the argument again, and say that no two people will use a brand to construct an identity in exactly the same way. There will be differences, even if they are subtle, allowing individualism to still shine through.

The point about individualism is also interesting to consider in relation to consumerism and choice. Most of us would agree that having an element of choice about what we buy is a good thing. We've considered how globalization has given consumers increasing choices. If we want to buy a pair of shoes, we can hop online and buy them from anywhere in the world. In the 18th century, people would have gone to the local shoemaker and had a very limited number of shoes to choose from. But at what point does too much choice become problematic and overwhelming? Do we benefit from having 500 pairs of shoes to choose from instead of two? Did Henry Ford do his customers a favour by telling them they could only have their Model T in black?

This argument can take another turn when we consider the role that algorithms and search engines play in our choices when we shop online. In just the same way that we only have access to the products that global marketers make available, **recommendation algorithms** serve us up what they think we're going to like. Is this true choice, or just an illusion of choice?

Loss of the local

The loss of the local is the final implication we will consider, and we will do so mainly through a case study illustrating the loss of local culture in Japan. The loss of the local can be considered from a variety of different perspectives. First, there's the degradation of local environments as local traders lose out to the likes of global online retailers such as Amazon. The effects of consumers shifting their shopping habits online can be seen in high streets all over the world. As consumers become increasingly dependent on the convenience and cost-effectiveness of online shopping, local shops struggle to survive.

Local tourism industries can also lose out. It's so easy and relatively inexpensive to travel abroad that people often don't explore their local area, therefore not contributing to the local economy in this way.

We might also argue that globalization has contributed to a breakdown of local relationships. While we are more connected than ever, our reliance on technology can have an impact on our ability and willingness to form true human connections with those geographically close to us. It's now so easy to send a WhatsApp or connect via a video call that we can stay in touch with people without leaving the house.

REAL-WORLD EXAMPLE   KFC in Japan

The American fast-food restaurant KFC specializes in fried chicken. It was founded in the US in the 1950s by Colonel Sanders (KFC, 2024), whose image is still used in the company's marketing today. The restaurant sells burgers and buckets of chicken that can be shared between family or friends.

It might surprise you to learn that KFC is big in Japan, especially at Christmas, when an estimated 3.6 million families choose to celebrate this Western, imported holiday with Western fast food – a bucket of Kentucky Fried Chicken (Barton, 2016). The queues start to form on 23 December and don't die down until the festive period is over.

In 1970, the first KFC opened in Japan in Nagoya. It reflected the huge interest in Western culture, fashion and food in Japan at the time. CNN Travel quotes Ted Bestor, a professor of social anthropology at Harvard University who was living in Tokyo at the time. Bestor recalls seeing globalization in action, with 'many foreign franchises popping up, such as Baskin-Robbins, Mister Donut and The Original Pancake House' (Springer, 2022). By 1981, the chain had opened 324 stores. According to Bestor, 'Suddenly, Kentucky Fried Chicken was everywhere.'

In 1974, four years after the first store opened, KFC launched a national 'Kentucky for Christmas' marketing campaign. The story goes that a group of tourists made their way to KFC on Christmas Day after an unsuccessful hunt for roast turkey. They visited the original store in Nagoya, where the store manager, Takeshi Okawara, heard what had led them there. Shortly afterwards, Okawara was inspired to start marketing a 'party barrel' to be sold at Christmas, marketing fried chicken as a traditional American Christmas food. It took off fast.

It is perhaps surprising that Christmas is recognized at all in Japan. The predominant religions are Shintoism and Buddhism and approximately only 1 per cent of the country identifies as Christian (Statista, 2024c). Christmas is not celebrated as a religious festival on a national scale. It is very much 'business as usual' throughout the Western festive period. According to Joonas Rokka, Associate Professor of Marketing at Emlyon Business School, 'It filled a void… There was no tradition of Christmas in Japan, and so KFC came in and said, this is what you should do on Christmas' (Barton, 2016). From then on it became a popular secular tradition and an extremely lucrative business strategy for KFC, reportedly pulling in 6.9 billion yen (roughly US$63 million) from 20 to 25 December in 2018 (Springer, 2022).

Even though this could be seen as the West infiltrating and dominating Japanese culture, you can also argue that the Japanese have very much interpreted this Western brand and tradition in their own unique way. It is the only place in the world where people will queue for hours on Christmas Day to get a bucket of fried chicken. As Bestor notes in the CNN Travel article, part of KFC's success in Japan could be due to how it aligns with Japanese cultural norms. According to Bestor, it's similar to a traditional Japanese chicken dish called karaage: 'Being able to share food is an important social practice in Japan. So a bucket of fried chicken both tastes familiar and fulfils this desire to eat together' (Springer, 2022).

Questions

- To what extent have the Japanese taken on a Western tradition, or have they created their own? Explain your answer.

- Would you queue to eat KFC on Christmas Day? Why, or why not? To what extent does your answer relate to the norms and traditions in your home country?

- Earlier in the chapter, we discussed the idea that globalization can change social relations, and in doing so, merge cultures in a way that erodes nations' identities. To what extent do you think Japan's adoption of KFC erodes the country's national identity?

CHAPTER SUMMARY

This chapter has explored globalization and marketing as separate concepts. We've considered what globalization means and the many different ways that the concept can be interpreted and defined. We've discussed its history, from before the 18th century up to the present day and considered the ways in which it has transformed society on a global scale. We've also considered other less popular perspectives of globalization including whether or not it really exists.

We've also discussed the concept of the Shrinking World (Dicken, 2015), which explains how advancements in technology and transport make the world feel like it's getting smaller. The world seems a much more manageable place to us today than it would have in the 18th century.

We ended the section on globalization with consideration of five key drivers: market, competitive, cost, government and technological.

In the second half of the chapter, we considered the rise of marketing and how it relates to globalization. We looked at how the marketing discipline has transformed from one that focused on persuading people to buy standardized offerings to one that, today, asks customers what they want and then caters to those needs.

We have also tackled the issue of Westernization, and the way that Western brands have infiltrated the rest of the world alongside some of the many implications of global markets and marketing.

In the next chapter, we delve a little deeper into the theory of marketing and globalization. In particular, we explore the concepts of global consumerism, standardization and something we have not yet encountered: glocalization.

CHAPTER REVIEW QUESTIONS

- How does globalization impact your daily life and activities? Illustrate your answer with examples.

- Do you view yourself as belonging to one nation, or do you view yourself as a citizen of the world? Explain the reasons behind your answer.

- To what extent would you agree that globalization began in the 1500s? Explain your thinking.

- Can you find any examples of global brands (aside from those mentioned in the chapter) which were launched before 1900? If so, to what extent is the success or failure of the brands that you have identified due to the so-called advances of globalization?

- What are the benefits and limitations of trade taking place 24/7? Consider the viewpoints of a variety of stakeholders in constructing your answer.

- To what extent has globalization heightened environmental awareness? Include specific examples in your answer.

- Dicken (2015) discusses the concept of the Shrinking World. What emergent technologies and other innovations do you think might make the world seem even smaller in the future?

- To what extent do you consider yourself to be a customer or consumer of: your local healthcare provider / your country's government / your university? Why?

- To what extent do you agree that Chinese luxury brands will begin (or have already begun) to permeate the Western market in the future?

KEY TERMS

Foreign direct investment (FDI): An FDI is an investment made by a government or organization into a foreign business or industry. It is fundamental to globalization and allows for the transfer of assets across economies.

Recommendation algorithms: An artificial intelligence algorithm that uses consumer data to make suggestions for future purchasing. These recommendations can be based on numerous data, such as past purchases, search history or demographics.

Time–space compression: Time–space compression is a concept which explains why and how advancements in transportation and communication can make the world feel as though it is getting smaller, despite the physical distance between places remaining the same.

References

Abrams, M (2019) China starts growing its own high jewelry designers, *New York Times*, www.nytimes.com/2019/03/22/fashion/jewelry-feng-ji-china.html (archived at https://perma.cc/8Y4N-RNKC)

Barton, E (2016) How a fast-food marketing campaign turned into a widespread yuletide tradition for millions, BBC, www.bbc.com/worklife/article/20161216-why-japan-celebrates-christmas-with-kfc (archived at https://perma.cc/T3PT-WXXD)

Bebar, J (1999) Wall St.'s record century, CNN Money, www.money.cnn.com/1999/12/31/markets/markets_newyork/ (archived at https://perma.cc/RQV2-XPJS)

Benyon, J and Dunkerley, D (2000) *Globalization: The reader* (1st ed), Routledge

Blue Ocean Strategy (2024) The Ford Model T, www.blueoceanstrategy.com/blue-ocean-strategy-examples/the-ford-model-t/ (archived at https://perma.cc/8XFJ-Y7QC)

Bray, R (2010) Vladimir Raitz obituary, *The Guardian*, www.theguardian.com/business/2010/sep/09/vladimir-raitz-obituary (archived at https://perma.cc/5ANE-L4TX)

Britannica (2024a) Telegraph, www.britannica.com/technology/telegraph (archived at https://perma.cc/A6GA-V6SZ)

Britannica (2024b) Athens 1896 Olympic Games, www.britannica.com/event/Athens-1896-Olympic-Games (archived at https://perma.cc/4HG6-VQG6)

Britannica (2024c) American Express Company, www.britannica.com/money/American-Express-Company (archived at https://perma.cc/PB53-NWPX)

Britannica (2024d) Concorde, www.britannica.com/technology/Concorde (archived at https://perma.cc/W35S-5JFM)

British Airways (nd) Explore our past, www.britishairways.com/content/information/about-ba/history-and-heritage/explore-our-past (archived at https://perma.cc/FWR4-9CG6)

CERN (2024) A short history of the web, home.cern/science/computing/birth-web/short-history-web (archived at https://perma.cc/78ED-TW5G)

Daniels, J D, Radebaugh, L H and Sullivan, D P (2015) *International Business: Environments and operations* (15th ed), Pearson

Dicken, P (2015) *Global Shift: Mapping the changing contours of the world economy* (7th ed), Guilford Press

Ford (2024) The Model T, corporate.ford.com/articles/history/the-model-t.html (archived at https://perma.cc/K2W7-DB5W)

Harvard Business School (2008) Harvard Business School sets out centennial activities, www.hbs.edu/news/releases/Pages/hbscentennial.aspx (archived at https://perma.cc/Y9XZ-HLFN)

Hirst, P (2000) The myth of globalization, in M Vellinga (2002) *The Dialectics of Globalization* (1st ed), Routledge

History.com (2024) Ford Motor Company unveils the Model T, history.com/this-day-in-history/ford-motor-company-unveils-the-model-t (archived at https://perma.cc/ST6K-G2G6)

KFC (2024) The KFC Colonel Sanders story, www.kfc.co.uk/colonels-story# (archived at https://perma.cc/5K2Q-AB4Y)

Latif, M I (2010) Globalization: Myth or reality? *Pakistan Horizon*, 63 (4), 33–49

Le Monde (2024) Shein and Temu products found to contain high levels of toxic chemicals, www.lemonde.fr/en/international/article/2024/08/14/shein-and-temu-products-found-to-contain-high-levels-of-toxic-chemicals_6715032_4.html (archived at https://perma.cc/D2M5-P5ZB)

Li, M (2022) Luxury brands look to China to supercharge fine jewellery, *Vogue Business*, www.voguebusiness.com/fashion/luxury-brands-look-to-china-to-supercharge-fine-jewellery (archived at https://perma.cc/7H99-RZ2V)

Lu, A (2023) First-ever mobile phone call made 50 years ago today, Vodafone, www.vodafone.co.uk/newscentre/news/first-ever-mobile-phone-call-made-50-years-ago-today/ (archived at https://perma.cc/D6VD-GQ5C)

NASA (2024) Model, Communications Satellite, Syncom A.M. Radio, airandspace.si.edu/collection-objects/model-communications-satellite-syncom-am-radio/nasm_A19750406000 (archived at https://perma.cc/X3VG-ZTAB)

Nescafé (2024) The history of coffee, www.nescafe.com/in/understanding-coffee/coffee-history (archived at https://perma.cc/4C52-4RC5)

Royal Museum Greenwich (2024) Ferdinand Magellan, www.rmg.co.uk/stories/topics/ferdinand-magellan (archived at https://perma.cc/YMU6-B6WF)

Springer, K (2022) How KFC became a Christmas tradition in Japan, CNN Travel, edition.cnn.com/travel/article/kfc-christmas-tradition-japan/index.html (archived at https://perma.cc/77S2-QP5X)

Stalzer, J (2019) Mastercard introduces the first taste of Priceless, Mastercard, www.mastercard.com/news/press/2019/september/mastercard-introduces-the-first-taste-of-priceless/ (archived at https://perma.cc/DB6P-K5EU)

Statista (2024a) Forecast number of mobile devices worldwide from 2020 to 2025 (in billions), www.statista.com/statistics/245501/multiple-mobile-device-ownership-worldwide/ (archived at https://perma.cc/C7WS-WRNL)

Statista (2024b) Number and share of merchants who use American Express as a payment solution on their website across various countries and territories in the world as of February 28, 2024, www.statista.com/statistics/1340265/american-express-use-among-merchants-in-the-world/ (archived at https://perma.cc/P9Z9-YGTD)

Statista (2024c) Japan: Religious affiliations in 2021, www.statista.com/statistics/237609/religions-in-japan/ (archived at https://perma.cc/SP83-LFAS)

Steger, M B (2003) *Globalization: A very short introduction*, Oxford University Press

The Coca-Cola Company (2016) Coca-Cola announces 'One Brand' global marketing approach, www.coca-colacompany.com/media-center/coca-cola-announces-one-brand-campaign (archived at https://perma.cc/3V7H-PBRR)

The Coca-Cola Company (2024) How did Coca-Cola grow as an international business? www.coca-colacompany.com/about-us/faq/how-did-coca-cola-grow-internationally (archived at https://perma.cc/8ZCM-WGE7)

UN (2024) International day for biological diversity, 22 May, www.un.org/en/observances/biological-diversity-day (archived at https://perma.cc/RVT4-PNQP)

UNEP (2021) Rebuilding the ozone layer: How the world came together for the ultimate repair job, www.unep.org/news-and-stories/story/rebuilding-ozone-layer-how-world-came-together-ultimate-repair-job (archived at https://perma.cc/GYZ3-LG5P)

UNRIC (2024) Goal 12: Ensure sustainable consumption and production patterns, unric.org/en/sdg-12/# (archived at https://perma.cc/NUB4-65SL)

World Bank Group (2024) Fixed telephone subscriptions (per 100 people), https://databank.worldbank.org/source/world-development-indicators/Series/IT.MLT.MAIN.P2 (archived at https://perma.cc/AU27-8L2C)

Yueh, L (2014) Can Huawei become China's first global brand? BBC, www.bbc.co.uk/news/business-29628044 (archived at https://perma.cc/46FZ-Q3YN)

3 | Theory and practice in the global marketplace

LEARNING OBJECTIVES

By the end of this chapter, you should be able to:

- describe different ways that marketing can respond to globalization
- explain different reasons for the rise in global consumerism
- describe the advantages and disadvantages of taking a standardized approach to marketing products on a global scale
- understand the local businesses' advantage over global businesses when developing and marketing offerings to local consumers
- articulate the importance of understanding cultural differences when marketing products to global audiences
- describe the benefits of glocalization as an alternative to standardization

Introduction

In this chapter, we build on the knowledge gained in Chapter 2 about marketing and globalization. In Chapter 2 we learnt that the spread of globalization changed the way that we think, relate to other people and consume on many different levels. This chapter considers what this means for marketing by examining two key theories: standardization and glocalization.

In Chapter 2 we learnt that globalization has given way to global consumerism, a phenomenon that can be used to explain our insatiable desire to buy more and more things. We begin Chapter 3 with a more in-depth exploration of this concept and how it can be defined and understood. Is it enough to conceptualize it purely in terms of people's desire to increase their material possessions, or is this too limiting a view? Are there other (perhaps more positive) reasons for the rise in global consumerism, such as people's perception of it as a hobby or as a fun way to pass the time?

Next, we move on to Theodore Levitt's 1983 theory of standardization, developed in response to his assertion that world markets are becoming increasingly homogenized. In basic terms, standardization means selling the same offering in many different target markets, and often to consumers worldwide. We look at examples of this in practice, including a case study of Disney's global expansion of its theme parks, and consider the benefits and disadvantages of the approach.

We also look at the advantages of being local and how this can translate into a deep understanding of consumer needs. We consider the role of cultural differences in defining consumer needs and preferences and question whether this dictates a need to move away from standardization.

We end the chapter with a discussion of a concept called 'glocalization', where companies think globally and act locally. By using this approach, companies can benefit from the positive aspects of standardization while adapting to local needs and preferences. To do this, we look particularly at a case study of Walmart's expansion into the Chinese market.

Global consumerism

As we already know, global consumerism relates to our seemingly never-ending desire to have more and more things. In 1996, Ger and Belk defined global consumerism as 'a widespread and unquenchable desire for material possessions'. To recap, consumerism and globalization are often considered together as related concepts. They promote production and consumption on a global scale and give rise to many implications of global marketing that we discussed in Chapter 2.

You might be able to relate to Ger and Belk's definition. Our inclination to consume and keep consuming means that most of us feel like we have too much stuff. Commentators have been saying for years that it's getting out of hand, and many people are experimenting with ways to cut down. For example, one mother in the UK didn't buy anything for a year and saved £25,000 (Holland, 2020). As we saw in Chapter 2, global consumerism has many downsides, both for the environment and for those who produce the endless products we want to buy.

There might be other varied reasons for the rise in global consumerism, aside from Ger and Belk's definition. We might, for example, choose to see it as a legitimate and valued activity. People like to shop, not just because they want things, but because they enjoy the experience. Before online shopping was so widespread, window shopping was a frequent and valid pastime. Many of us engage in forms of 'window shopping' online. We like to browse what is on offer and, sometimes, we buy what we see. In this way, consumerism can be viewed as a sort of hobby or pastime, and something to be enjoyed. While you could argue that this is still an addiction of sorts, it remains that consumers are not necessarily driven solely by an insatiable desire to acquire new things, but by a desire to pass their time in a way that makes them feel happy.

We might also decide to view the rise in consumerism as a means to reach a particular status. Owning certain possessions or sets of possessions can make people feel like they belong to a certain group, or have reached a social position that they aspire to inhabit. This might mean owning a certain television, smartphone or car. Advertising's job is to persuade consumers that they will feel, look or be a certain way if they buy a particular product. For this reason, advertising and product packaging often portray people in certain situations that businesses hope will tap into consumers' deep desires. According to this idea, people consume in order to reach an ideal portrayed by marketers. This links to our discussion in Chapter 2 that global marketing allows consumers to construct an identity based on the things that they buy, albeit that identity is limited by the products that marketers give us access to.

We might also suggest that a further reason for the increasing emphasis on global consumerism can be seen in the rise of global consumer culture, which we consider in detail in Chapter 5. Global consumer culture positions purchasing products as a cultural practice. Ultimately, this suggests that people all over the world should have the same opportunity to purchase the same goods. However, while we could debate the ethics of such desires themselves, our focus here is on how organizations can attempt to keep up with consumer needs and demands in an increasingly globalized, and arguably Westernized, world market.

ACTIVITY

How do you view your own consumerism?

Can you relate to Ger and Belk's definition? Do you buy things because you have an insatiable desire to accumulate belongings? Or do you relate more to one of the alternative reasons for the growth of global consumerism?

Levitt's theory of standardization

We will now delve a little more into the theory of standardization, which we touched on in Chapter 2. To do this, we will focus on the ideas of Theodore Levitt, who is widely regarded as one of the founders of modern-day marketing and a key proponent of standardization theory. His ideas attempted to answer one way in which organizations could keep up with customer needs in a globalized marketplace.

In 1983, Levitt published his essay 'The globalization of markets' in the *Harvard Business Review*. In it, he put forward the idea of standardization as the future of global marketing, referring to Ford's Model T as an exemplar of the practice.

He posits that technology is 'a powerful force', driving the world together and encouraging people to become more alike. Applied to consumer wants and needs, technology could therefore be seen as creating a 'converging commonality' across world markets: 'Almost everyone everywhere wants all the things they have heard about, seen or experienced via the new technologies.'

This, Levitt argues, opens up new opportunities for global organizations looking to increase their profit margins. It allows them to take advantage of the 'emergence of global markets for standardized consumer products on a previously unimagined scale of magnitude' and produce higher-quality products at lower cost. Levitt distinguishes between multinational and global corporations, suggesting that while a multinational takes account of local needs and preferences, adjusting its practices and products for each country that it operates in 'at high relative costs', a global corporation sells 'the same things in the same way everywhere'.

According to Levitt, multinationals go wrong because they 'falsely presume that marketing means giving customers what they say they want rather than trying to understand exactly what they would like'. This results in products that are customized to local wants and needs but at a cost that is too high to allow the organization to be competitive on the global stage. Global organizations, on the other hand, respond to the new era of 'homogenized demand' and apply a standardized approach to what they sell and how they operate, therefore benefiting from huge **economies of scale**. This, in turn, enables them to drive down prices and increase sales, thereby upping their profit margins and 'decimating' their competitors.

Levitt's theory effectively suggests that organizations should attempt to operate as if the world is one large market. They should try to ignore superficial regional or national differences that may arise in the different markets that they enter across the globe. Elements of Levitt's theory are a far cry from the marketing practices we are familiar with today, as he confidently proclaims that successful global organizations 'will never assume that the customer is a king who knows his own wishes'.

Interestingly, Levitt's concept of standardization is particularly applicable to the product, but also holds relevance for other elements in the marketing mix: for example, Coca-Cola's global Taste the Feeling campaign discussed in Chapter 2.

Levitt suggests that cultural differences such as preferences, national tastes and standards are 'vestiges of the past' and not something that organizations need to concern themselves with. He further suggests that organizations should only deviate from standardization as a last resort, after exhausting all possibilities to stick to it. And if they do need to deviate, they should push to reinstate it.

Simply put, Levitt suggests that the use of standardization in the creation of organizational offerings can save the organization both time and money. On the other hand, adapting products to suit separate markets is much more costly. Remember that, while enormously influential at the time, this paper was published in 1983, before the 1990s and 'the decade of marketing' when more customer-centric practices took hold (see Chapter 2).

ACTIVITY

Is the world one homogenized market?

Take a moment to consider Levitt's view of the world as one homogenized market. Given what you learnt about customer-centric marketing in Chapter 2, what do you think are the downsides to this point of view?

(Dis)advantages of standardization

Levitt's views may appear somewhat dated to us now, but his influential essay marks a pivotal point in the evolution of modern-day marketing. Whatever you might think of Levitt's ideas of standardization, there are, of course, advantages and disadvantages to his approach for organizations that choose to apply it. We'll aim to summarize the main ones below.

Advantages of standardization

There are four main advantages of standardization to be aware of:

1 **Economies of scale:** As mentioned above, organizations that successfully use standardization as an approach can expect to gain economies of scale. This forms a primary part of Levitt's argument. Mass-producing exactly the same product is cheaper than designing diversified products to cater for specific customer needs. Sourcing and buying separate components for bespoke products is also relatively expensive. These economies of scale don't only apply to the product itself but to other elements of a business's operations, such as marketing communications or logistics. Think of the economies of scale Mastercard achieves through its Priceless campaign (see Chapter 2).

2 **Attractiveness to international customers:** As we discussed in Chapter 2, Westernized brands and products are in demand all over the globe. Cultures around the world are becoming increasingly Westernized. This might suggest that a standardized approach could be what global customers desire. Rather than

having Westernized products adapted to their local needs, some consumers might prefer the standard Western offering.

3 **Access to larger segments across the globe:** Organizations that use standardization as an approach might therefore have access to larger segments of consumers across the globe. These segments are increasingly viable due to the continued spread of Westernized culture.

4 **Higher-quality products:** Quality is another of Levitt's key arguments. Organizations that only develop one version of a particular product can spend more money on research and development than if they developed several versions of that product. Standardization also means that the product in development must be created to the highest standards of all the markets in which the organization intends to sell. An obvious example is product safety. While most legal frameworks across the world incorporate product safety regulations, the rigour of the frameworks varies. This means that consumers in countries with less rigorous standards benefit from a product produced to and tested against the highest standards. A greater number of customers will have access to a better-quality product. The functionality of such offerings is also likely to be improved, as the organization will have spent time and money to ensure that the standardized offering will work well for its intended purpose across every market in which it's sold.

Disadvantages of standardization

There are three main disadvantages of standardization:

1 **Local competitors are better placed to understand their customers:** There is a strong argument that local companies are often better suited to serving local areas because they can have a greater understanding of their consumers' wants and needs. We delve into this in more detail below. Not only can products fall wide of the mark, but promotional campaigns too. Language use is a common stumbling block as global companies often don't have sufficient insight into idiomatic expressions, colloquialisms and cultural nuances to promote their standardized products effectively in different markets. There have been enough mishaps for us to know that translating taglines and other marketing messages word for word without considering cultural nuances is not a reliable approach. For example, when KFC launched in China, it translated its well-known tagline 'Finger-lickin' good' directly into Chinese. It didn't work as intended, as the translation read 'Eat your fingers off'. When Pepsi entered the Chinese market in the 1960s a similar thing happened. Pepsi's slogan at the time was 'Come alive! You're in the Pepsi generation'. In Chinese, it read 'Pepsi brings your ancestors back from the grave' (Houston, 2022).

2 **Missing the target:** The kind of linguistic mistakes described in point 1 can be catastrophic to a global brand's reputation and credibility in local markets. They can also be incredibly costly to fix. But global organizations don't have to make such glaringly obvious howlers to get it wrong. There are many aspects of localization that, if not considered, can result in an organization missing the mark. An example is Disneyland's expansion into European and Chinese markets, which we discuss in detail later in the chapter. Disney missed the mark on a cultural level and paid the price. Another common example is failing to localize digital products or product websites by using incorrect date formats, currency or units of measurement. All these things can affect an organization's positioning in a local market. Small errors or a lack of consideration for cultural nuances can mean that organizations fail to appeal to all consumers they target.

3 **Over-standardization:** Above we touched upon the idea that the requirement for organizations to meet the highest market standards could be seen as an advantage of standardization. The flip side is when these standards are too rigid for a product to be sold in all markets. Take, for example, car dimensions. Many governments have regulations stipulating a maximum width for cars. For example, the maximum width for cars produced in the US might be greater than for cars produced in the EU. If a company wanted to produce a car that would work for all markets, it would need to do it to the maximum width. This might result in a wider car than a European customer would like. What may work well for one market might not work so well for another. Due to such reasoning we can say that, in actuality, 100 per cent standardization is a very rare thing.

ACTIVITY

Does standardization equate to better quality?

To what extent could a standardization strategy result in better-quality products for consumers? Give reasons for your answer.

The benefits of being local

We'll now dig a little deeper into the importance of adapting to local markets' different needs and cultural contexts. We'll look at how some of the theories we discussed above have been put into practice by various organizations, with varying degrees of success.

We'll return particularly to one of the main disadvantages of standardization listed above – failing to adapt to local differences sufficiently, missing the target and seeing sales and profits suffer. Catering to local differences can be understood as 'localization'. To understand the importance of local differences, we'll begin with a case study demonstrating some of the successes and failures of The Walt Disney Company's global expansion of its theme parks.

REAL-WORLD EXAMPLE   Getting it right and wrong: The Walt Disney Company's global expansion of its theme parks

---

Disneyland is often cited as an example of how organizations can miss the mark with local consumers. There are seven Disney theme parks across five countries. It all began in the US when the original Disneyland resort opened in California in 1955. In 1971, a much larger resort, the Walt Disney World Resort, opened in Florida (Disney Experiences, 2023).

Disney's ideas for global expansion were a long time in the making. The company planned for many years before any further parks became a reality. In 1983, the first Disney theme park outside America opened in Tokyo. It was a resounding success. According to Chen, the success was due to 'the high level of cultural identification with the US' and the fact that the park adopted a franchise model. A Japanese real estate company bought the rights to run the park, so operations aligned with local lifestyle and consumption habits (Chen, 2022).

Disney's luck began to change when it opened further theme parks. The company had planned to take Disney to the European market for some time. Both Spain and France were considered as possible locations and Paris was chosen, partly due to the transport links and proximity to the UK market. Euro Disneyland opened its doors in 1992 (Disney Experiences, 2023).

When the Paris location was first announced in a televised address, the CEO of The Walt Disney Company, Michael Eisner, said that the resort would 'be different in that it will not only take advantage of, but have respect for, the French culture' (Kasulke, 2024). The intent to align with a European demographic was there from the beginning and some adaptations were made. One was to design the park with the European climate in mind. Parisian winter can be cold and wet, and it often snows. It's very different from winter in Florida, or even California. For this reason, the park was designed with more indoor spaces and covered walkways than the US parks (Sylt, 2019). Another was to design Sleeping Beauty's castle in a more fantastical way than those in the US theme parks. It was thought that European visitors would be accustomed to seeing gothic castles dotted around the countryside (Offhand Disney, 2018).

However, when the park opened, it became clear that The Walt Disney Company had not delivered on their promise to respect French culture. Many nuances had been overlooked. Critics saw the park as the embodiment of cultural imperialism and felt it would 'encourage an unhealthy type of American consumerism in France' (Offhand Disney, 2018). Visitor numbers suffered. Only 50,000 people went through the doors in the first quarter – a far cry from the expected 500,000. According to Chen, 'huge cultural differences made the French feel disrespected', and visitors stayed away (Chen, 2022).

Michel Serres, a French philosopher, stated, 'It is not America that is invading us. It is we who adore it.' Euro Disney's chairman Robert Fitzpatrick responded to the criticism by saying, 'We didn't come in and say OK, we're going to put a beret and a baguette on Mickey Mouse. We are who we are' (Loveman and Schlesinger, 1993).

Euro Disney was at the point of bankruptcy when several important changes were made to adapt the park to local needs. These included:

- **Changing the name:** The park was renamed from Euro Disney to Disneyland Paris. This gave locals a greater sense of belonging and ownership over the park.

- **Changing the décor:** Much of the décor was redone to align more with French tastes. A notable example was changing the paint colour of many spaces from purple to alternatives that were not associated with the Catholic Church. Painting indoor spaces purple would have been seen as disrespectful by many (Kasulke, 2024).

- **Changing the restaurants and menus:** While Americans tend to like to eat casually, often while ambling along, the French prefer to take a proper break to eat their meals. They like to sit down and enjoy a relaxed lunch. The park therefore changed its operations and made more space in restaurant areas for visitors to sit down. It added more French cuisine to the menus. Perhaps most importantly of all, it added alcohol to the menu. Alcohol was banned in Disney's US parks, and initially it was banned in Paris, too. But for the many French diners, a meal is incomplete without a glass of wine. According to Chen, 'One of the most prominent points of the culture clash was the ban on alcohol in Disneyland restaurants.' So Disney reversed this ban.

- **Cut ticket prices:** Finally, Disney lowered ticket prices in 1995. Visitor numbers increased by 33 per cent and the park became profitable for the first time (Chen, 2022).

Interestingly, although The Walt Disney Company seemed to learn some lessons in Paris, it got it wrong again when it opened Hong Kong Disneyland in 2005 (Disney Experiences, 2023). According to Chen, the company adopted the same marketing strategy that had been so successful in Japan. But Japanese culture has far more in common with US culture than Hong Kong. Chen explains that this led to a consumer backlash against the park's 'crude copycat model'. Visitor numbers fell far short of the target and it was criticized for 'chaotic park operations, lack of respect for local legislation, exploitation of workers, and [for being] a crass supporter of Americanism' (Chen, 2022).

Put together, these three examples of globalization could illustrate that, while taking a standardized approach may work for organizations in some markets, it's dangerous to assume that a blanket approach will work everywhere. While Disney's standardized approach worked well in Tokyo, its attempts to replicate the business model in France and Hong Kong were less of a success.

Questions

- What adaptations did Disney make to its parks to suit the needs and wants of consumers in the various countries the organization entered?
- To what extent might we suggest that Disney's park expansion was a success? Explain your answer using examples.
- Would you suggest that Disney should move towards standardization or adaptation if they were to open a new park in another country?
- As the case study notes, Disney's efforts in France and Hong Kong were not deemed to be particularly successful. Are there any further adaptations that you might have suggested to encourage further connections with consumers in these locations?

Local success stories

It's possible to argue that Disney's lack of success in Paris and Hong Kong may be due to its status as a non-local organization in those markets. There are several benefits to being local, including having a deeper understanding of the micro preferences of the customers on your doorstep. A local organization's actions and operations can be closely tailored to consumer wants and needs.

Does this mean that true success can only belong to very local (and therefore small) businesses such as high street shops and farmers' markets selling offerings to customers in their immediate vicinity? It doesn't. There are numerous examples of larger organizations marketing successfully to 'local' cultures on a national level.

Take, for example, CavinKare Pvt Ltd, which is headquartered in the southern Indian state of Tamil Nadu. The company has consistently kept innovation and customer preferences at the heart of its strategy, allowing it to diversify its product offering from purely personal healthcare to fast-moving consumer goods. One of its most resounding success stories is the supply of Chik shampoo in sachets, which it sells to the Indian market. The market need in India for products in small sachets was first identified in the 1970s by Chinni Krishnan, an Indian entrepreneur. He had a farming background and understood the needs of low-income communities in the country. He noticed that these communities didn't buy personal care products such as Epsom salts and talcum powder as they were sold in large, unaffordable quantities. He therefore started to sell these products in small packs and sachets to cater directly to the needs of those on lower incomes. The idea was a huge success. His son, C K Ranganathan, ran with it, founding Chik India and launching a 'Chik' brand of shampoo named after his father. He later renamed the company CavinKare (Srinivasa and Hari, 2022).

The success of CavinKare Pvt Ltd means that it is seen as direct competition for the likes of global organizations such as Procter & Gamble and L'Oréal in India. There has been a continuing need for shampoo sold in small sachets in the market as it's continued to be an attractive option for those on lower incomes. It's also easy to store and results in minimal waste as consumers don't use more than they need to. As a result of this success, global competitors such as Dove, Pantene and Head & Shoulders also began to produce sachets of shampoo for sale to the Indian market.

A further local success can be seen with the company Tencent QQ, the free Chinese messaging service we discussed in Chapter 2. Tencent QQ launched in 1999 under the name of OICQ. By 2008, it had more than 100 million users in China and 80 per cent of the market (Coonan, 2008). This was despite direct competition from Microsoft, which launched MSN Messenger in the Chinese market in 2005. The company's success has continued, with monthly user numbers peaking at 899 million in 2016 (Statista, 2024a). According to Statista, the success of QQ 'was based on its user ID which had numbers and not alphabets. Most Chinese users found numbers easier to remember and share.'

The flow of information might be viewed as strictly controlled in China, so the service appeals directly to its customers by focusing on entertainment. It offers free chatrooms, games, virtual pets and ringtone downloads, along with the ability to use personalized avatars and purchase outfits for them using real money (Coonan, 2008). Tencent QQ has become so popular that the term 'QQ me' is now a verb. This is a perfect example of how a local company can win over a global behemoth such as Microsoft. The company's deep understanding of the Chinese market's desires and needs gave it a clear advantage over Microsoft's global dominance.

ACTIVITY

Local business success stories

Can you think of any further examples of local companies that could be used as evidence that ignoring cultural preferences because they are 'vestiges of the past' is a bad idea?

Patterns of consumption

Culture can be seen to play a large role in understanding consumption patterns and the purchasing decisions of consumers in different countries. Cultural indicators such as **patterns of consumption** are one way to understand differences in local and regional preferences. These statistics can give us insight into how culture is played out in consumer behaviour, or, in other words, what consumers in different countries or regions spend their money on.

Take, for example, cut flowers. Understanding statistics such as the number of stems sold per person, per year and per country will give us an indication of how popular cut flowers are in certain countries. To understand food preferences, we might look at the weight of certain foodstuffs sold per person per year and per country. This might tell us that seafood is popular in countries such as Japan, Spain and France but not so popular in countries with little to no coastline such as Germany or Austria. Looking at how much wine is consumed per person per year and breaking that down by country might demonstrate that wine is very popular in France (remember the Euro Disney wine ban disaster?) but not so popular in Japan. You could go further and break these statistics down by region, if you wanted to.

Let's now look at some actual statistics by considering the retail sales of Fairtrade International products in countries across the world. We touched on the sale of Fairtrade products in Chapter 2. Products with the Fairtrade seal of approval usually meet stringent social and environmental standards and, because of this, they can carry a higher price than standard products. Buying Fairtrade products is one way that Western consumers can attempt to ameliorate some of the negative effects of globalization, such as unfair working and pay conditions. Statista gives us estimated retail sales of Fairtrade International products in selected countries in 2017. Out of 17 countries, the United Kingdom spent by far the most, at €2,014 million. Germany and the United States also scored highly, spending €1,329 and €994 million respectively. Japan, Norway and Italy were the three countries with the lowest consumption of Fairtrade International products, with Japanese consumers spending €94 million (Statista, 2024b).

Such statistics can be useful indicators of culture as they help to suggest the preferences, likes and dislikes of consumers in different countries. They also suggest that the world might be less of a homogenized market than Levitt suggested back in 1983.

So far in this chapter, we've considered the benefits and downsides of standardization and looked at the advantages of organizations taking a more localized approach. We've also considered how cultural differences can be seen to affect purchasing decisions in different countries, which goes against Levitt's idea that cultural differences are ideals of the past. Bearing all of this in mind, it makes sense that organizations hoping to market their products on a global scale need to understand whether a standardized approach might work, or whether a more localized one is necessary. Questions need to be asked such as: 'Would our standardized offering be a good fit?' or 'Would a product in this market only succeed if supplied by an organization with in-depth local knowledge?'

Fortunately for organizations seeking to expand into global markets, there is a third option that combines the benefits of global standardization and localization strategies. Numerous global organizations have achieved success by applying the theory of 'glocalization'. We will go on to consider this now.

Glocalization

Glocalization represents a third way. A strategy adopted by many organizations, it is what it sounds like – an incorporation of local elements into global products and services.

Glocalization was popularized by Roland Robertson in 1995. According to Robertson, the term itself was coined by Japanese economists to describe global marketing strategies in Japan. These economists had modelled the idea on the Japanese agricultural principle of *dochakuka*, which refers to adapting farming techniques to local conditions. Robertson argues that global products or services have more chance of succeeding if they are altered to cater specifically to each local market or region in which they are introduced. He also emphasizes that glocalization does not necessarily need to occur in the offering itself. It can also be applied to other elements, such as marketing communications or in the locations from which consumers can purchase the product. Whichever element of the marketing mix glocalization is applied to, the aim is to gain interconnection and interaction between the global and the local. With glocalization, homogeneity and centralization appear alongside heterogeneity and decentralization.

In our case study earlier in the chapter, Disney reversed its Euro Disney crisis by applying principles of glocalization. The company also did this in Hong Kong after the disappointing opening there. It reduced prices, adapted to local visitors' customs, changed the décor and settings and adapted labour practices. It was a very similar story to what had happened in Paris and the park has since proved to be successful, with healthy attendance and revenue growth (Matusitz, 2011).

Glocalization strategies have helped numerous companies to drive global growth. Let's return to Mastercard's globalized Priceless campaign which we discussed in Chapter 2, where the strapline was the only necessary change from market to market. This is a very basic example of applying glocalization principles to marketing communications. The adverts were standardized, but the strapline was adapted as necessary for each market.

Apple successfully uses glocalization by adapting its innovative and globally recognized products and marketing campaigns to local needs and preferences. For example, it introduced more affordable models in India to cater to price-sensitive customers. The company has also partnered with local businesses in India and China to expand its customer base, distribution reach and payment options. It has also localized its products, marketing campaigns and customer support in both these regions, including providing a Hindi language version of its software for the Indian market (Accelingo, 2024).

There are countless examples of glocalization across numerous industries. Take the toy industry and Barbie. When the doll was first released in the 1960s, she was famous for her blonde hair and blue eyes. Her lack of diversity was something that the doll's maker, Mattel, faced increasing criticism for until it released a series of Barbie dolls to appeal to different local markets to suit their ethnicities.

McDonald's is often used as an example of a company that has achieved huge global expansion by successfully applying glocalization principles to its products and marketing strategies. Since its founding by the McDonald brothers in San Bernardino, California in 1940, McDonald's has opened restaurants all around the globe. At the beginning, the ambition was only to open 1,000 restaurants across the US, but in 1967 the first McDonald's restaurants outside the USA opened in Canada and Puerto Rico, and the country's global expansion continued from there (Goodall, 2021). According to Statista, McDonald's has 'retained annual growth in its restaurant count for almost two decades', and at the end of 2023 it had over 41,000 restaurants in about 120 different countries across the globe (Statista, 2024c).

McDonald's offers standardized products in many of its markets. You can buy a Big Mac, cheeseburger and hamburger in most countries (McDonald's, 2024). But McDonald's also moves away from standardization to adapt its products to suit local tastes and traditions when the market demands it. For example, customers can buy teriyaki or rice burgers in Japan, bratwurst in Germany or McSpaghetti in the Philippines. In India, the beef in a Big Mac is replaced with chicken in a Maharaja Mac to cater for the predominantly Hindu population. Vegetarian customers can choose a Masala Grilled Veggie Burger. Some McDonald's locations, particularly in Europe, serve beer (World Population Review, 2024). The company also introduces special menus for local holidays, such as Prosperity Burgers for Chinese New Year (Foodie, 2024).

(Dis)advantages of glocalization

The main advantages and disadvantages of glocalization are listed below. You might notice that many of the advantages build on the advantages of standardization that we considered earlier in the chapter, while at the same time cancelling out the main disadvantage of standardization – that local wants and needs are ignored. You might also notice that many of the disadvantages of glocalization are similar to those we discussed in Chapter 2 in relation to the disadvantages of globalization.

Advantages of glocalization

There are five main advantages of glocalization to be aware of:

1 Adapting products and marketing campaigns in line with local consumer wants and needs means that organizations can reach a bigger audience and increase

sales. At the same time, companies can exploit their economies of scale and large supply chains to minimize costs. Organizations therefore have a better chance of successfully expanding into new markets, gaining greater market share and higher profit margins.

2   Glocalization allows organizations to demonstrate respect for local cultures and build trust in markets with significant opportunities for growth. Although their motivations are primarily financial, this can help to enhance a brand's reputation in global markets if the business really demonstrates that it understands local needs, cultures and traditions and is willing to adapt as necessary. Getting it wrong can have very damaging consequences, as we saw in the Disneyland case study earlier in the chapter.

3   Businesses such as McDonald's, Disney or KFC can provide increased employment opportunities for local people, although efforts need to be made by the employing organization to understand local employment law and practices. When Euro Disney first opened, 3,000 workers left within one month due to its labour policies. Not only were staff required to use English as their first language (rather than French), but Disney enforced strict rules about how workers should dress, dictating such things as type of nail polish, earring length and mascara colour. Once Disney reversed these rules as part of their glocalization strategy, staff turnover was reduced (Chen, 2022).

4   Increased competition from global organizations offering quality products can encourage local businesses to up their game, improving the quality of their products and/or reducing their prices. This can result in a wider range of better-quality, lower-cost products for consumers.

5   Glocalization can be employed by organizations as a risk mitigation strategy. By diversifying their offerings and operations to adapt to local needs, organizations reduce their dependency on single markets. This makes them less vulnerable to economic fluctuations in those specific markets.

Disadvantages of glocalization

There are four main disadvantages (or challenges) associated with glocalization:

1   Companies looking to expand into foreign markets face a high chance of failure and rejection by the local community. As we have seen throughout this chapter, companies can get it wrong and make unintentional cultural faux pas. Local cultures can be unforgiving, especially towards Western brands. Disney showed that it's possible to recognize the need to adapt to local consumers, but still fail to do it sufficiently.

2   Implementing successful glocalization strategies takes significant financial and time investment. Understanding local requirements takes money and effort.

Organizations need to research diverse cultures and traditions at a deep level, to understand how different cultural nuances could affect their chances of success. They also need to research local laws and regulations, such as employment laws. Finding the right local employees and training them also have a high time and financial cost.

3 Organizations that have built a strong brand identity will want to maintain it in international markets while adapting to local preferences and needs. There can be tension between maintaining brand authenticity and identity and making necessary adaptations to suit local needs.

4 When international organizations succeed with glocalization, it can mean that local businesses suffer. While competition from global organizations can encourage local businesses to adapt and become more competitive, it can also wipe them out. We discussed many of the implications of the loss of the local in Chapter 2.

The different levels of glocalization

So far in this chapter, we have discussed localization and glocalization predominantly on a national level. We have considered how well Disney adapted to the French market, how CavinKare introduced products for Indian consumers, how Tencent QQ recognized the needs in China and how McDonald's adapts according to the needs of different nations. Some theorists suggest that this is not, in fact, true glocalization. They suggest that true glocalization can only be seen in changing offerings to suit very local areas, for example regions or cities, rather than changing products to suit whole countries. This can be thought of as glocalization on a sub-national level, rather than a national one.

One way to understand this would be to imagine if, in the UK, McDonald's sold oatcakes in Stoke-on-Trent and oysters in Kent. In this way, McDonald's would be aiming to appeal to the wants and needs of consumers in local towns and cities by considering specific cultural traditions and practices in those areas.

It is certainly true that attempting to understand culture and preferences on a national level is often not enough. A good illustration of this is Walmart's expansion into China, explained in the following case study.

REAL-WORLD EXAMPLE   Walmart in China

Walmart can be characterized as one of the world's largest retailers. In 2023, the company's retail revenue was $635 billion. It operates over 10,000 stores across 19 countries (Capital One Shopping, 2024). Walmart began in 1950 in Oklahoma City, US. It expanded throughout America and by 1988 was operating in 27 states. In 1991, the first Walmart outside the USA opened in Mexico City and, in 1995, the company successfully expanded into South America by opening stores in Argentina and Brazil (Walmart Digital Museum, 2024).

By 1996, the company felt ready to enter the Chinese market and introduced its first store in Shenzhen, a city in the Guangdong province in southeastern China (Walmart Digital Museum, 2024). Walmart has achieved significant success in the country since, with 365 stores in operation in 2023, albeit this number is down from a peak of 424 stores in 2018 (Statista, 2024d). Despite this reduction, China is still one of Walmart's largest overseas markets and 'one of its few foreign success stories' (Shoulberg, 2022).

As a general rule, Walmart represents fast service and cheap, high-quality products, all of which point towards standardization. The company typically attempts to refrain from glocalization, but realized it had to adapt its operations in China due to significant differences in Chinese consumer needs and preferences compared to typical US consumers. It therefore made several adaptations to its stores and product lines in China. You might find the following differences in Walmart stores in China compared to other countries such as the US:

- Shoppers expect meat and seafood to be fresh. They select live fish and seafood from tanks containing fish, frogs, eels and turtles. They use nets to catch what they want before handing it over to have it killed and cleaned. Meat aisles might contain rows of fresh pig heads or crocodiles.

- Consumers in China tend to shop frequently – sometimes daily – and only buy in small quantities. This may be because they have smaller apartments and refrigerators than people in many other countries, such as the US. Chinese consumers don't tend to buy in bulk, so stores tend to stock less merchandise than in other countries.

- Frequent shopping habits and China's high population mean that stores can get very crowded, with customers having to push through crowds to get where they want to go. This can give Walmart a very different feel in China to elsewhere in the world, particularly in the US.

- Rice is stored in giant, open tanks so that customers can reach in and scoop out what they want (Walpole, 2014).

Walmart has had to overcome several hurdles in China. When it first entered the Chinese market, the company struggled with the logistics of truly catering to local needs. China is a big country. There is a large variation in consumer tastes and preferences from region to region. It therefore wasn't simply 'Chinese' consumer needs that the company needed to get to grips with, but regional needs that could vary from city to city. It struggled to identify the right product mix to sell nationwide and needed to apply glocalization strategies on a subnational basis, not simply a national one. Inventory needed in one city might not necessarily be needed in another. For example, while consumers in Beijing may need pollution masks to deal with the smog, the same might not be true for consumers in Shenzhen, which has lower pollution levels than the country's capital.

Building trust among local Chinese consumers has been crucial to Walmart's success. Speaking in 2016, Sean Clarke, CEO of Walmart in China, who was based in Shenzhen and had previously worked in Britain, Japan, Germany and Canada, described China as 'easily the most challenging market to operate in... There is a huge level of distrust' (D'Innocenzio and Wisemanap, 2016). He was referring to the common practice in China of cutting corners, incorrectly labelling products or selling substandard goods. China has had some food scares, and consumers can be wary. In fact, Walmart found itself at the centre of one such food scare when donkey meat (a delicacy in China) was found to contain traces of fox meat. The problem occurred after Walmart gave local managers more leeway to run their stores, in an attempt to instil local practices to appeal to local consumers.

To overcome this, Walmart reduced its suppliers and took back some control from local managers. It also increased investment in food safety and introduced a 'Worry Free' slogan in 2012, implying that customers could rely on being able to buy quality, low-cost items at its stores (D'Innocenzio and Wisemanap, 2016). Demonstrating that the company understood customer needs at a subnational level has also been important in building and maintaining this trust.

Walmart didn't only need to think about how to adapt its products and product mix to local needs. It has also needed to give careful consideration to its employment policies. One example is employee unions. According to Reuters, 'None of Walmart's roughly 4,700 US stores have unionized despite decades of attempts by labor unions' (Wiessner, 2024). Interestingly, China is the only country where the organization has allowed employees to be unionized, after significant pressure from the government (CLB, 2015).

While Walmart has adjusted its products and operations to effectively retail in China, we can still see the negative effect of a global organization entering the market. For example, local retail outlets have struggled because consumers have chosen to spend their money at Walmart rather than with local businesses. We can also see the effect of Walmart paying lower wages than local competitors. While this drives down costs for Walmart, it potentially leads to a lower standard of living for its employees. Of course, the effects of such practices do not stop there. To compete with Walmart, other organizations are likely to have needed to lower their wages too, further adding to a reduction in living standards for local people.

Questions

- Why did Walmart adapt its approach for the Chinese market, and in which ways do we see this adaptation being portrayed throughout the case study?

- To what extent can we see glocalization practices in Walmart's approach to business in the Chinese market?

- What are the implications of Walmart's entry into the Chinese market for customers, employees and local competitors?

CHAPTER SUMMARY

This chapter has covered the theory of standardization as put forward by Levitt (1983) and has explored some of the many cultural differences that perhaps challenge standardization's usefulness in the global marketplace.

We've looked at some examples of companies that have got it right, such as CavinKare and Tencent QQ successfully marketing to their home markets, as well as other global (and Western) brands that have missed the mark, such as when Disney opened Euro Disney in 1997. We've also considered many Western brands that have successfully applied Robertson's concept of glocalization as an alternative to standardization, such as McDonald's. The 'local' element of glocalization can be understood at either a national or subnational level, and organizations that consider the level they need to operate at will have the most success in the markets they wish to enter.

While glocalization may cost organizations more in terms of the resources required to meet consumers' wants and needs at a local level, it is arguably better to invest upfront than risk damaging brand reputation and having to rectify costly mistakes. As we've seen in this chapter, Disney's reputation suffered when the company didn't adapt its operations sufficiently when entering different global markets.

Let's now turn to our next chapter, during which we will further build on the notion of culture, including via an exploration of key definitions of culture. Furthermore, we will examine and apply key cultural theories as they relate to marketing activities and scenarios, noting indicators of culture (such as the country-of-origin effect and the different interpretations of colour that consumers across the globe hold) which impact consumption practices across the globe. We will also pick up on the brief discussions hinted at in this chapter with regard to whether local or global organizations are best suited to meet the needs of customers and consumers in specific geographical areas.

CHAPTER REVIEW QUESTIONS

- Explain Levitt's (1983) view of standardization. Do you agree that standardization is always the best approach for global organizations to take?

- To what extent is global consumerism an activity that you enjoy? Do you see this as a pastime, or are your consumption practices just a means to an end?

- Explain the concept of glocalization, and what is meant by 'true' glocalization. Illustrate your answer with examples.

- Can you provide any examples of glocalized products? Does this make you more or less keen to purchase the offering? Why?
- How does the concept of culture link to glocalization, and why should marketers be aware of this connection?

KEY TERMS

Economies of scale: Cost advantages that companies can achieve when production levels increase and processes become more efficient.

Localization: The process of adapting an offering to meet the needs and desires of a specific market.

Risk mitigation strategy: A strategy put in place by organizations to reduce the likelihood of certain risk events occurring and the impact they might have if they do.

Subnational: Occurring below the national level, perhaps at a city or regional level within a nation.

References

Accelingo (2024) Apple's global strategy: Simplicity, innovation, and adaptability, www.accelingo.com/apples-global-strategy/ (archived at https://perma.cc/NU2C-9TZD)

Capital One Shopping (2024) Largest retailers, capitaloneshopping.com/research/largest-retailers/ (archived at https://perma.cc/CC9P-WLPE)

Chen, R (2022) Disneyland Paris: A case study of glocalization operational strategies, in *Proceedings of the 2022 International Conference on Economics, Smart Finance and Contemporary Trade (ESFCT 2022)*, Atlantis Press, www.atlantis-press.com/proceedings/esfct-22/125980595 (archived at https://perma.cc/7D8L-QFPL)

CLB (2015) Walmart workers in China push for genuine trade union elections, clb.org.hk/en/content/walmart-workers-china-push-genuine-trade-union-elections (archived at https://perma.cc/GG8R-PLBJ)

Coonan, C (2008) QQ craze holds key to China's internet market, *Independent*, www.independent.co.uk/news/world/asia/qq-craze-holds-key-to-china-s-internet-market-769128.html (archived at https://perma.cc/2HXU-SGE8)

D'Innocenzio, A and Wisemanap, P (2016) Wal-Mart seeks overseas success by going native in China, *AP News*, apnews.com/57f8b5259a38420292cfe726ab0c6aea/wal-mart-seeks-overseas-success-going-native-china (archived at https://perma.cc/C8RN-3DZD)

Disney Experiences (2023) Disney history: Navigating the timeless magic of Disney parks, www.disneyconnect.com/disney-history/ (archived at https://perma.cc/D996-BZLE)

Foodie (2024) McDonald's Prosperity Burger series returns for Chinese New Year with Hello Kitty theme, www.afoodieworld.com/blog/2024/01/12/mcdonalds-chinese-new-year-burgers/ (archived at https://perma.cc/Y5ZC-WRMD)

Ger, G and Belk, R W (1996) I'd like to buy the world a Coke: Consumptionscapes of the 'less affluent world', *Journal of Consumer Policy,* 19 (3), 271–304

Goodall, R (2021) The story of McDonald's, theboar.org/2021/12/story-of-mcdonalds/ (archived at https://perma.cc/PXP9-4V5C)

Holland, P (2020) Savvy mum-of-two who saves £25,000 in just one year shares how she did it, *The Mirror*, www.mirror.co.uk/money/savings-banks/savvy-mum-two-who-saved-23072918 (archived at https://perma.cc/YZ2S-2PHA)

Houston, A (2022) Lost in translation: 10 times brands got it wrong when going global, *The Drum*, www.thedrum.com/news/2022/10/10/lost-translation-10-times-brands-got-it-wrong-when-going-global (archived at https://perma.cc/33RB-SSUF)

Kasulke, E (2024) Euro Disneyland: When glocalization goes wrong, storymaps.com/stories/ef34dbc732d14074aea32c0a4f789a60 (archived at https://perma.cc/K8DN-EG22)

Levitt, T (1983) The globalization of markets, *Harvard Business Review*, 61 (3), 92–102

Loveman, G W and Schlesinger, L A (1993) Euro Disney: The first 100 days, Harvard Business School Case 693–013, www.hbs.edu/faculty/Pages/item.aspx?num=22227 (archived at https://perma.cc/6JHX-E96E)

Matusitz, J (2011) Disney's successful adaptation in Hong Kong: A glocalization perspective, *Asia Pacific Journal of Management*, 28, 667–81, link.springer.com/article/10.1007/s10490-009-9179-7#citeas (archived at https://perma.cc/QDB3-CWFB)

McDonald's (2024) Are there any elements of your menu that are standardised globally? www.mcdonalds.com/gb/en-gb/help/faq/are-there-any-elements-of-your-menu-that-are-standardised-globally.html (archived at https://perma.cc/RY2Z-3J32)

Offhand Disney (2018) Saving Euro Disney, www.youtube.com/watch?v=5q2gLy9ssyM (archived at https://perma.cc/9EH9-MS2B)

Robertson, R (1995) Glocalization: Time-space and homogeneity-heterogeneity, in M Featherstone, S Lash and R Roberson (eds), *Global Modernities*, Sage Publications

Shoulberg, W (2022) How big is Walmart's China problem?, *Forbes*, www.forbes.com/sites/warrenshoulberg/2022/01/19/how-big-is-walmarts-china-problem/ (archived at https://perma.cc/R9JE-3RUN)

Srinivasa, B and Hari, T N (2022) CavinKare – shampoo sachet that was the true pioneer of Middle India market, *The Print*, theprint.in/pageturner/excerpt/cavinkare-shampoo-sachet-that-was-the-true-pioneer-of-middle-india-market/1209049/ (archived at https://perma.cc/U44V-BUJU)

Statista (2024a) Number of monthly active smart device users of Tencent QQ from 2014 to 2023, www.statista.com/statistics/227352/number-of-active-tencent-im-user-accounts-in-china/ (archived at https://perma.cc/4PE6-U72H)

Statista (2024b) Estimated retail sales of Fairtrade International products in selected countries in 2017, by leading country, www.statista.com/statistics/247459/estimated-sales-of-fairtrade-products-in-selected-countries/ (archived at https://perma.cc/FXF4-XXXT)

Statista (2024c) Number of McDonald's restaurants worldwide from 2005 to 2023, www.statista.com/statistics/219454/mcdonalds-restaurants-worldwide/ (archived at https://perma.cc/KTM7-B23X)

Statista (2024d) Number of Walmart stores in China 2013–2023, by type, www.statista.com/statistics/752119/china-walmart-store-number/ (archived at https://perma.cc/GH3N-GTZA)

Sylt, C (2019) Michael Eisner reveals the magic touch that gave a glow to Disneyland Paris, *Forbes*, www.forbes.com/sites/csylt/2019/09/09/michael-eisner-reveals-the-magic-touch-that-gave-a-glow-to-disneyland-paris/ (archived at https://perma.cc/C6MC-427Q)

Walmart Digital Museum (2024) Timeline, www.walmartmuseum.com/content/walmartmuseum/en_us/timeline.html (archived at https://perma.cc/X3U7-AJQF)

Walpole, J (2014) Walmart in China: Dramatically different than in the US, *The American Genius*, theamericangenius.com/walmart-china-dramatically-different-u-s/ (archived at https://perma.cc/VWP6-8ZB2)

Wiessner, D (2024) Walmart engaged in illegal union busting at California store, US agency says, Reuters, www.reuters.com/business/walmart-engaged-illegal-union-busting-california-store-us-agency-says-2024-01-25/ (archived at https://perma.cc/3GHK-UAKQ)

World Population Review (2024) Countries without McDonald's 2024, worldpopulationreview.com/country-rankings/countries-without-mcdonalds (archived at https://perma.cc/5242-DY4X)

4 | Culture and the global marketplace

LEARNING OBJECTIVES

By the end of this chapter, you should be able to:

- understand and explain several definitions of culture
- apply several cultural theories to global marketing activities and scenarios
- explain the relevance of differentiators such as colour and the country-of-origin effect for consumer behaviour
- critically discuss whether local or global organizations are best suited to meeting the needs of consumers in specific geographical locations

Introduction

The intent of this chapter is to introduce the concept of culture, along with a number of relevant cultural theories, via which marketers might better understand their intended audiences, along with their wants, needs and desires, across the globe. This, of course, suggests a contrast to our earlier discussions of elements such as standardization, in which a unified approach to marketing (including products, communications, and so on) is applied. When we instead consider marketing activities at a global level in concert with culture, our findings will often (if not always) suggest that some type of adaptation is required to provide what customers in varied geographical locations actually desire.

In efforts to showcase the relevancy of culture in the global marketplace, and its significance to marketers, the chapter introduces the lens of culture via discussions of key theories and concepts such as cultural universals (Murdock, 1940), sources of culture (Usunier and Lee, 2005), the country-of-origin effect and cultural difference signifiers. Signifiers, in this case, might be taken as referring to elements such as colour preferences and/or consumption patterns. Other chapters, however, also include points in relation to culture (such as with discussions of Hofstede's dimensions of culture in Chapter 5), as culture is interlinked with many of the concepts and theories discussed in this book.

It is also key to keep in mind these theories and viewpoints as they, much as with standardization, might be used to frame thinking throughout the remainder of the text, and as such you are encouraged to keep the views presented in this chapter in mind throughout the rest of your reading.

Defining culture

As with most concepts we might discuss in the marketing discipline (and beyond), **culture** might be explained via a multitude of definitions. Indeed, writing in 2009, Taras and Steel noted that their Google search for 'culture' provided over half a billion hits, and the same search on Yahoo! generated more than two billion. In providing additional explanation as to the extent of these results, Taras and Steel suggest that these result numbers are much higher than those generated for other popular terms (e.g. 'politics', 'war', 'the environment'). Such discussions and the figures generated by online searches position culture as a topic much under discussion. But how might we actually define the term itself in this sea of information?

Culture itself, by its very nature, suggests a move away from the principles of standardization that we have discussed in this book so far. Culture, instead, demands that we examine the differences between people, locations and more (as we will see in continuing throughout this chapter). This can be useful in helping global organizations to move away from the so-called negative elements associated with the use of standardization on a global scale, such as with local competitors being better suited to serving the needs of local areas, a lack of universal appeal and the rigid nature of standardization itself (such arguments might also be applied on an international level, rather than only pertaining to discussions of a truly global nature).

De Mooij (2004) defines culture as 'glue' that binds individuals to each other, noting that, without culture, people would have difficulty living with and alongside others. If we accept culture as a form of 'glue', we might see the concept as allowing individuals to operate from a foundation of understanding, facilitating the reconciliation of differences into similarities so that people can interact with the world around them (Earley, 2009). In summarizing, Jones and George (2019), writing with the organizational perspective in mind, provide a perhaps more extensive definition of culture, noting that the term relates to a 'shared set of beliefs, expectations, values, norms and work routines that influence how individuals, groups, and teams interact with one another and cooperate to achieve organizational goals'.

Culture, however, does not only relate to organizations. For instance, UNESCO (2024) paints the picture of culture as encapsulating a range of elements such as historic monuments, museums, living heritage practices and art. As such, culture enriches people's lives by enabling them to build inclusive, innovative and resilient communities. It is with such definitions in mind that we seek to progress throughout the remainder of this chapter. The intersection between organizations and their culture, discussions of which might also be broadly assigned to people living in particular geographical areas, in concert with the cultural elements (as with those described by UNESCO), all pull together to form our interpretations and understandings as relates to culture.

With this in mind, we might then suggest that culture is the sum of values, beliefs, rituals, symbols, the way people think, and so on. It is learnt, in that culture might be taken as equating to what life is like in the geographical area in which we live, along with what others who also live in the area think, feel and do. We can learn culture, with our impressions and understandings being moulded by those who came before us, but also by those who are newer to the world than ourselves, and who may understand things in different ways due to their generational norms and values.

Finally, culture can also be conscious and unconscious. It can underpin the meanings that we associate with images and symbols and what they represent to us as a member of our culture. With such discussions in mind, it seems clear that to be a successful marketer on a global scale, one must also be a successful student of global culture, understanding those inherent differences that might be encountered in targeting different cultures across the globe.

Theories of culture

Let's now turn our attention to several theories of culture, via which we might begin to apply our understanding of 'culture' to marketing activities across the globe. It is also important to note here that there are many theories of culture, and this chapter is not meant as all-encompassing but rather to introduce to you, the reader, to just some of the core theories via which marketers might begin to understand the global marketplace and therefore reduce their reliance on a standardized approach to their activities and operations.

Cultural universals

In 1940, Murdock published his seminal paper 'The cross-cultural survey', which posited that all cultures have much in common, despite their differences and diversity. These commonalities are known as the cultural universals. In further explaining this viewpoint, Murdock suggests seven basic assumptions about cultures across the globe. In adapting this work somewhat, we might suggest that Murdock's work argues for the commonality of universal themes, regardless of a culture's geographical location. For instance, these themes might be described as:

- **Economy:** We might see the economy as being played out in many of the elements that constitute our daily lives. For instance, in this category we might reference clothing, food, shelter, communication, jobs and transportation.

- **Institutions:** Institutions can make significant contributions to what life is like in a particular culture. Here, institutions might, for example, be taken to include education, government, religion and family.

- **Arts:** Here, we relate to the more creative side of culture, with elements such as music, theatre and literature.

- **Language:** Language might be expressed verbally within a culture, or via the written use of an alphabetic system. However, other forms of language, such as body language, can contribute to the cultural norms in particular geographical locations.

- **Environment:** The environment relates to elements such as the landscape itself, the climate and the wildlife that lives in a particular geographical area.

- **Recreation:** Recreation relates primarily to activities that we do for fun in a particular culture, such as holidays, media and games.

- **Beliefs:** Beliefs, our final of the universals suggested here, include elements such as the values, morals and traditions that may be prevalent in a culture.

The general idea here, then, is that wherever we are in the world (or, in other words, as relates to whichever culture we are currently exploring), we will see elements pertaining to these seven criteria. Let's take food, as a simple example. If I am in the UK, I might be thinking of eating fish and chips or an English breakfast. If I visit France, I might eat a croissant or some cheese. If my travels then take me to Japan, I'm probably going to eat some sushi – you get the picture. The locations and therefore cultures that we visit may have different favourite dishes and meal options, but they all do have those options, with food being available regardless of our geographical location. Similarly, if we consider the wildlife native to a particular culture or geographical location, we might find coatis in Mexico, hedgehogs in the UK, brown hares in Germany and turtles in the Seychelles. Again, these animals (or elements of culture) are different, but they are there nonetheless, regardless of where we are across the globe.

Sources of culture

Another way in which we might begin to see the formats and entities via which culture takes shape is **sources of culture** (Usunier and Lee, 2005). Usunier and Lee suggest several ways in which culture might be illuminated, including the following:

- **Language:** Language can be verbal, or it may take other forms such as body language, both of which can deliver significant clues to an individual's culture. For example, despite meaning different things in different geographical locations, certain words might be used to describe the same item. If we take verbal differences in language between the US and the UK, for example, we can see such instances with differing terms like 'chemist' and 'pharmacist', 'crisps' and 'chips' or 'biscuits' and 'cookies'. We might also consider written language and symbols to be of importance in this category and as a significant indicator of culture. For instance, in some areas of Japan, you will find interesting signs in public areas directing individuals not to stand on toilet seats, and even not to be sick in the street!

- **Religion:** This might be in the form of how intensely religious principles followed by a particular culture are adhered to and appear in everyday life. For instance, this might relate to dietary restrictions upheld by followers of certain religions.

- **Education:** Education might be seen as shaping the outlook and desires of individuals residing in specific cultures. Equally, however, we must also remember that systems of education will vary between countries, as will other elements such as literacy rates and the percentage of individuals seeking higher education.

- **Nationality and culture:** Here, we relate to the culture of an individual's home country, along with that of the culture of the country in which that individual chooses to live.

- **Family and social class:** This category of culture sheds light on the various roles played by individuals, as they can have a big impact on the ways in which a culture operates and is perceived. For example, here we might concern ourselves with the number of women in employment, divorce rates, same-sex relationships and marriage, the percentage of one-person households, approaches to childcare, the use of convenience foods, the role of extended family and so on.

Cultural knowledge

Despite the fundamental purpose of this chapter being to explore culture as it pertains to the environments (and the people living in them) that marketers may choose to target, we would be remiss if we did not also briefly explore culture as it relates to organizations themselves.

For instance, Schein's (2010) work suggests that culture can be viewed and understood at several levels, using 'level' to mean the extent to which cultural phenomena are visible to the observer. With this conceptualization in mind, Schein suggests that culture might be viewed and performed at three different levels.

Schein's first level of culture is artifacts (everything that you can see, hear and feel). This, for example, might include visuals such as the aesthetics and design of a space, what people wear and other visuals such as branding or logos.

The second level of culture, according to Schein's discussion, relates to espoused beliefs and values, which suggest that all group learning ultimately reflects someone's original beliefs, values and sense of how things should be (which is not the same as what 'is'). We might, for example, find espoused beliefs and values in an organization's mission or goal statements. Importantly, this level of culture relates to how we might describe such elements rather than to how we might actually see them in practice.

Schein's third and final level of culture is that of basic underlying assumptions, which are now so taken for granted that there's little to no variation within the community. Schein continues to explain that such assumptions may be particularly difficult to articulate given that they encompass underlying understandings that may be held and yet not explicitly discussed by members of a certain culture. For example, in an organizational setting, the view of the customer might be that the organization's purpose is to provide a specific product line or service, whereas for insiders of that same organization, the underlying assumption is that the organization exists to make a profit for its shareholders.

With an adapted version of Schein's layers of culture in mind, we might suggest that culture in an organization can be seen as pertaining to three different layers, all of which contribute in some way. As mentioned earlier on in the chapter, one might also apply much the same principles and categories to wider efforts to examine culture, for instance at the geographical rather than the organizational level.

In our efforts to do so, we might visualize levels of culture as displayed on a pyramid structure, with the lowest level of the pyramid relating to basic assumptions, the middle to daily enactment, and the highest level equating to surface knowledge. If we then populate the layers of our pyramid with information that we know about a particular organization, we start to see a picture of the organization's culture appear.

In layer 1 of Figure 4.1 we see surface knowledge about an organization, which may be illustrated by elements such as the building housing the organizations, the office layout, the dress code used by employees and the activities that they are expected to undertake. In layer 2, daily enactment, we are concerned with the language and vocabulary used in an organization, who holds status and the way that things are typically done in that environment. Conscious awareness also has a role to play

Figure 4.1   The cultural knowledge triangle

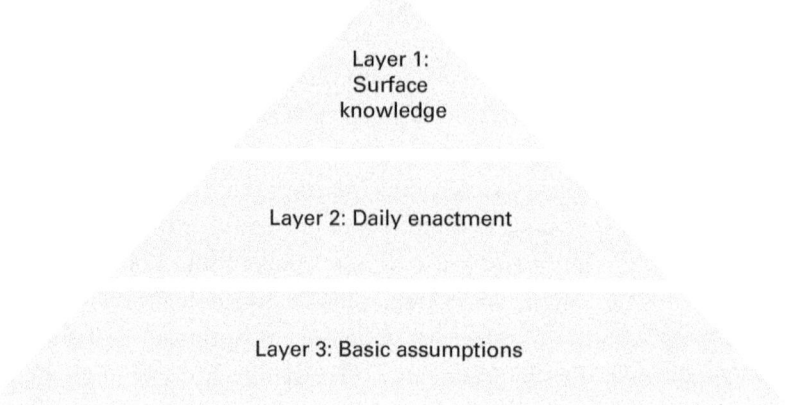

Layer 1:
Surface
knowledge

Layer 2: Daily enactment

Layer 3: Basic assumptions

here, as the elements that fall under the daily enactment layer are aspects that most if not all members of an organization's culture will be fully aware of.

The final layer, that of basic assumptions, speaks to the assumptions made about the nature of the world and of the people who live in it. While discussed in the organizational context for this and the following example, we might also consider the use of such layers when exploring cultures more broadly, for example in efforts to characterize the culture of a specific geographical location.

REAL-WORLD EXAMPLE   A new job?

Imagine that you have just graduated from university, and that you are looking for a new job. You narrow down your choices to two organizations. Organization 1, 'Sell2You', is a UK-based call centre, which deals in outgoing calls only. If you take the opportunity to work at Sell2You, your new role would require you to convince the target audience to purchase advertising space in a magazine which is produced by Sell2You's in-house publishing team. Your second choice is to work as a faculty member at Squirrel University, also located in the UK. Your role at Squirrel University would require you to undertake research, to teach classes and to undertake some citizenship responsibilities.

While both job roles appeal to you, you want to make sure that you will be a good fit for whichever organization you choose. Luckily for you, you have friends in high places. Mia, your friend from school, works at Sell2You, and Finn, a former colleague, now works at Squirrel University as a faculty member.

You decide that, in order to choose which organization would be the best fit for you, and to allow for you to be successful in your new job role, you will need to learn more about the organizations' cultures. Mia and Finn offer to help you via a discussion of the different types of cultural indicators that they have observed while working for their respective organizations. The easiest way to do this, they suggest, is by demonstrating their knowledge via the three layers of culture that might be seen as making up cultural knowledge.

Surface knowledge

- **Sell2You:** Mia tells you that layer 1 of the pyramid is concerned with surface knowledge. This, she says, can be seen in some of the visual elements that you might see on a daily basis, along with the typical activities that take place during the working day. Mia notes that Sell2You's operations take place on two floors of a typical office-style building, with staff expected to dress for a smart business role in suits or dresses. These are visual indicators, giving hints as to the culture of the organization. Mia, however, also mentions the morning and afternoon meetings that all staff members are expected to attend. The meetings are designed to encourage staff to 'let off some steam', with boisterous team challenges and activities, designed to make staff feel energized to sell advertising space.

- **Squirrel University:** Finn tells you that the surface knowledge as pertains to Squirrel University differs as you move across campus, typically depending on the discipline or role in which employees work. For example, he says, employees in Squirrel University's Business School typically wear smart clothing such as suits, while those working in the University's School of Philosophy have a much more relaxed style of dressing. The University's campus is large, featuring a number of buildings reflecting different styles. Unlike Sell2You, morning and afternoon meetings do not happen every day, with employees given a higher degree of autonomy over their daily activities, although, Finn tells you, employees are expected to attend frequent meetings related to specific topics, including those which may impact their professional practice such as with teaching.

Daily enactment

- **Sell2You:** Mia now moves on to discuss level 2 of the pyramid with you, relating to daily enactments. Here, she tells you that a mixture of professional language and swearing is typical in Sell2You's office environment on a daily basis. Status is also a key component of Sell2You's organizational culture, with managers and 'top' sellers being perceived as holding status, and those who fail to make many sales being seen as holding less power and influence in the organization. Mia also mentions that Sell2You has a very intense and fast-paced way of doing things, with employees always expected to be manning the phones and attempting to make sales. Furthermore, Mia emphasizes that, as part of daily enactment in Sell2You's culture, employees are expected to consistently consider their own actions, for example with pressure to constantly be talking, and to sell.

- **Squirrel University:** Finn again notes the degree of autonomy afforded to colleagues at Squirrel University when talking about daily enactment. He suggests that professional language and terminology is the norm, and that swearing would generally not be expected or condoned in the workplace. Finn tells you that all members of the faculty hold status, but that higher levels of status might be seen as colleagues progress during their careers, with professors holding a higher level of status, for example, than a teaching fellow might be expected to obtain. The speed of working differs at Squirrel University, with some tasks such as research being intense and fast-paced, while other activities such as teaching and course content development taking place at a slower rate. Much as with Mia's discussions of Sell2You, Finn suggests that employees are expected to consider their own actions, but that these might vary depending on the individual employee's timetable and responsibilities.

Basic assumptions

- **Sell2You:** In giving some guidance about Sell2You's organizational culture, Mia decides to talk to you about the basic assumptions that stakeholders, including the organization's managers and employees, make about the nature of people and the world as it pertains to Sell2You's operations. Mia tells you that the nature of people in the call centre differs dramatically, with top sellers and managers often being seen as 'cut-throat' due to their aggressive sales tactics. On the other hand, Mia also notes that some colleagues are very supportive, and are keen to help new hires to make sales and therefore succeed in the organization. The nature of the work is also important, which is time-sensitive due to the need to publish the magazine and therefore the paid advertising content by a specific date, according to Mia.

- **Squirrel University:** Finn notes that at Squirrel University there is a heavy emphasis on developing colleagues and acting in a supportive manner towards new colleagues. This, he suggests, may reduce as those new colleagues progress in their roles, but he does insist that there is usually a more experienced member of staff available to help when needed. The nature of the work is still time-sensitive, but rather than a heavy emphasis on sales, this emphasis is often placed on making sure that students are well prepared to submit their assessments on time, or on meeting research deadlines.

Questions

- After reading through the case study, what is your impression of Sell2You's culture? What is your impression of Squirrel University's culture? Explain the reasons behind your answer.

- Do you think the culture of Sell2You or Squirrel University would be a better fit for you personally? Explain the reasons behind your answer.

- Choose an organization with which you are familiar (for example, you may wish to use your university, or a current or previous place in which you have been employed). Discuss the indicators of the selected organization's culture in terms of surface knowledge, daily enactments and basic assumptions.

ACTIVITY

What does culture look like?

To be completed following reading of the case study 'A new job?'

After talking to your friends Mia and Finn, you decided that neither the role at Squirrel University nor the one at Sell2You had an appealing organizational culture. You decided that, instead, you would try a completely different career.

As a result, you have been working as a junior hairstylist at Luscious Locks hairdressing salon in the UK for the past year. Your friend Julia is also considering working in the hairdressing industry, and luckily Luscious Locks is hiring. But, much as you did with your previous job search, Julia decides that she wants to find out more information about the organization's culture before applying for the role.

In response, you send Julia an email telling her about your day at work:

Hi Julia,

How are you? It was great to see you today and to hear that you are considering joining me at Luscious Locks!

As promised, here's how my day went at work, along with a bit more information about the salon.

So, this morning I chose my work outfit for the day, black jeans and a white t-shirt. It really annoys me having to wear only black and white for work, but it's the Luscious Locks uniform; they don't care what we wear though, as long as it's black or white. It's so nice to wear trendy clothes for work every day!

Today the appointments book was nearly full, so it was a really busy day with the other stylists having lots of clients booked in and no time for walk-in appointments. Everyone knows what they have to do, though; the junior stylists like me were busy washing clients' hair and mixing and applying colours, the stylists were busy cutting clients' hair and applying foils and perms, and the managers were mostly taking more bookings and talking to clients, dipping into other roles as they were needed. Luscious Locks is nice in that way, everyone helps each other out. We do have a hierarchy, but it's generally quite a relaxed and supportive environment, and the stylists do take time (when they have it to spare) to teach me new skills. After all, this helps them too, when I can pick up some of their tasks during the really busy periods.

We didn't have much time to stop and chat with one another today, and lunch was a bit of a rush, as always. It's actually quite rare that we sit down and eat together, there's always something that needs to be done, so if you do join us at Luscious Locks, be prepared to eat your sandwich on the run...

There were a few ups and downs today; one client didn't like the colour of her hair after some foils, so we had to try to placate her by offering a discount. The other clients seemed very happy though, and there were a lot of jokes shared between the staff, clients and managers. We were all pretty tired by the end of the day, but a few of us went out for a drink to catch up after making sure that the salon was ready for the next morning.

I should probably also tell you about the salon itself as you've yet to visit. It takes up two levels of a building on the high street, and is quite similar to our uniform, in that the decorations are mainly black and chrome. The ground floor has these huge floor-length glass windows that let other people see the stylists cutting and styling clients' hair, which I think is a good advertisement for the services that Luscious Locks offers. The backroom downstairs houses three washbasins, which we use for washing clients' hair and for taking off colours. This area is not visible to the public, which is probably a good thing as who wants other people to see them when they're having their hair washed?!

The upstairs of the building is split between a treatment area for the Luscious Locks in-house beautician and a small staff room. We don't tend to go upstairs very much during the day though (there's never time to sit down for long!), only really to put our bags into the staff room and to get fresh towels from the salon's dryer.

Overall, it's a nice place to work. Hopefully see you there soon!

Bye for now.

Questions

- Where can you see surface knowledge in the description of Luscious Locks salon's culture?

- Where can you see daily enactment in the description of Luscious Locks salon's culture?

- Where can you see basic assumptions in the description of Luscious Locks salon's culture?

- How do the elements of Luscious Locks' culture differ to those described in the case study for Sell2You and Squirrel University?

Colour

A further indicator of culture might be seen in the ways in which individuals respond to colour. What we find beautiful and pleasing varies, just as do the colours that we like and dislike. This is due to the attachments that we may have to colours due to their cultural, symbolic or even historical backgrounds.

For instance, we might suggest that some colours have universal meanings, such as blue (linked to trust and safety) or red (linked to danger or excitement), whereas other associations are more specific (Fussell, 2024). For example:

- Yellow:
  - connected to royalty in China
  - suggests optimism in the West
- Red:
  - related to love and romance in the West
  - linked to mourning in South Africa
  - denotes good fortune in China
- Orange:
  - related to spirituality and sacredness in Southeast Asia
  - linked to autumn and Halloween in the West
- Green:
  - linked to magic and myth in Ireland
- Purple:
  - considered to symbolize bad fortune and mourning in Brazil and Italy
- Black:
  - related to elegance but also to mourning in the West
  - linked to the supernatural and to being skilled in the East
  - connected to life (as opposed to death) for the Ancient Egyptians

The country-of-origin effect

Aside from elements such as colour impacting the way that particular cultures may view or respond to certain offerings and other stimuli, we might also look to the **country-of-origin effect** to help us to understand how culture, and our understandings of it, can play a significant role in the ways that we view offerings, and ultimately what we choose to purchase and from where.

The country-of-origin effect relates to the impressions that we have about a particular country or culture, and how these are ascribed to the offerings produced by that country. To include a stereotypical example where budget is not a key concern: if I want to purchase a new luxury wristwatch, it's likely that I would purchase the offering from a Swiss watch brand (due to associations with luxury and high quality) rather than a Chinese watch brand (for which I may hold lower impressions of quality and reliability).

There are a number of indicative examples that we might use here, as to where we might look to purchase specific products. For example, we might choose to purchase cars from Germany, luxury fashion from Italy, and electronics and technology from the US, Japan, China or South Korea, due to the associations we have of the cultures in question.

Local versus global: Meeting consumer needs

As keen readers will likely have realized on reaching this point in the book, culture can play a significant role in global marketing efforts. Indeed, this is a notion that we see time and time again, throughout the remaining chapters of this text. With that being said, culture does also present us with the potential for some interesting critical discussions, primarily relating to the global organization's choice as to whether to standardize or adapt their global offerings and operations. While we might debate the best route for each organization or even offering to take in such a critique, we must also question the impact for other stakeholders, and in particular customers and consumers.

With this in mind, we might consider whether global organizations can ever truly gain a thorough understanding of a multitude of cultures, given that unless one is a member of that culture, one is essentially still an outsider. As such, we might question whether some of the nuances associated with cultural understandings, perceptions, history and so on might be lost to those who do not strongly identify with a particular culture. If this is indeed the case, marketers and global organizations seeking to engage with particular cultures may face an incredibly difficult challenge in making sure that they are successful.

Such concerns may also lead us to question whether global organizations are actually best suited to meeting the needs of customers and consumers. If understanding culture is such a challenge, would local organizations be better suited to meeting customer and consumer needs, given that they likely have a strong understanding of the culture through their geographical location?

REAL-WORLD EXAMPLE   Hunter wellington boots make a splash
in America

Hunter is a British brand founded in 1856, with its now somewhat infamous Hunter wellington boots being introduced to the market in 1956. While the brand offers a range of apparel and footwear for men, women and children, they are arguably best known for their signature wellington boots. Hunter suggests that its products are practical, steeped in heritage, and merge functionality with fashion (Hunter, n.d.).

Stocked in the UK by the likes of department stores such as Harrods and Selfridges, Hunter wellington boots remain a popular choice for UK consumers. However, perhaps surprisingly, they also appear to be a popular choice for American consumers, in spite of America having its own set of highly regarded brands offering wellington boots, such as Ariat, Red Wing and Thorogood.

Celebrity endorsement appears to have been a useful tool for Hunter in reaching consumers across the pond, with a host of well-known individuals being spotted wearing Hunter's products. These include American stars Rachel Bilson, Mila Kunis, Kendall Jenner and Reese Witherspoon, and English celebrities like Kate Moss and Kate Middleton.

Aside from being worn by the current Princess of Wales, Hunter boots also hold further connections to the British monarchy, with the then soon-to-be Princess Diana appearing at her engagement photoshoot in a pair of green Hunter wellington boots in 1981 (Coster, 2009), and with Hunter one of a select few British brands to hold two royal warrants. Taking a slightly different tack, Hunter's boots have also featured in political relations between the UK and America, as in 2010 UK Prime Minister David Cameron delivered US President Barack Obama's children pairs of Hunter wellington boots on a visit to the country (Klara, 2018).

Hunter is also no stranger to collaborations with other well-known brands, with the likes of Stella McCartney, Jimmy Choo, Peter Rabbit and Target working with the brand. In addition, a further interesting collaboration can be seen between Hunter and BBC's popular *Killing Eve* television show, with one of the show's main characters, Villanelle, being pictured in the boots (Mackenzie, 2022).

Questions

- What factors have made Hunter wellington boots popular in America, despite the strong presence of American wellington boot brands in the country?

- What role does the country-of-origin effect play in the popularity of Hunter's wellington boots for consumers in the UK and America?

- Hunter have used celebrity endorsement to promote their products. How successful do you think this has been?

- What other marketing actions and tactics could Hunter use to make sure that its brand remains popular with American consumers in the future?

CHAPTER SUMMARY

This chapter began with efforts to showcase some of the many definitions of culture in the academic literature and beyond. Key theories of culture such as the cultural universals (Murdock, 1940) and sources of culture (Usunier and Lee, 2005) were introduced, providing to some extent a framework via which we might seek out elements of culture regardless of where we are in the world. Our focus also temporarily shifted to the organizational perspective in relation to culture (Schein), while other elements such as colour and its different meanings around the globe were also explored to illuminate the different impressions that different cultures may have of the same entity, element or phenomenon.

The latter section of this chapter sought to explore the connections between culture and the country-of-origin effect, lending focus to implications for consumer behaviour. This section of the chapter also encouraged you to question whether, due to presumed better understandings of culture, local organizations might be better suited to meet the needs of customers and consumers than global organizations.

Let's now move on to the next chapter, which discusses the role of global marketing communications and whether these should be standardized or adapted for different audiences across the globe. In doing so, we explore key differentiators aligned with culture, such as understandings of various emotions, humour and what may cause offence to individuals in certain cultures or geographical areas.

CHAPTER REVIEW QUESTIONS

Culture

- How would you define culture?
- Which of the cultural theories discussed in the chapter do you feel best represents your understanding of culture? Why?

Cultural universals

- Do you agree that there are elements of culture that we might expect to find present in any culture across the globe? Explain your answer using supporting examples.
- Describe how culture is played out in your home town or city with regard to each of the seven cultural universal categories (economy, institutions, arts, language, environment, recreation and beliefs).
- Next, consider how the cultural universals might be applied to the further geographical location that you have previously visited.
- Were the answers that you gave different for each location's culture? If so, in which ways? Why might this be the case?
- If you could add an eighth cultural universal, what would this be? Why?

Colour

- Revisit the meanings associated with different colours for various cultures across the globe, as discussed in this chapter. Consider your own culture and perceptions of colours noted. Do you agree or disagree with the associations listed?

- Are there other colours that hold particular meanings for you as a result of your culture?

- To what extent would you agree with the following statement: 'The associations of colour that we hold due to our culture play a significant role in our decisions to purchase one product over another'? Explain the reasons behind your answer.

The country-of-origin effect

- Consider the following products. Which country would you choose to purchase these offerings from if given the choice? Which country would you not want to purchase the products from? Why?

  o coffee

  o tequila

  o wine

  o perfume or aftershave

  o cosmetics

  o modern art

  o furniture

  o a television

- Does the amount of money you consider the average item in the list to cost impact your answer? Why, or why not?

- How important do you think the country-of-origin effect is when customers select the brands from which they purchase?

- How important to your own purchasing behaviour is the country-of-origin effect? Do you think that this will change in the future? Why, or why not?

Theories of culture

- What are the key differences between the categories proposed in the sources of culture (Usunier and Lee) and the cultural universals (Murdock)?

- Do you think the sources of culture or the cultural universals would be most useful for marketers trying to understand contemporary culture? Why?

- Consider the categories proposed by both the sources of culture and the cultural universals. Would you include any further categories? If so, what might these be?

Local vs global

- Are global organizations or local organizations best suited to meeting the needs of customers and consumers when we consider the significance of culture? Why? Use examples to further your response.

KEY TERMS

Country-of-origin effect: The characteristics and positive or negative attributes that consumers and customers assign to a brand or an offering due to its country of origin.

Cultural universals: Murdock (1940) suggested that there are seven universal elements of culture that we might expect to find anywhere in the world. These are economy, institutions, arts, language, environment, recreation and beliefs.

Culture: The term 'culture' has many definitions. However, we might suggest that culture could be defined as consisting of elements such as values, beliefs, activities, traditions, rituals, symbols and so on that are the same for a particular group of people in a given culture.

Sources of culture: Usunier and Lee (2005) suggested elements such as language, religion, education, nationality and culture, and family and social class as ways in which we might view and understand culture.

References

Coster, H (2009) A brand re-booted, *Forbes*, www.forbes.com/global/2009/0330/021-celebrities-brand-rebooted.html (archived at https://perma.cc/ALM3-XHSK)

de Mooij, M (2004) *Consumer Behaviour and Culture: Consequences for global marketing and advertising*, Sage Publications

Earley, P C (2009) So what kind of atheist are you? Exploring cultural universals and differences, in C Nakata, *Beyond Hofstede: Cultural frameworks for global marketing and management*, Palgrave Macmillan

Fussell, G (2024) The significance of color symbolism in different cultures, Shutterstock, www.shutterstock.com/blog/color-symbolism-and-meanings-around-the-world#color-symbolism-around-the-world (archived at https://perma.cc/76XY-RYDA)

Hunter (n.d.) Hunter history, www.hunterboots.co.uk/pages/hunter-history (archived at https://perma.cc/6P8M-9ZCG)

Jones, G R and George, J M (2019) *Contemporary Management* (11th ed), McGraw-Hill Education

Klara, R (2018) The Hunter wellington: How an English duke and the invention of vulcanized rubber gave us the ideal boot for April showers, *ADWeek*, 59 (9), 22

Mackenzie, L (2022) BBC *Killing Eve*: Get Villanelle's look with these Hunter Boots from the show, *Watford Observer*, www.watfordobserver.co.uk/leisure/20059885.bbc-killing-eve-get-villanelles-look-hunter-boots-show/ (archived at https://perma.cc/86GY-DHPW)

Murdock, G P (1940) The cross-cultural survey, *American Sociological Review*, 5 (3), 361–70

Schein, E H (2010) *Organizational Culture and Leadership* (4th ed), Jossey-Bass

Taras, V and Steel, P (2009) Beyond Hofstede: Challenging the ten commandments of cross-cultural research, in C Nakata, *Beyond Hofstede: Cultural frameworks for global marketing and management*, Palgrave Macmillan

UNESCO (2024) Culture, www.unesco.org/en/culture (archived at https://perma.cc/QAP6-YQ67)

Usunier, J-C and Lee, J A (2005) *Marketing Across Cultures*, Pearson Education

5 | Global communications

LEARNING OBJECTIVES

By the end of this chapter, you should be able to:

- critically evaluate whether a standardized or adapted approach to global marketing communications is most appropriate in a variety of global marketing situations and scenarios
- explain the concepts of encoding and decoding, along with their significance to marketers and consumers
- discuss successful and unsuccessful global marketing communications efforts as they relate to concepts such as humour, emotions, miscommunications and causes of offence

Introduction

This chapter builds on existing discussions of Levitt's (1983) notions of standardization, but this time with an emphasis on the standardization of global marketing communications. In order to further understand some of the significant difficulties associated with marketing communications on a global scale, discussions include exploration of key concepts, such as encoding and decoding marketing messages, along with explorations of how our own consumer perceptions can make a big difference to what we actually understand from the messages presented to us by marketers and, as a result, whether we understand the message as it was originally intended or draw a different meaning from the communication's content.

To further solidify our understandings of perception and the differences that may be required when considering marketing communications via a global lens, the chapter next explores Hofstede's (2003) dimensions of culture, outlining the various dimensions via which we, as marketers, might seek to further understand the appropriateness of our marketing communications for various intended audiences around the globe.

Furthermore, the chapter introduces several types of appeals that might be made by organizations in their global (or local) marketing communications, focusing on emotional frames in addition to elements such as music. One such appeal comes in the form of humour, which is also explored in more depth at a later point in the chapter. Humour, as we will see throughout the chapter, can be a difficult beast to tame, with consumers understanding humorous marketing communications in different ways depending on elements such as their backgrounds, culture and geographical locations. When marketing communications mishaps do take place, organizations may ultimately cause offence to their audience. Thus, the chapter explores the notion of miscommunication, along with some of the potential outcomes for global organizations when they cause offence through their marketing activities.

As astute readers will note, this chapter perhaps contains the highest number of organizational and real-world examples of any in this book as a whole. Through these examples the intention is to show you, the reader, how marketing communications including content such as humour, causes of offence and so forth might be seen in practice. You are also encouraged to think of your own experience of marketing communications as you read through the chapter, considering any adverts that you have seen which might fit under the chapter's headings. Furthermore, you may wish to explore some of the adverts mentioned online, to put the discussion into perspective.

Global communications and standardization

As discussed in Chapter 3, Levitt (1983) is a great proponent of standardization, with this thinking also being applicable to global communications.

When considering global communications, a standardized approach can bring a host of potential benefits such as cost savings and simplified logistics. However, this assumes that, due to standardization, an organization will use the same message and the same message execution across the globe. Added to this is the requirement for organizations to ideally unify their approach to marketing communications in terms of their slogans, visuals, images, language, spokespeople, the offering's features and uses and so on. The growth of global media and technology has arguably made efforts in this arena more fruitful, with additional opportunities to target consumers across the globe being created.

REAL-WORLD EXAMPLE   Mastercard's Priceless campaign

In the 1990s, financial brand Mastercard was in big trouble. This trouble came in the form of a decline in business, due to a problem of perception. *Marketing Week* (Vizard, 2019) explained that, in some ways, Visa's stronger brand pull was stopping people from using Mastercard products, and as such the Mastercard brand had its work cut out in attempting to address its perception in the minds of customers.

Following a stint of brief advertising campaigns and a change of CEO, the brand moved to the Priceless campaign, designed to run on a long-term basis, rather than as just another short-term campaign like those previously run by the brand. Such efforts appear to have come to fruition, with the Priceless campaign still being seen as core to the organization as of 2019 (Vizard, 2019).

Mastercard launched the campaign in 1997 via television advertising, which, according to the brand, 'captured the hearts of people around the world' (Mastercard, 2022). The first television advert was actually the work presented in the advertising agency's pitch to Mastercard, featuring 'a father and son attending a baseball game' (Vizard, 2019). With its now infamous slogan, 'There are some things money can't buy. For everything else there's Mastercard', the premise of the campaign was to place value on family and relationships rather than materialism, which perhaps seems a strange focus for a financial brand at first glance. However, considering all of the countries in which Mastercard operates, the introduction of a universally popular theme and a standardized approach to the advertisements (i.e. family and relationships) allowed the Priceless campaign to reverberate through the audience's consciousness and to resonate across generations and cultures, right to the present day (Mastercard, 2022).

Visit the Mastercard website now, and it remains clear that the Priceless theme still prominently adorns Mastercard's brand. The organization boasts that it now connects 'individuals, businesses and organizations in more than 210 countries and territories' (Mastercard, 2024), ultimately suggesting that the campaign certainly had a Priceless impact for a brand struggling in the 1990s.

Questions

- What did Mastercard get right with their Priceless marketing campaign?
- How does the campaign transcend geographical and cultural boarders?
- Does the campaign's slogan appeal to you as a customer? Why, or why not?
- Mastercard's efforts with Priceless are presented as a highly successful yet standardized marketing campaign. What made this campaign so successful?
- What might Mastercard do to keep their Priceless campaign relevant moving forwards?

Encoding and decoding

While Mastercard represents a highly successful example of a standardized global communications campaign, we must also turn our attention to the ways in which messages are conveyed to customers, and how, in turn, customers might understand them.

This can be explained via **encoding** and **decoding**. Encoding relates to an organization's choice of elements to be included in a marketing communications message. This may include elements such as words, music, visuals and so on. The message must then be put into a format that can be accessed by the intended audience (for example, a television or radio advert), known as encoding.

Regardless of the elements chosen, it is vital that the message includes everything that the intended audience requires in order to understand the communication properly. This understanding from the audience's perspective is called decoding. Decoding relates to the process undertaken by a customer or other stakeholder who views the message, during which they will attempt to interpret the elements into thoughts. This understanding is typically informed by the receiver's background, prior knowledge and experiences.

Indeed, communication is a delicate thing, and if customers cannot decode or understand the message there is a host of potential negative implications for the organization. For instance, customer inability to decode the message suggests that the organization has missed its target and, as such, may suffer reduced purchase intention, sales and profits. When messages are misunderstood by consumers we might see a range of potential outcomes. In some instances such misunderstandings may provoke confusion or even humour for the intended audience, but the results of such misunderstandings can also be distinctly negative. For example, a message may be misconstrued as offensive, as not resonating well with culture, and so on.

Importantly, if decoding is not successful, it is likely that, regardless of how many times a potential customer views a message, it will not result in any action towards the brand or offering on the part of the customer. Furthermore, organizations must

Figure 5.1   Old woman, young woman

NOTE This optical illusion first appeared on a German postcard in 1888.

be particularly careful with the messages that they encode in the global arena, as cultural difference, for example in relation to emotions or symbolism, can have a damaging impact if not understood correctly.

However, encoding and decoding messages can be a difficult thing to accomplish, as consumers may understand the same communication in a plethora of different ways. For example, consider Figure 5.1. Do you see an old woman or a young lady? Or can you see both?

If you asked another person what they see in the image, their answer may be different to yours, despite you both looking at the same image. This is because our own perceptions, backgrounds and culture play a role in determining how we understand the communications we receive. If you, for example, could see the young lady in the image and then tried to explain your view to someone who could only see the old woman, you may find it difficult to get your perspective across. This may result in negative feelings, such as anger or frustration.

In other words, decoding messages often requires negotiation and interpretation. This can be problematic for organizations seeking to distribute global communications as customers are likely to hail from a variety of backgrounds, countries and cultures, and as such may have very different views, perceptions and understandings of the same communication. Regardless, meanings between the encoder (typically the organization or marketer) and the decoder (typically the consumer or customer) need to overlap. Where this is not the case, it is unlikely that the intended message will be properly understood by the audience. One way in which marketers can attempt to ensure that their communications messages are decoded by the audience as intended is to pay close attention to culture.

Hofstede's dimensions of culture

Hofstede's seminal 2003 work outlines five key dimensions of culture underpinning values in more than 50 countries, exploring the ways in which they impact how we, as humans, act, feel and think, along with the implications of this for organizations. Adding to the cultural dimensions over time, Hofstede suggests that cultures in particular countries, and as a result those individuals and organizations residing in those geographical locations, will fall somewhere between these opposite descriptors:

- **Power versus distance:** This explores how less powerful members of institutions accept and expect that power is unequally distributed.

- **Uncertainty avoidance:** This relates to how comfortable or uncomfortable the members of a particular culture feel in unstructured situations. Hofstede describes these unstructured situations as 'novel, unknown, surprising, different from [the] usual' and as concerned with 'the degree to which a society tries to control the uncontrollable'.

- **Individualism versus collectivism:** By their very nature, individualism and collectivism are opposites. Individualism speaks to how individuals are supposed to look after themselves, whereas collectivism is more concerned with the ways in which individuals integrate into groups (e.g. families).

- **Masculinity versus femininity:** Hofstede describes these opposing poles as 'the distribution of emotional roles between genders' (in his view, 'tough' masculinities are opposed to 'tender' femininities).

- **Long-term orientation versus short-term orientation:** This relates to how people accept delayed gratification of their needs (material, social, emotional, etc.).

- **Indulgence versus restraint:** The indulgence versus restraint dimension relates to 'people's attitude towards happiness, pleasure, and pleasure-seeking, and towards the importance of fun' (Heydari et al, 2021).

Message appeals

When global organizations choose to construct a new advertising campaign, there are a number of different ways in which they might decide to share their message(s). For instance, common techniques used by organizations in their marketing messages might be to provide factual information, a slice of life, a demonstration or a comparison.

When organizations choose to use a factual appeal to consumers, they tend to provide a high level of information, using a logical and rational approach, whereas with a slice of life-style appeal, the emphasis is instead placed on providing the audience with a scenario, typically featuring the organization's offering, to which they might be able to relate. If an organization chooses to use a demonstration in its marketing communication efforts, the central idea is exactly as it sounds – to provide a demonstration of how the offering might be used to solve a particular issue (common examples, for instance, might include everyday products related to pain relief, cleaning, and so forth). Finally a comparative appeal simply seeks to show the organization's offering as superior to those offered by its competitors.

Emotional messaging

The ways in which organizations attempt to appeal to their intended audience via their marketing communications messages can also take on an emotional perspective. Here, however, organizations must be careful not to go too far, particularly when their efforts involve promoting negative emotions as a consequence of viewing advertising.

Fear, for example, might be seen in marketing communication efforts via the communication of the threat of physical danger, or via the threat of social disapproval. Organizations using this type of emotion in their marketing efforts must take care, however; if the adverts are too extreme, or provoke too high a level of negativity for the audience, that same audience may take pains to avoid seeing the advert altogether. Equally, if an advert's contents are deemed too extreme by the audience, they may also consider its contents to not be applicable to them personally.

Humour, while further outlined in the discussions later on in this chapter, is also a frequently (if not always correctly) used emotion in advertising efforts. Having been used in advertising for more than 100 years, brands attempt to include humour in their advertising approaches to create positivity in their intended audience, along with the hope of gaining consumer interest and attention. However, brands must also take care here; if the advert is deemed too funny, it may ultimately cause the audience's attention to shift from the offering and/or brand to the advert itself.

Our next emotion seen in advertising is shock, which makes a point to deliberately startle and offend (Venkat and Abi-Hanna, 1995). Typically, marketing communications messages including the shock factor do not conform to social norms, but they are attention-grabbing and memorable for the intended audience. In addition, shock can have the knock-on effect of increasing word-of-mouth discussion surrounding an advert, again potentially leading to further attention for the brand and its offerings.

Taking a slightly different tack, animation can also be used in advertising messages and is often seen as particularly useful for low involvement offerings to increase an audience's levels of attention and engagement. The addition of animation (often in the form of cute kittens, puppies or similar) serves to encourage differentiation of the brand and its offerings in what is often a crowded sea of alternative products and services. Why, you might ask, would organizations work with animated animals rather than the real thing? Simply put, much as with the old adage of working with children, trying to get real animals to act in particular ways can be a difficult task!

Finally, we must also mention the role of music in marketing appeals. Music can be a valuable asset, setting the scene for a variety of moods and messages. If the intended audience likes the music, or if it is in some way catchy, the chances of recall are generally good, which can of course lead to additional positive outcomes such as increased purchase intention. For instance, Fill and Turnbull (2016) note that commanding background music might be seen as equating to power, prestige and affluence in luxury car advertisements.

Regardless of the type of appeal an organization decides to include in its approach to marketing communications, one thing remains clear – that is, that if an advert is standardized and as such is intended for a global audience, very careful consideration must be given to ensure that the correct message is communicated in the correct way. As with discussions throughout this chapter (and many others throughout this book as a whole), elements such as fear, humour, shock and so on might be understood in very different ways by audiences belonging to different geographical locations and cultures. Therefore, one might argue that it is the role of the marketer to properly understand their intended audience(s), and to adjust their standardized advertisements and marketing campaigns accordingly.

Miscommunications

When little attention is paid to the composition of marketing messages and how they will land with a prospective audience, global organizations may find themselves in a bit of a predicament. While global organizations undoubtedly do their best to ensure, when using a standardized approach to marketing communications, that the messages they want their audience to receive are appropriate, mistakes are still made. For example, consider the following list of brands and their marketing communication mishaps. While some may seem at first glance to be amusing, in certain cultures, such errors can have significantly detrimental implications for organizations and ultimately cause offence to consumers.

Language

First up is stationery brand Parker Pens' efforts to market ballpoint pen products in Mexico. The intention of the brand's adverts was to inform consumers about the product range, and they stated: 'It won't leak in your pocket and embarrass you' (Marketing Profs, n.d.). However, the brand thought that the Spanish word *embarazar* meant 'to embarrass', and used the term in its marketing campaign. *Embarazar* actually means 'to make pregnant', thus giving the brand's advertising a different meaning entirely.

Another communication gaffe thanks to poor translation can be seen with dental brand Colgate's efforts to introduce its 'Cue' toothpaste in France. Unfortunately, *Cue* was the name of a French pornographic magazine (Marketing Profs, n.d.). Scandinavian vacuum manufacturer Electrolux did not fare much better with its foray into the American market, thanks to its advertising campaign centred around the slogan 'Nothing sucks like an Electrolux', while the Schweppes tonic water brand managed to translate its own name into 'Schweppes Toilet Water' in the Italian market (Marketing Profs, n.d.).

Equally part amusing/part offensive is car manufacturer Ford's campaign which tried to suggest that 'Every car has a high-quality body', which actually turned out to translate to 'Every car has a high-quality corpse' for Belgian consumers, and Green

Giant's (a frozen and tinned vegetable brand) mascot, the Jolly Green Giant, typically a fun and encouraging character, being translated badly to 'the far more threatening "intimidating green ogre" telling [Arabic-speaking children] to eat their veg' (Houston, 2022).

Furthermore, the Coca-Cola brand hit a snag in China, with the brand's name first being 'rendered as Ke-kou-ke-la', which 'means "bite the wax tadpole", or "female horse stuffed with wax", depending on the dialect' (Marketing Profs, n.d.). Coca-Cola is not the only brand to suffer translation issues in the Chinese market. Car brand Mercedes-Benz also hit issues, with the brand's name being initially translated as 'Bensi', which actually means 'rush to your death', and Pepsi's iconic 'Come alive! You're in the Pepsi generation' tagline was rendered as 'Pepsi brings your ancestors back from the grave' (Houston, 2022).

For a final example of the mistranslations of Western brands in the Chinese market, we might look to the somewhat amusing, somewhat disturbing case of KFC, whose famous 'Finger Lickin' Good' slogan was translated as the unappetizing 'Eat your fingers off' (Houston, 2022).

Use of colour

Words are not the only source of miscommunication mishaps that organizations may face when communicating with global markets. Colour can also play a large role in an audience's understandings of a message, due to elements such as local and cultural interpretation and meanings assigned to particular colours.

For example, telecommunications brand Orange ran a highly successful advertising campaign in the 1990s, featuring the slogan 'The Future's Bright – the Future's Orange'. While the slogan and campaign were broadly successful, an exception was seen in Northern Ireland, where people strongly associate the colour with the Orange Order, a religious and political entity (Wooten, 2011).

In addition to its blunders with verbal and written language, drinks brand Pepsi have also made some missteps with their use of colour. Specifically, Pepsi reportedly lost a significant share in the beverage market in at least one Southeast Asian country when it changed the colour of its vending machines to ice blue. This colour is often associated with death in the region (Wooten, 2011).

So, while one might not reasonably expect the intent of global organizations to upset, anger or alienate their potential and current customers and consumers, the examples noted above show that such mistakes can and do take place. Thus, whether in consideration of language, colour or other elements, global organizations must tread very carefully indeed in their efforts to communicate on a global scale.

ACTIVITY

Communications mishaps

Aside from those outlined in the chapter, can you think of any other examples of brand miscommunications?

REAL-WORLD EXAMPLE   Christmas: Marketing, symbolism, Westernization and interpretations across the globe

Christmas, originally a Christian festival celebrating the birth of Christ whose message is focused on love and anti-materialism, is often depicted to consumers in the West via marketing messages of 'happiness, peace and goodwill... festive food, family gatherings and gift giving' (Lapperman et al, 2020). Does this image sound reminiscent of your own festive traditions? Even if it is perhaps not the picture-perfect rendering of your own past experiences, Christmas is a concept acknowledged and celebrated each year, even in regions where Christian traditions aren't acknowledged.

While many who do acknowledge the Christmas tradition will recognize well-known festive figures and symbols such as Santa Claus, elves, snowmen, Christmas trees and their decorations, such as tinsel and stars, other symbols of the festive period are perhaps more geographically specific. For instance, the Monarch's Christmas speech in the UK, a tradition started by King George V via radio broadcast in 1932 and moved to television in 1957 by Queen Elizabeth II, remains a beloved tradition steeped in history for some of the British public, who sit down with their families to watch the broadcast on Christmas Day (Schmidt, 2023). Such a tradition, however, might be seen as puzzling for American consumers. Equally, the UK's joke-laden Christmas crackers and party hats are seen as a confusing festive prop by some consumers in Belgium and France, while America's Black Friday tradition may also seem perplexing to consumers in other parts of the world.

To take the Western perspective in exploring the meanings associated with the festive period (and in consideration of the spread of such Western perspectives across the globe), it is perhaps fair to note that while Christmas used to be primarily about spending time with family and friends, undertaking annual traditions such as decorating the Christmas tree, in recent years we have seen a shift in this area. Namely, rather than focusing only on these elements of unity (as is key for Afrocentric consumers), Western marketing messages have arguably led to an increased focus on 'consumerism, materialism and individualism' (Lapperman et al, 2020).

That is not to say that we do not still see differing versions of festive traditions based on culture and consumer backgrounds. For instance, in South Africa, Lapperman et al report symbolic alterations, such as Santa Claus ditching the reindeer and sleigh and instead arriving 'on a truck collecting gifts to give to children and the needy', therefore becoming a 'symbol of charity' and removing some of the consumeristic and materialistic associations of the central Christmas figure that we might see from a more Western perspective.

However, that is not to say that the Western construct of Christmas (along with other holidays) falls flat on its face in every other country across the globe; only that, instead, it is somewhat modified. For example, Waldmeir (2014) writes that 'Christmas lost its soul in the west around the time that I stopped believing in Rudolph', but that 'in China, the holiday never had much soul to begin with. That's what makes it such fun.' Christmas in China as reported by Waldmeir does certainly put a different spin on the celebrations, with older generations not celebrating the event at all, and a lack of the Americanized additional festive period elements, such as Black Friday, also being apparent.

However, while China may not be overtly concerned with the more traditional and historical views of Christmas, Chinese consumers do certainly have their own ways of celebrating; Waldmeir notes that it is unashamedly about money and fun rather than tradition and gifting, and that Mainlanders will celebrate with shopping, eating out and karaoke. While at first glance China may seem to have discarded all of the elements of Christmas and the festive period that may be seen as causing stress and discomfort for Western consumers, this disconnect to tradition (in the Western sense) has led to a rather interesting phenomenon. Instead of focusing on Christmas gifting, Cupid and Santa seem to have interbred to give Christ's birthday a romantic flavour. For example, reports suggest that in previous years aspiring blind daters at a matchmaking evening in Shanghai were encouraged to tell Santa who they fancied.

China's interpretation of Christmas, then, might be seen as a far cry from the religious, historical and child-centric focus of the West, with younger generations of Chinese consumers who may wear reindeer antlers on a date but leave decorating to restaurants and shopping malls. Such conceptions lead Waldmeir to conclude that 'China shopped in the cultural supermarket and decided to import them all'. Thus, we see varied interpretations not only of the festive period, but also of other holidays and at least in part their meanings (if we take Chinese consumers' desire to spend time with one another during the festive period as akin to Western families spending time together at Christmas, although reinterpreted).

Moving back to our discussion of the festive season itself, Lapperman et al provide some interesting analysis in relation to Afrocentric consumers residing at the bottom of the pyramid (see Chapter 11), along with their impressions of the festive period and its associated figures, traditions and symbols. Lapperman et al speak to a 'cultural blending', with a divided set of consumers residing in South Africa, both at the top and bottom of the pyramid. This has resulted in a sense of cultural colonization and 'convergence towards Western culture, and many marketers targeting emerging markets [using] these Western, festive season symbols in festive season marketing messages'.

However, Lapperman et al argue that Western conceptions of the festive period pushed by marketers, along with the traditionally Western values of materialism and individualism, may not fully resonate with South African consumers (particularly those at the bottom of the pyramid) due to the differing focus on people and culture, rather than consumerism.

When considering marketing communications, as might any organization attempting to communicate on a global scale, there is a requirement to consider how 'different languages, non-verbal behaviour and cultural backgrounds can impact the communication process, thereby [potentially] causing misunderstandings or unnecessary conflict'. Such potential issues are further compounded in the South African case, with previous colonialization in the area creating 'an environment of corporate mistrust' (Lapperman et al, 2020).

Indeed, South Africa's history and culture did appear, in the case of Lapperman et al's study at least, to have some significant implications for the ways in which consumers decoded the marketing messages being presented to them during the festive period. For instance, participants in the study discussed positive conceptions of the Santa Claus character, noting the positive role played in bringing presents and sweets to children. While this may sound similar to Western conceptions of Santa Claus, the study's South African consumers noted that the figure 'was not strongly linked to Christmas. Rather, Santa Claus has a stronger association with retail and festive season spending.'

Christmas trees were another festive symbol under discussion in the study, with South African consumers suggesting that they bring people together, acting as a place to gather with family and friends, to tell stories, and also as a reminder of the festive period in the home. But some South African consumers felt that having a Christmas tree at home was not actually that important. This feeling was related to the placement of gifts (often traditionally placed under the Christmas tree in the West), as some South African consumers spoke of placing presents either inside or outside. As Lapperman et al suggest, having a Christmas tree in their homes held low significance for many, leading to 'hints at convergence' with Western cultures via its inclusion in the festive period's celebrations.

A final area of consideration in terms of the marketing messages and Western symbols of Christmas to be explored is that of consumption, in relation to both food and gifts. On food, Lapperman et al suggest that, for South African consumers, enjoying food together during the festive period is an important act, with the study's interviewees highlighting that unity has an effect on how they decode marketing messages, specifically ones that focus on family gatherings given the importance of joint celebrations.

The marketing messages during the festive period, and consumer responses to those messages, also present an interesting element for discussion. South African consumers participating in Lapperman et al's study (particularly those at the bottom of the pyramid with low disposable income levels) suggested that advertisements promoting gifts actually reminded the audience that they couldn't buy the gifts advertised. Here, we might link to elements such as affordability, but also, potentially, to feelings of guilt or shame when consumers are not able to provide what they may see as a gift equal to that of another gift giver (a concept that will also likely be recognized by many other consumers across the globe).

To get around such feelings, and arguably linking back to the Afrocentric values assigned to South African consumers described earlier, we see the notion of providing collective rather than individual gifts, resulting in a collective rather than individual decoding of marketing messages (Lapperman et al, 2020). This presents an interesting notion, in that, although South African consumers do take on board some of the Western ways of thinking about the festive period (such as having Christmas trees in their homes), they might be seen as decoding marketing messages differently (collectively), due to affordability, but also, at least in part, due to their adherence to South African culture and values.

As a result, Lapperman et al call for 'marketers to acquire further understanding of the South African market when creating marketing messages targeted there', not only due to the different cultural values and norms held by consumers, but also due to the need to understand the differences brought about by varied levels of urbanization in South Africa. This type of thinking, we might argue, could also be reasonably applied to the activities of marketers in targeting consumers across the entirety of the globe.

Questions

- Explain the symbols and traditions that you associate with Christmas in your home country. Why are the elements identified important to the way in which you construct your views of the festive period?

- Lapperman et al discuss the inclusion of Christmas trees in South African consumers' homes. Discuss the ways in which this inclusion – or lack thereof, in some cases – contributes to discussions about the spread of Westernization.

- To what extent are concepts such as consumerism, materialism and individualism prevalent across the globe during the festive period? Explain the reasons behind your answer.

- To what extent is China's focus on romance during the festive period a 'cultural blending'?

- Where festive figures such as Santa Claus are arguably recognized across the globe, should organizations standardize or adapt their marketing communications? Explain your answer.

Humour

Humour, or the lack of it, in advertising can also have significant implications for consumer engagement with adverts. Furthermore, the appropriate use of humour, when done well, can lead to positive brand associations and increased consumer purchase intention, among other such benefits. Simply put, humour both increases tension and releases tension, rewarding the attention of the audience (Gregory et al, 2019).

As Gregory et al explain, humour is ever-present in global media, and advertisers are aware of audiences' desire for entertainment, hence many choosing humorous advertisement campaigns. However, when considering humour and advertising (or marketing communications more broadly), we might still question whether the notion of something universally funny actually exists. Indeed, Gregory et al note that humour can be difficult to translate across cultures.

Such difficulties become increasingly apparent when we consider the entry of global organizations and brands into new international markets, often at pace due to increasing levels of competition for the attention of consumers in developing countries. However, in doing so, global organizations open themselves up to the 'risk of using inappropriate humorous techniques due to cultural unfamiliarity' (Gregory et al), particularly where standardization in advertising is required due to fast entry into some geographical areas and, as such, opportunities for marketers to thoroughly understand different cultures and what they may find funny may not be possible before an advertising campaign takes place.

To avoid any negative connotations that may result from ignorance, a lack of understanding, or time, when developing adverts for new markets, Gregory et al argue that marketers need to understand how to apply humour mechanisms and humour types in different cultural zones.

With such arguments in mind, let's now turn to a few humorous advertisements. While reading the following discussion, consider whether you think the adverts are amusing and, if so, why. Equally, consider whether these advertisements would increase your purchase intention as a consumer, and why this may or may not be the case.

Metro Trains Melbourne's 2012 campaign 'Dumb Ways to Die' sought to reduce the number of accidents taking place on its railway network. The advertising video is comprised of cartoon characters singing an incredibly catchy song (apologies in advance to those who decide to search for this advert online and spend the remainder of the day singing it) which 'runs through all the stupid ways a person could die' (Mulcahy, 2019). These 'dumb ways to die' provide quite the range of methods via which a person might accidentally die, but the tail end of the advert focuses specifically on 'dumb ways to die' involving Metro's transportation network. Thus, we see a very serious message being portrayed in a humorous, catchy and memorable way.

Our next example comes in the form of Burger King's Whopper Neutrality advert, as an effort by the fast-food brand to explain issues of internet neutrality, as it relates to the equal treatment of data on the internet. The advert shows customers trying to buy a Whopper, but being told to wait if they won't pay more: this leads to customer anger and questioning of staff on the injustice of wealthier customers getting better service. It is then revealed that the Whoppers are a metaphor for staff to educate the customers (Mulcahy, 2019). While most will likely sympathize with the plight of consumers shown in the video, via shared recollection of long wait times at food outlets and restaurants, the advert provides an amusing spin on a serious issue, with real customers becoming almost incensed at the injustice facing them via the decision to wait longer or to pay more for their Whopper burger.

Fast-food chain KFC also made the headlines with its humorous advertising in 2018 after facing social media backlash from customers due to chicken shortages resulting from a change in its supplier, which ultimately led to restaurant closures. In response to customers' negative feedback on social media, the brand used a clever play on the KFC lettering implying a four-letter swearword, as an apology to customers (Mulcahy, 2019).

Next up is Swedish homeware brand Ikea's paper-based advertisements for its range of children's cribs. These had a hidden pregnancy strip, and prospective mothers were invited to urinate on the ad and wait for the results. 'If the result was positive, customers could then take the ad into their nearest Ikea and buy a brand new crib at a discounted price' (Mulcahy, 2019).

Our final example relates to Spotify's Wrapped campaign, which made efforts to showcase the strange habits of customers using the streaming platform. One might argue that this campaign was fraught with risk due to its publicization of elements of users' data. However, it seems this was a campaign worth that risk. The campaign highlighted, for example, a playlist called 'I love gingers' featuring 48 Ed Sheeran songs. It even revealed that one user had played the Justin Bieber song 'Sorry' 42 times on Valentine's Day (Mulcahy, 2019).

Causes of offence

When global marketing communications are not properly understood as intended by an organization, it can result in very negative implications. For example, when an organization gets their communications really wrong, it may cause offence. This may be due to a number of factors, such as cultural values, which can negatively impact the audience's response to the communication. This can be particularly troublesome for global organizations when standardization is viewed as the platform from which identical or highly similar marketing communications emerge to help to fulfil the so-called homogeneous wants, needs and desires springing from global consumerism.

Chan et al (2007) conducted a useful study on causes of offence, specifically exploring different interpretations of and responses to offensive advertising for consumers located in Germany and China. It is perhaps useful to note at this point that at the time of Chan et al's study both China and Germany were 'among the five biggest advertising spenders worldwide'. While irritating, offensive and plain old an-noying advertising efforts have been much debated in the extant marketing commu-nications literature, one might still question whether global organizations use such offensive advertising due to genuine cultural insensitivity, or whether such an ap-proach is simply a brazen attempt to capture attention in an increasingly cluttered global marketing arena in which consumers are bombarded with advertisements every day.

Chan et al provide some useful context with regards to examples of advertise-ments that had previously been found offensive by consumers. For instance, in China, a McDonald's television advert featuring a Chinese man kneeling down to get a discount was charged with insulting consumers. The advertisement was felt to present 'unequal power distribution between the Chinese consumers and the [likely American] advertiser', hinting at 'American imperialism' (Chan et al, 2007).

Switching focus to consumers in Europe, Chan et al discuss the now infamous Benetton campaign that showed blood-covered clothes, a boat with refugees jump-ing into the sea and people with tattoos reading 'HIV positive'. A further offending advertisement, this time by luxury brand Dolce & Gabbana, sparked protests across Europe because it showed an ad suggestive of a gang rape of a woman by four men. Here, we might link back to the question posed earlier in this section of the chapter: whether global brands publicizing offensive adverts are simply looking to cut through the clutter of advertisements available for consumer consumption, or whether it is a genuine case of cultural ignorance. This question perhaps seems more pertinent, given the examples just outlined...

Regardless, these examples do illustrate that offensive advertising has and argu-ably continues to take place. For instance, in 2017 soft drinks brand Pepsi issued an apology following its controversial advertisement featuring Kendall Jenner. Pepsi's advert, whether inadvertently or not, had 'borrowed imagery from the Black Lives Matter Movement' with backlash against the advert and brand, suggesting that they had 'trivialized the widespread protests against the killings of black people by the police' (Victor, 2017). With such examples in mind, perhaps many readers would agree with Chan et al's call for global organizations to be required to 'gain a deeper understanding of their impact on consumers'.

There are, of course, a number of reasons why a consumer might find an adver-tisement offensive. To further compound the examples explored above, we might suggest that a consumer's individual background and links to culture, along with the traditions and norms that are the standard in their geographical location, might make up some of the reasons behind their response to particular adverts. However, the adverts themselves also play a large role in whether they are perceived to be of-fensive (or, to be fair, funny, amusing, sad, happy, or any other descriptor we might assign here). Chan et al, however, note that advertisements will often be found to be offensive by consumers because the product itself, the advertising execution or the type of advertisement being seen as appropriate for a particular medium. Chan et al further highlight sexism and racial discrimination as key causes of offence in the Western perspective, while in the Asian context the authors note 'sexist themes, fear, nudity, and cultural insensitivity' as key determinants by which an advertisement might be judged to be offensive.

Chan et al's own study of offensive advertisements as they pertain to Chinese and German consumers ultimately found that Chinese respondents considered the advertisements offensive or uncomfortable more often than German respondents, whereas German respondents were more likely to consider them irritating or ridiculous, and often found them creative. Furthermore, the study found that Chinese consumers appreciated advertisements more if they were informative or, in other words, if the adverts helped them to better understand the brand. Conversely, German consumers only regarded advertisements as informative if they provided factual details (Chan et al, 2007).

Ultimately, if a marketing communications effort, or advertisement, is viewed as offensive, there is the possibility of the advert being rejected in a particular country or countries, with backlash possible or even likely for the brand. Indeed, the cause of offence from a particular marketing communication does not necessarily have to be the same in various geographical locations. But, importantly, it also does not necessarily have to be confined to only one advert or advertising campaign – negative impressions brought on by advertising campaigns that have not been well thought out can spread like wildfire to the brand as a whole. This can result in negative future impressions and interactions (if these still take place) with the brand, leading to low purchase intention and a host of other negative connotations.

With this in mind, global organizations (and also local organizations) will need to consider how they convey their messages to the intended audience. Such considerations may take into account the variations of media that are available to the organization, along with how available these media are to the intended target audience. For example, an organization may wish to use social media for their global marketing communications; however, they must also consider whether their intended audience will have frequent (or any) access to the internet in order for them to be able to view the advert.

Intensity is also a key determinant here, as the organization may wish the audience to view the communication a particular number of times. However, to use our previous social media example, this may not be possible if the intended audience has very limited access to the internet. Spend will also be a significant determinant of the type of marketing communications used, but, regardless, the organization must take into consideration the different stages of infrastructure in the different geographical locations it intends to target with its communications, along with the cultural backgrounds and associations held by its intended audience.

REAL-WORLD EXAMPLE   Breaking up with Bumble?

Bumble describes itself as 'a platform for connection', aimed at consumers looking for romance and those simply looking to make some new platonic friends (Bumble, 2024). The brand's unique selling point lies in its user requirement that women are empowered 'to make the first move', whereas '[i]n same-gender matches, either person has the power to make the first move'. Thus, to a certain extent at least, Bumble might be seen as making inroads in challenging the traditional gendered power dynamics that one might encounter on online dating apps.

However, Bumble's reputation took a turn for the worse thanks to its 2024 billboard campaign which derided celibacy and abstinence (Encinas, 2024). This provoked criticism that the adverts shamed women who were not sexually active (Sherman, 2024) for the purpose of enticing them to (re)become active users of its platform, without considering the reasons why users might choose to remain celibate. While celibacy is not a new concept, abstaining from sex and decentring men has been a path chosen by many women in recent times (Cherelus, 2024). Indeed, the general feeling for Bumble's campaign was rather bluntly encapsulated by the *New York Times*' article headline: 'Bumble to users: You need sex. Users to Bumble: Get lost'.

Given that a cornerstone value of the brand is supposed to be the empowerment of women, consumers were quick to point out that the ads suggested anything but. For instance, *USA Today* reported that the majority of people reacting online felt insulted by the insinuations of the ad. There can be little wonder why, when messages such as 'You know full well a vow of celibacy is not the answer' and 'Thou shalt not give up on dating and become a nun' were being publicized by the campaign.

While Bumble has since acknowledged that the adverts did not land as the humorous success that they were intended to be, this begs the question as to whether the brand's apology will be enough to draw users back to the Bumble platform. In penance, Bumble has since removed the adverts and has taken actions such as donating to organizations like the National Domestic Violence Hotline and others that support 'women, marginalized communities and those impacted by abuse' (Encinas, 2024).

Questions

- What mistakes did Bumble make with its advertising campaign?
- To what extent do you, as a potential consumer, find Bumble's advertising campaign offensive? Explain your answer.
- What might Bumble have done differently to gain a more positive reaction from critics?

Standardization versus adaptation

Drawing this chapter to a close, it seems pertinent to reprise the discussion of standardization versus adaptation, with a specific focus on the marketing communications campaigns outlined in this chapter.

While discussions of this ilk are perhaps not surprising to readers (see Chapter 3 for an earlier discussion in relation to standardization and adaptation) given the nature of this book as a whole, marketing communications are arguably a reasonably easy area in which global organizations can get things right. And yet, as we have seen with several examples throughout the chapter, global organizations do not always manage to do so. To be clear, by 'easy', I do not mean that culture is an 'easy' thing to understand and enact in marketing communications – far from it, in fact. However, what I refer to here is the basic premise of not causing offence to the intended audience. Marketing communications campaigns that ultimately cause offence might be seen in two ways: as evincing a genuine ignorance of a location's culture, or as being too lazy to understand culture and to adapt communications to meet the specific needs of a particular geographical area's consumers.

In such cases, we might defer back to the question of whether standardization for global organizations' marketing communications is always a good thing, or whether, at times, a firmer focus on adaptation would be more appropriate.

CHAPTER SUMMARY

This chapter has explored the role of global marketing communications from a standardized perspective. In particular, emphasis has been placed on the importance of the encoding and decoding processes required for marketing communications to be successful, along with the potential consequences when the intended meaning of a marketing communication is not properly understood by the target audience.

Further to this, the chapter sought to shed light on the variety of emotions that might be used in marketing communications campaigns, along with some of the consequences for organizations when they do, and do not, get things right. For instance, the chapter closely explored the notions of humour and causes of offence stemming from the advertising efforts of several organizations, with varied measures of success being noted.

The next chapter explores the role of brands and branding in the global marketplace. Specifically, we define what a brand actually is, following which we explore how brands are seen as representing value in the value chain. The chapter also introduces some critical discussion of concepts such as Aikido brands and the alternative meanings held by consumers in various geographical locations in relation to particular global brands.

CHAPTER REVIEW QUESTIONS

Causes of offence

- Can you think of any adverts that you have found to be offensive? Try to deconstruct your understanding of the advert to determine what made this offensive to you. Consider to what extent this offence stems from your own geographical location, culture and background.
- To what extent should marketers concern themselves with Hofstede's cultural dimensions when attempting to avoid causing offence with their advertisements?
- Consider the examples of offensive adverts outlined in the chapter as per Chan et al (2007). Has your impression of the brands changed since reading the chapter? Would you be happy to make a purchase from these brands? Explain your answer.

Humour

- Which adverts do you find funny? Why?
- Consider the Spotify Wrapped campaign example. Would you have found this advert funny if it was your data being anonymously shared?

Communications mishaps

- Aside from those outlined in the chapter, can you think of any examples of brand miscommunications?

Standardization versus adaptation

- Would you agree that all global marketing communications should be standardized? Why, or why not?

KEY TERMS

Encoding: The ways in which a sender (such as an organization) compiles and presents its intended communications messages to the intended audience. This may include elements such as words, music, visuals and more. The message must include everything that the intended audience would require to properly understand the message.

Decoding: The process undertaken by the intended audience, or receiver, of an encoded marketing communications message. Decoding is concerned with the receiver being able to understand the message(s) included in the communication by the way that it has been constructed by the sender.

References

Bumble (2024) What is Bumble? www.bumble.com/en-us/help/what-is--bumble (archived at https://perma.cc/5ZTF-2YT6)

Chan, K, Li, L, Diehl, S and Terlutter, R (2007) Consumers' response to offensive advertising: A cross cultural study, *International Marketing Review*, 24 (5), 606–28

Cherelus, G (2024) Bumble to users: You need sex. Users to Bumble: Get lost, *New York Times*, www.nytimes.com/2024/05/14/style/bumble-celibacy-ad-apology.html (archived at https://perma.cc/59CW-WHMD)

Encinas, A (2024) Bumble drops controversial ad poking fun at celibacy, abstinence, issues apology, *USA Today*, https://eu.usatoday.com/story/money/2024/05/14/bumble-ad-backlash/73677916007/ (archived at https://perma.cc/RNJ3-N552)

Fill, C and Turnbull, S (2016) *Marketing Communications: Discovery, creation and conversations* (7th ed), Pearson

Gregory, G D, Crawford, H J, Lu, L and Ngo, L (2019) Does humour travel? Advertising practices and audience efforts in the United States and People's Republic of China, *International Journal of Advertising*, 38 (7), 957–78

Heydari, A, Laroche, M, Paulin, M and Richard, M (2021) Hofstede's individual-level indulgence dimension: Scale development and validation, *Journal of Retailing and Consumer Services*, 62, 1–10

Hofstede, G (2003) *Culture's Consequences: Comparing values, behaviors, institutions and organizations across nations* (2nd ed), Sage Publications

Houston, A (2022) Lost in translation: 10 times brands got it wrong when going global, *The Drum*, www.thedrum.com/news/2022/10/10/lost-translation-10-times-brands-got-it-wrong-when-going-global (archived at https://perma.cc/AT7Y-MUZ4)

Lapperman, J, Zornitta, C and Mowzer, Z (2020) Decoding Western festive season symbols and rituals in marketing messages: A bottom of the pyramid consumer study in South Africa, *Communication*, 46 (1), 61–86

Levitt, T (1983) The globalization of markets, *Harvard Business Review*, 61 (3), 92–102

Marketing Profs (n.d.) Lost in translation: 8 global marketing gaffes (Part 2), www.marketingprofs.com/4/delany15.asp (archived at https://perma.cc/S95C-NTNJ)

Mastercard (2022) Marketing 25 years of Priceless, www.mastercard.com/news/perspectives/2022/priceless-25-year-anniversary/ (archived at https://perma.cc/PXU8-PLFK)

Mastercard (2024) About Mastercard: Always moving forward, www.mastercard.us/en-us/vision/who-we-are.html (archived at https://perma.cc/KXD9-XDKZ)

Mulcahy, E (2019) Humor marketing: Five ads that got consumers laughing, *The Drum*, www.thedrum.com/news/2019/06/27/humor-marketing-five-ads-got-consumers-laughing (archived at https://perma.cc/VG69-KYGD)

Schmidt, A (2023) 9 British Christmas traditions that probably confuse Americans, *Business Insider*, www.businessinsider.com/uk-christmas-traditions-vs-american-2018-12 (archived at https://perma.cc/R4G8-FG6T)

Sherman, N (2024) Bumble apologises for anti-celibacy ad after backlash, BBC News, www.bbc.co.uk/news/articles/cz4xx2rw0leo (archived at https://perma.cc/9Z4A-VN8P)

Venkat, R and Abi-Hanna, N (1995) Effectiveness of visually shocking advertisements: Is it context dependent? *Administrative Science Association of Canada Proceedings*, 16 (3), 139–46

Victor, D (2017) Pepsi pulls ad accused of trivializing Black Lives Matter, *New York Times*, www.nytimes.com/2017/04/05/business/kendall-jenner-pepsi-ad.html (archived at https://perma.cc/M464-MDX9)

Vizard, S (2019) 'We were pinching ourselves': How 'Priceless' helped Mastercard save a brand 'in a mess', *Marketing Week*, www.marketingweek.com/mastercard-priceless-campaign/ (archived at https://perma.cc/L9N4-Z8DY)

Waldmeir, P (2014) China has all the gifts but no guilt at Christmas, *Financial Times*, www.ft.com/content/a755f754-8217-11e4-a9bb-00144feabdc0 (archived at https://perma.cc/BYY4-SS2L)

Wooten, A (2011) International business: Color meanings can be lost and found in translation, *Deseret News*, www.deseret.com/2011/1/21/20368525/international-business-color-meanings-can-be-lost-and-found-in-translation/ (archived at https://perma.cc/H2N5-FZKT)

6 | Global brands

LEARNING OBJECTIVES

By the end of this chapter, you should be able to:

- explain the concept of branding and the value of building strong brands
- describe the concept of a value chain and explain where most value sits in the chain
- explain the repercussions of organizations moving their production to the developing world in relation to branding
- explain how brands tap into emotions and symbolism to influence consumer decision making
- articulate three key dimensions consumers use to evaluate global brands and make purchasing decisions
- explain the kind of activities brands might undertake once they have achieved global status
- understand some of the reasons for consumer backlash against global brands

Introduction

This chapter considers the importance and value of global brands. We build on concepts we have touched on in previous chapters. Before you read this chapter, make sure you understand the concepts we discussed in Chapter 4, particularly the cultural universals. In this chapter, we will build on this by considering the influence of cultural norms and expectations on our purchasing decisions.

The first part of the chapter is concerned with how branding works. We begin by exploring the concept of branding and the perceived value of brands. We look at how two similar objects can have vastly different price tags if one is branded and the other is not. Next, we consider three elements of Kaplinsky and Morris's value chain: design, production and marketing. We think about which of these three activities, or stages in the value chain, holds the most value, and whether that value has shifted over time. To help us answer this question, we consider Nike's evolution since its beginnings in 1962.

Next, we look at what happens in our brains when making certain brand choices, particularly when considering well-known global brands. We explore the idea that brands only exist in our minds – a vital concept to understand when we progress to consider the power of emotional value and symbolism.

The second part of the chapter explores branding in the global arena. We begin by considering three key dimensions that have been found to inform consumer choices between global brands: quality signal, global myth and social responsibility (Holt et al, 2004). We consider some interesting views about these dimensions that demonstrate the power and value of global brands. We delve a little deeper into social responsibility to reflect its increasing importance on the global stage. To help us, we consider a company well known for its social responsibility activity: Camper Shoes.

Next, we look at what brands can do once they have achieved global status. Some might opt to grow through mergers and acquisitions, while others might diversify their offerings to provide brand-based experiences to hook consumers in further. We end the chapter by considering some alternative, more negative perspectives of global brands, exploring the types of brand backlash that may occur when branding goes wrong.

But first, we'll begin with a simple way of understanding the impact branding can have on the value of a product.

Branding and value

When I teach my students about branding, I like to begin by asking them to look at two images. One shows simple rows of coloured dots on a white background while the other shows a more random pattern of dots on a blue background. While they have their slight differences, they are essentially the same thing – images of coloured dots on coloured backgrounds. I then ask my students to guess the difference in value between the two images. I am normally met with the same response each time I ask the question – that there is probably very little difference in their value. When I let my students know that one of the images is painted by the famous English artist, Damien Hirst, and the other is taken from a children's book that retails at £3.99, most revise their opinion. But few rarely come close to guessing the true difference in value.

Over 1,000 spot paintings exist by Damien Hirst, which he painted between 1986 and 2011. They range in value but typically sell for between £4,000 and £50,000 (MyArtBroker, 2024a). The artist explains their popularity by saying: 'It's an assault on your senses. They grab hold of you and give you a good shaking' (Hirst and Burn, 2002). But they are, effectively, just dots.

The reason for this enormous difference in value is branding. Damien Hirst was one of the leaders of the Young British Artists (YBA) movement in the 1990s.

Alongside the likes of Tracey Emin and Sarah Lucas, Hirst produced artworks using unusual materials and processes, many of which were intended to shock. He is particularly well known for preserving animals in formaldehyde. The highest price ever paid for a Hirst was £10.3 million for his work *The Golden Calf* – a bull in formaldehyde with 18-carat hoofs, horns and a golden disc on its head (MyArtBroker, 2024b). While his spot paintings are not in this category of value, their worth is nevertheless driven by Hirst's personal brand and the global brand of the YBAs (Tate, 2024).

As we will learn throughout this chapter, branding is important for all sorts of reasons. Indeed, due to brands' ability to form powerful connections with consumers, they are arguably organizations' most important and valuable assets.

What is branding?

Naomi Klein is the author of a hugely influential book called *No Logo*. It was published in 2000 at a time of significant public protest against global corporate brand dominance. Klein defines branding, in its simplest form, as 'the process of marking a product with a consistent logo, image or mascot that sends a message of consistency and quality to the consumer' (MEF, 2003). She goes on to explain that the importance of branding increased at the turn of the 20th century when mass industrialization meant that consumers who were accustomed to buying their goods from local shops had to get used to seeing them coming off the back of a train or truck from a factory. Companies needed to foster trust directly with the consumer, so early examples of brands feature comforting images of people: for example, Quaker Oats' Aunt Jemima or Minnesota Valley Canning Company's introduction of the Jolly Green Giant in 1928 (Hennepin History Museum, 2018). According to Klein (2000), these images were intended to create 'surrogate relationships' to replace those that consumers had with their local shopkeepers.

The importance of branding is now indisputable. Brands help consumers to make choices. They help to build trust between consumers and organizations. If a consumer trusts a brand, they are more likely to buy from it. As such, brands can reduce the amount of time it takes consumers to make decisions. As we will discover later in the chapter, brands often evoke an emotional response in consumers. As we will also see, many of us use brands to help form our identities or project an image of ourselves that reflects how we want others to view us and our values.

Brands and branding, therefore, hold immense power and value. But it hasn't always been this way. We'll use Kaplinksy and Morris's concept of the value chain to explain how and why many organizations have shifted their priorities away from production and towards marketing and branding.

The value chain

The concept of a **value chain** was first put forward by Michael Porter in his book *Competitive Advantage* (1985). For Porter, the value chain can be used to understand the organizational activities necessary to deliver value to customers and gain a competitive advantage. Organizations make choices about how the activities in the value chain are configured and linked together. These choices, Porter believes, form the foundation of an organization's strategy (Harvard Business School, 2024).

Porter's value chain has been used by organizations around the world since he published *Competitive Advantage*. Kaplinsky developed the idea of value chains further in the early 2000s by focusing on how they could be understood alongside increasing globalization and the outsourcing of Western corporations' activities to the developing world.

According to Kaplinsky and Morris (2001), a simple value chain can be defined as 'the full range of activities which are required to bring a product or service from conception, through the different phases of production… [to] delivery to final consumers, and final disposal after use'. The full value chain has four separate components:

1 design and product development

2 production

3 marketing

4 consumption and recycling

For this chapter, we will focus on the first three components, as demonstrated in Figure 6.1. These components are included in the value chain in the order that they would naturally occur if an organization produced a real-life offering, be that a physical product or a service. It would first be designed, then produced and then marketed to the target audience.

The central purpose of most organizations is to make as much profit as possible, partly so that they can grow and gain more market share (therefore achieving competitive advantage, as explained by Porter, 1985). With this in mind, Kaplinsky and Morris's value chain can be helpful for companies seeking to understand how to maximize returns for the organization. Organizations can ask questions such as:

• Which stage of the value chain holds the most value?

• Where should we focus our efforts to maximize our profits?

• Where should we innovate and seek to be different to stand out from our competitors?

• Will the design, production or marketing of our offerings determine our success or failure on the global stage?

Figure 6.1   The first three components of Kaplinsky and Morris's value chain

Adapted from Kaplinsky and Morris, 2001

Increasing globalization has meant that, for most Western organizations, the most valuable component of the chain has changed over time. In many Western countries, including the UK, value used to sit in the production stage of the chain. Manufacturing used to be scarce. In Chapter 2, we briefly discussed how the Industrial Revolution began in the United Kingdom in the 18th century and spread to other nations such as the United States and Western Europe in the 19th century. For hundreds of years, industries such as textiles and coal added huge value to industrially advanced countries like the United Kingdom. For businesses operating in these countries, production was the most profitable component of Kaplinsky and Morris's value chain.

However, lowering production costs in developing countries such as China has led to a significant shift. For example, economic reforms in China in the late 1970s and early 1980s opened the country's economy to foreign investment. A combination of factors including low labour costs meant that many companies began to outsource their manufacturing (Atkins, 2023). These price pressures and changes in competition meant that production was no longer the jewel in the crown for Western businesses. For instance, Staffordshire (UK) was once famous for manufacturing shoes and boots, while Stoke-on-Trent (UK) was home to a number of manufacturers centred around the pottery, coal and steel industries. However, due to changes such as the benefits of outsourcing manufacturing, production was no longer viewed as the most profitable element of Kaplinsky and Morris's value chain, and the majority of production sites closed in Staffordshire and Stoke-on-Trent due to the relocation of manufacturing processes.

ACTIVITY

Where do you think most value sits?

If the most value can no longer be found in the manufacturing stage of a product, where is it? Do you think more value exists in the design stage or the marketing stage?

The question posed in this activity can be difficult to answer. You may have heard the famous quote: 'Cars rust. People die. Buildings become dilapidated. What lives on are the brands.' It is often attributed to Hector Laing, a prominent British businessman and chairman of United Biscuits. (He is also reputed to have said that he would die a happy man if he could hear the sound of a billion Chinese people munching on digestive biscuits – a clear sign of his global ambition (Brewerton, 2010).) If it really is brands that live on, above all else, that might suggest that marketing is now the most valuable component of Kaplinsky and Morris's value chain. To help you consider this point further, read the following case study, highlighting how Nike shifted away from a focus on product (trainers) and towards a focus on marketing and branding.

REAL-WORLD EXAMPLE   Nike discovers the value of marketing and branding

---

In her book *No Logo*, Klein quotes Nike's co-founder, chairman and CEO, Phil Knight: 'There is no value in making things any more. The value is added by careful research, by innovation and by marketing' (Klein, 2000).

Nike is one of the most successful global brands of our time. As we noted in Chapter 2, the Nike Swoosh logo is so well known that it's likely to be the first thing you think of when you hear the brand's name. But building and marketing a powerful brand have not always been the company's priority. In a *Harvard Business Review* article published in 1992, Phil Knight, the co-founder, chairman and CEO of Nike, explains how and why the company shifted its focus from production to marketing the brand (Willigan, 1992).

Nike was originally Blue Ribbon Sports and was set up by Knight and his running coach in 1962. At the beginning, it distributed shoes for a Japanese company, before shifting to design its own shoes and outsourcing the production of them to Asia. In 1978, the company changed its name to Nike and achieved significant success by developing innovative running shoes and getting famous sportspeople to wear them when they competed in global events. This was the extent of Nike's marketing at the time. The shoes incorporated features that no other running shoe had, and this was enough to see sales rise year on year. This, coupled with a focus on keeping manufacturing costs down by outsourcing production to Asia (when competitors like Puma and Adidas were still making their shoes in Europe), contributed to Nike's early success.

This strategy only worked for so long. By the mid-1980s, various factors such as increased competition from the likes of Reebok meant that Nike's sales began to plummet. In 1985, the company was in the red for two quarters and in 1987 sales dropped by $200 million. The focus on the design and manufacture of the product was no longer enough, and Nike instead put consumers in the spotlight: Willigan terms this learning 'marketing oriented'.

From that point on, Nike introduced marketing operations and shifted its focus to the consumer. It started to sell a lifestyle, demonstrating how it gives consumers what they need to be the best versions of themselves. Their marketing is inspirational, aspirational and supportive. Their famous tagline 'Just Do It' was introduced in 1987 and has been followed since by others such as 'Find Your Greatness' and 'Run Anywhere' (Wieden, 2024).

The 'Find Your Greatness' campaign in 2012 featured normal people stretching themselves to their limits. It showed that Nike's products were not just the preserve of elite athletes. The ads featured a young girl doing backflips in her front garden, a child with limb deficiency excelling at baseball, kids skateboarding in their neighbourhood and volleyball being played on a rooftop. These were ordinary people, pushing their boundaries, exercising and staying healthy (Crimmins, 2012).

Today, Nike continues to keep the consumer at the heart of its company. It has built an exceptional brand and continues to innovate through its marketing to sell a lifestyle to consumers and build brand loyalty. For example, it encourages user-generated content and liaises with its customers through social media.

Questions

- What does Nike's story tell us about where value lies in Kaplinsky and Morris's value chain?
- What do you think is a more lucrative career? If the most value can be found in design, intellectual property rights and branding, who is more rewarded, those who work in manufacturing or those who work in product design or marketing and branding?

The downside of the value shift

Due to Nike's beginnings as a distributor of a Japanese company's shoes, it was familiar with Asia's economic landscape. It understood the benefit of offshoring its manufacturing operations to Asia earlier than many Western companies. Therefore, the company's shift to becoming more customer-centric didn't instigate an outsourcing of its production. It was already doing it, and it was one of the reasons for its success in the early days.

For many other organizations, however, the shift to customer-centric marketing and brand building set in motion a critical shift surrounding the production element of the value chain. They realized they could capitalize on low-cost manufacturing in developing countries while keeping the more valuable functions of Kaplinsky and Morris's value chain – design, marketing and branding – in developed, high-income countries. Offshoring manufacturing to countries with much cheaper production allowed organizations to spend more time and money on the more profitable areas of the chain.

As we touched on in Chapter 2, the disposal of an organization's own production facilities and its offshoring to lower-wage countries can have many consequences for various stakeholders. People in developed nations may lose their jobs, while those in developing nations can be forced to work in sweatshops for little pay. Notably, the lack of ownership that organizations have over the production element of the value chain leads to a lack of responsibility surrounding sustainability and ethics in the production process.

ACTIVITY

The consequences of global brands shifting production to developing nations

Klein's *No Logo* (2000) was published at a time when people were beginning to demonstrate against global brands' dominance. The world was entering a new phase of globalization, where brands such as McDonald's, Starbucks, Microsoft and Coca-Cola were seen by many to be trampling over workers' rights, local laws and civic opposition, so they could pursue profit. Western outsourcing was understood to be 'crashing against the shores' of emerging economies and leaving misery and environmental ruin in its wake (Hancox, 2019).

What do you think has been the worst consequence of shifting production to developing nations? Give reasons for your answer.

How do brands work?

According to Oswald (2020), brands are 'sign systems that form the identity of specific products or services and distinguish them from other brands in a product category'. This definition is a helpful starting point for understanding how brands work. They are a system of signs which communicate meaning to a brand's interpreter. This meaning may be intentional or unintentional but, fundamentally, the individual interprets the signs in their own way to form their own idea of, or identity with that brand.

This suggests that brands exist in our minds. They are a perception rather than a reality. How consumers view a brand is crucial to building brand loyalty and, ultimately, the success or failure of that brand. Brands aim to tap into the minds of consumers and align themselves with their values, wants and needs.

It can therefore be helpful to think about brands as intangible. We can't touch them. They exist only in our awareness. When we purchase an offering from a brand, we don't get any tangible benefit other than the offering itself. However, their intangible nature does not mean that they lack power. The fact that brands form connections in our minds makes them very powerful indeed, as we consider later in the chapter.

This leads us to an important suggestion made by Duncan and Moriarty (1998) that 'perception is more important than reality'. While this assertion was made some time ago, it has formed the bedrock for our understanding of how brands work. In the context of branding, Duncan and Moriarty's statement suggests that our perception of a particular brand is perhaps more important than the brand itself. The building and management of brands are, in fact, the building and management of perceptions.

To help us understand this further, it's useful to be aware of a study published back in the early 2000s. Schoenberg et al published interesting research on using functional magnetic resonance imaging (fMRI) to study what happens in people's minds when choosing between different brands. The researchers found that 'strong brands activate certain areas of the brain independent of product categories' (Radiological Society of North America, 2006). Volunteers were presented with logos of well-known and lesser-known brands. They were asked to press buttons to signify their level of agreement with certain statements intended to evaluate perceptions of the brand. The fMRI scanner took images of the volunteers' brains while they were being shown the logos and responding to the statements.

The researchers found that strong brands 'activated a network of cortical areas and areas involved in positive emotional processing and associated with self-identification and rewards'. In other words, they saw activity in the part of the brain that processes emotions while the individuals made certain choices between different brands. They also found that it's easier for our brains to process strong, well-known brands. Weak brands showed 'higher levels of activation in areas of working memory and negative emotional response' (Radiological Society of North America, 2006).

This study further confirms Duncan and Moriarty's suggestion about perception and reality, particularly regarding how important consumer thoughts and feelings about brands are in making purchasing decisions.

ACTIVITY

Take the Coca-Cola taste test

Have you ever tried testing different brands of products blindfolded, and tried to tell the difference? For example, when we drink cola, we are simply drinking a fizzy, coloured and flavoured liquid. Can we tell the difference between Coca-Cola, Pepsi and generic versions if we have no idea what brand we are tasting?

You can do this with anything: cola, tortellini, cereal bars, sliced bread, cheese or bottled water. Choose a product from a well-known brand and one from a supermarket brand. The supermarket brand is highly likely to cost less, but does it taste inferior to the product from the well-known brand?

It can also be illuminating to test similar products from different supermarkets. In the UK, this might involve tasting a comparatively expensive product from Waitrose or Marks & Spencer against a similar one from Aldi or Lidl. There will be a price difference, but is there a difference in taste? And which do you prefer: the one that costs more, or less?

Experiments such as these can help to open our eyes to the power of branding and how we have formed our own perceptions of certain brands. It can be interesting to challenge ourselves and really think about where our preferences stem from. Are they real, or do they just exist in our minds?

There's one extra thing you can think about. If you decide, blindfolded, that one version of a product tastes better than a branded version you would normally opt for, is that realization enough to make you change your purchasing habits? Or are the connections you've formed with certain brands so strong that you would choose them again, regardless of what you've discovered?

Emotional value

Whether you think that you could or couldn't identify different products without being able to see their branding, we can suggest that the emotional values that we attach to brands may play a role in our purchase decisions. Brands strive to evoke an emotional response from consumers and build powerful connections so that people will repeatedly buy their offerings. In this way, brands can transcend functional value, rational thinking and cognitive processes. Put simply, we make purchase decisions based on our emotions towards particular brands rather than on the product's attributes.

Brands can also evoke emotional memories, which in turn can affect which products we choose to purchase. For example, if you have happy memories of drinking Coca-Cola with your family growing up, and you remember the logo on the can or bottle, you might subsequently make Coca-Cola your cola brand of choice as an adult. You may not necessarily realize that this emotional association is why you're choosing Coca-Cola over Pepsi or any other brand, but it may feel like the natural thing for you to do.

Hochschild's feeling rules

Sociologist Arlie Hochschild developed the concept of 'feeling rules' in 1983. This is the idea that societal norms dictate our emotional responses in different contexts. Hochschild suggests that these rules play into how we manage our emotions and conform to societal and cultural expectations in certain situations. Each situation will require a different response: feeling rules guide emotion, engendering feelings of entitlement or obligation that drive emotional exchanges (Hochschild, 1983). These rules dictate what emotion to feel, when to feel it, how strongly to feel it and how long to feel it for. Feeling rules can also help people to express, experience and regulate their emotions. A very simple way to understand this is to think about how we are expected to feel sad at a funeral, but happy at a birthday party.

How can we apply Hochschild's feeling rules to brands? Could this suggest that our brand choices are culturally dependent, with cultural and societal contexts dictating how we respond to certain brands? As consumers, do we try to feel (and therefore make choices) according to what we think is appropriate in any given social situation? To consider this point further, try the following exercise.

ACTIVITY

Do feeling rules impact your brand choices?

Can you think of any situations where Hochschild's feeling rules have influenced your purchasing decisions? Do you feel a certain way when you wear or use particular products? For example, have you ever bought a certain brand of clothing or trainers to fit in with your friends, or to meet the expectations of others by looking 'socially acceptable'? If so, has this decision been guided by a certain emotion?

Alternatively, would you consider yourself a nonconformist? Are you aware of feeling rules; in other words, what you could do to conform, but intentionally decide to go against them? If so, why do you think that this might be the case, and what does this tell us about your approach to brands?

Symbolism

Symbolic meaning is another crucially important element of branding and perception. By choosing a certain brand, individuals can reaffirm their own perception of themselves and how they want to be perceived by others. The symbolic meaning of a brand can also be seen as a 'brand myth'. For example, someone might choose to buy luxury items to symbolize their status and wealth, both to themselves and to others. Someone else might buy an electric car to convey their concern for the environment. It could reinforce how they want to see themselves and how they want others to see them. In this way, symbolism and branding can be seen as culturally dependent, as is the case with Hochschild's feeling rules. As we can see from these examples, brands communicate symbolic meaning in two different ways.

Self-symbolism

Self-symbolism relates to how we understand ourselves through our use of brands.

With self-symbolism, an organization communicates a message about the brand which the consumer uses to understand themselves. For example, someone concerned with personal fitness might use a smart ring such as Oura to track their sleep and wellness metrics. They can download an app to receive their health information in real time and use it to make choices about their day, such as how hard to work out at the gym. Using a ring such as this can help to shape a person's self-perception and how they want to be – healthy, rested and physically strong. Using products with symbolic meaning can help to construct and/or improve a person's sense of self, and brands can seek to align themselves with what they believe to be their consumers' ideal self-perception.

Social symbolism

Social symbolism relates to how we use brands to reflect a certain image of ourselves to others. By associating ourselves with certain brands we can communicate how we want others to think of us. Buying Nike socks might suggest we are fashion-conscious, while buying Ecover cleaning products might suggest we care about being sustainable. Using a meditation app such as Headspace might suggest we are keen to prioritize mental health. Our purchasing choices provide us with ample opportunity to symbolize who we want to be to other people.

Lévi-Strauss (1991) sums these ideas up nicely, suggesting that consumer goods are offerings that we might use in constructing our thinking, and as proxies via which we might speak. With this comment, we might refer to the potential for identity creation and projection through the use of brand. As a result of this, we can suggest that advertising can be seen as a source of symbolic meaning, allowing organizations to ascribe particular attributes to certain brands through the stories they present to their consumers.

The three key dimensions of global brands

The elements of branding that we've discussed so far are all applicable to brands in the global arena. However, there are three key value dimensions of global branding that we have not yet considered. In the early 2000s, Harvard Business School and a market research company called Research International conducted joint research into the factors that make consumers choose one global brand over another (Holt et al, 2004).

The research was done at an interesting time for global brands. It was published in 2004, just a few years after the anti-globalization protests mentioned in an earlier exercise and four years after Naomi Klein had published her global bestseller *No Logo*. It was a time when transnational brands like McDonald's and Coca-Cola had become 'lightning rods for anti-globalization protests'. People were truly beginning to understand global brands' power, 'capable of doing great good and causing considerable harm' (Holt et al, 2004).

The project involved 3,300 consumers across 41 countries. It found that consumers all over the world associate global brands with three key characteristics, and they evaluate brands against these dimensions to guide their purchasing decisions. These characteristics are:

- quality signal
- global myth
- social responsibility

We will go on to consider them now.

Quality signal

Global brands are considered to be of higher quality than their local counterparts. They are also perceived to be more innovative and to introduce newer, better products more frequently than brands operating at local or national levels. They are assumed to have more rapid technological innovation than local brands, which, in comparison, are often considered to provide static, unexciting and lower-quality products.

Due to the perceived quality and innovative nature of global brands, consumers expect them to come with a higher price tag than local or national brands. They consider this to be a price worth paying, due to the uptick in quality and other benefits like more favourable guarantee policies.

It's worth pointing out that these are assumptions, and they will not always necessarily be true.

Global myth

Consumers view global brands as 'symbols of cultural ideals' (Holt et al, 2004). Global myth refers to how consumers use brands to construct an imagined global identity to connect with consumers across the world and foster a shared sense of belonging. (Remember we considered the notion of a collective global identity in our discussion of the meaning of globalization in Chapter 2.) With this assumed global identity, consumers view themselves as citizens of the world, and as 'part of something bigger'. For example, from a consumption perspective, we might suggest that purchasing from a local brand shows who we are, while purchasing from a global brand shows who we want to be.

Linking back to the first dimension of quality signal, local brands can be seen as lacking in terms of technological advancement and innovation, whereas global brands can be seen as the opposite. As such, in the case of the global myth, consumers may wish to align themselves with a global identity, to project themselves as technologically advanced and innovative.

Social responsibility

Consumers can hold global brands to higher standards than local brands when it comes to social issues. Global brands are judged on their willingness to tackle social problems such as poverty or climate change. At the same time, smaller organizations or those operating at only a local or national level are not seen to hold the same responsibility.

For example, think about the placement of unhealthy snacks and sweets in supermarkets. In the UK, since 2022, large supermarkets have been required by law to place foods high in saturated fat, sugar and salt (HFSS) in less conspicuous locations in their stores. Until the legislation came in, these products were typically placed at the till points, meaning consumers stood next to them while queuing to pay, making unplanned purchases far more likely. Crucially, HFSS foods were often placed in children's eyeline, so they had ample opportunity to pester their parents for sweets, chocolate bars and crisps. The legislation is intended to tackle the obesity crisis in the UK and applies to organizations of over 50 people that sell food and drink. Smaller local shops, such as corner shops, are not held to the same standards (Food Active, 2023).

ACTIVITY 🔗

Global brands and their greater level of social responsibility

Why do you think both consumers and governments hold larger, global brands to higher social responsibility standards than smaller, local organizations? Could it be the size of the organization, its higher profit levels or its greater level of influence on the global stage? Give reasons for your answer.

As Holt et al (2004) explain, taken collectively, the three dimensions 'together explain roughly 64 per cent of the variation in brand preferences worldwide'. In other words, the considerations outlined above can impact the consumer decision-making process regarding their choice of brand by up to 64 per cent. This significant number emphasizes the important power that global brands hold. Consumers consider them to be in a special category of their own.

It also demonstrates the importance of managing these three dimensions carefully to gain consumer loyalty and trust. This is easier said than done, perhaps especially in the third dimension of social responsibility, which is arguably becoming increasingly important to consumers, and many organizations have been accused of '**greenwashing**'. In 2021, Hall & Partners published a 'Value Shift' report which discussed the rise of the 'conscious consumer'. It stated that over half of consumers (57 per cent) believe that brands need to do more to positively impact society.

The shoe brand Camper recognized the importance of social responsibility relatively early and has kept it at the forefront of its brand messaging since the early 2000s. This is explained in more depth in the following case study.

REAL-WORLD EXAMPLE   How Camper turns glocalization
                          on its head

Camper provides us with an interesting example of global branding. Camper is a Spanish footwear company that has grown from a family business to a global business over four generations. In 2001, the company decided to develop a marketing campaign that would reflect the 'true spirit of the company, that could add culture to products while humanising the message' (Camper, 2024). It launched a campaign with the tagline 'Walk, don't run', which was meant to embody a link between the company's rural origins and the urban market. It created The Walking Society, which it describes as 'a cultural declaration' (Camper, 2024).

Camper adverts were, and still are, very different to the typical Westernized advertising we are used to. Camper prefers to emphasize the local way of life in Spain (and the Mediterranean more broadly) rather than tapping into the 'global cool'. Each campaign 'travels through a different location, with specific people and their customs' (Camper, 2024). The company draws on ideas of life in Spain and some of its key characteristics, such as people hanging out on hay bales stacked in a field, sitting at cafés or standing by the seaside. Each is intended to reflect a slower pace of life. Some adverts have also put environmental concerns at the forefront, with taglines such as 'If you don't need it, don't buy it' (Fulleylove, 2015).

With this in mind, we can suggest that Camper turns ideas of glocalization (where you think global and act local – refer to Chapter 3) into 'locbal' (where you think local and act global). Their adverts effectively turn the glocalization concept on its head.

As we've seen, Camper should be viewed in contrast to other global brands. Global brands often seek to be seen as cool and placeless, rather than Camper's focus on being small, friendly, authentic and traditional, as well as emphasizing their sustainable product attributes.

A large part of Camper's success on the global stage comes down to this recognition of its cultural background. It enhances brand authenticity and makes them stand out from the crowd. Today, Camper continues to emphasize its originality and sustainability focus. Its ESG policy occupies a prominent position on its website, and its environmental and social responsibility messaging is front and centre.

Questions

- How do the Camper adverts in question differ from typical Western-style adverts? Why is this significant?
- How do Camper's adverts link to glocalization? What about globalization?
- Would you suggest that other global organizations might be successful in taking a similar approach to their advertising as seen in Camper's adverts? Explain your answer, and provide supporting examples to further your discussion.

Getting to be a global brand is not easy, but global status is considered by many to be a key milestone in a longer game plan rather than an end destination. We'll now consider what brands can do to maintain and enhance their status once they have managed to become global. What can they do beyond branding? What are the next steps? How do they grow? How do they maintain and deepen customer loyalty over time?

Beyond branding

For many brands, becoming global is not the end goal. Global status acts as a gateway to further growth and the diversification of product offerings, including things like **brand-based experiences**. Many of these strategies have one goal in mind – to forge stronger relationships with customers, deepen customer loyalty and strengthen their positive feelings and emotions towards your brand.

How global brands can grow

Once brands reach global status, many seek to use their newfound position and influence to grow further. This often happens through **mergers and acquisitions** (M&A) activity, when two companies either merge together or, typically, a large company buys a smaller one and absorbs it into its operations. M&A activity can offer interesting opportunities for expansion and gaining market share. For example, The Walt Disney Company has completed at least 20 acquisitions with an average acquisition value of US\$8.71 billion (Tracxn, 2024). In 2019, the company acquired the television and film company Twenty-First Century Fox Inc. The deal offered Disney the chance to bring together 'talented leaders in television and movie production, major cable properties and a vast network of local sports cable channels to fold into Disney's... programming' (Schwartz, 2019). It also meant that Disney now owned characters such as Marvel's X-Men and Fantastic Four, putting it in a better position to take on the likes of competitors such as Netflix.

These types of acquisitions have been happening for decades. Indeed, Twentieth Century Fox Film Corporation was formed after a merger of Fox Film Corporation and Twentieth Century Pictures in 1935 (Britannica, 2024). In 1996, Time Warner bought Turner Broadcasting, the parent company of CNN. This not only resulted in Warner Bros, but it allowed for cross-promotion between magazines and films on CNN, which ultimately kept cash in the corporate family (CNN Money, 1996).

Such cross-promotion creates a synergy that is mutually beneficial for collaborators and extends brands' reach to maximize impact. Cross-promotional brand experiences are another way that global brands can extend their reach once they have become global.

Brand-based experiences

Brand-based experiences occur when brands branch out to offer a complete lifestyle package to consumers. Brands can go further than the branding itself. Disney is a great example of how this can be done. Consider the company's use of branded stores, amusement parks, multimedia, merchandise, coffee bars and food. Together, these brand elements create a brand-based experience where consumers have the opportunity for Disney's brand to infiltrate many different facets of their lives. Such brand-based experiences can become a 'branded loop', making it increasingly difficult for consumers to escape. Disney perhaps created the ultimate branded loop by building its own town in Florida. See the following case study for more details.

REAL-WORLD EXAMPLE   Disney's Celebration town, Florida

Celebration is a town designed and built by The Walt Disney Company in the late 1990s (AFP, 2012). It was built like a Disney film set, embodying many of the brand's key characteristics. Front gardens were lined with picket fences, while pristine public spaces and neoclassical architecture gave it a traditional, cosy feel. Celebration was the embodiment of 'days gone by'. A Disney-appointed residents association worked tirelessly to keep it that way, ensuring that strict rules were adhered to by all residents. Gardens had to be free of weeds, external paintwork had to be maintained, and patios jet-washed until they looked perfect.

In return, residents could live in a Disney dream world, complete with year-round Disney fun such as fake snow at Christmas time in the Florida heat. Residents didn't just buy a house, they bought a lifestyle. As Klein wrote in *No Logo* (2000), 'For the families who live there, year-round, Disney has achieved the ultimate goal of lifestyle branding; for the brand to become life itself.'

Questions

- What do you think it would be like to live in a branded town such as Celebration? Can you think of any other examples of people choosing to live such branded lives?

- Interestingly, in a town that was itself an embodiment of a brand, there was no evidence of any brands in it. No Walmarts, no Starbucks, not even Disney-branded products. In Klein's words, it was 'a celebration of brandlessness' (Klein, 2000). What do you think The Walt Disney Company was trying to achieve by taking this approach?

The negative side of global brands

So far, we've considered some of the overwhelmingly positive aspects of global branding from the perspective of organizations. We've also touched on some of the more negative repercussions of global brands switching their production to the developing world in order to achieve and maintain dominance on the global stage. We've discussed reasons for consumer backlash against global brands, particularly in the 1990s when globalization was entering a new phase. There are some further critical issues to be aware of in relation to global brands. We will end this chapter by considering some alternative meanings that consumers can ascribe to global brands.

Infidel brands

In 2012, Izberk-Bilgin published an influential article entitled 'Infidel brands'. Its focus was to unveil alternative meanings of global brands, particularly concerning globalization, consumer culture and Islamism. The study looked at how the religious ideology of Islamism informs brand meaning among low-income Turkish consumers and therefore impacts the marketplace.

Izberk-Bilgin found that global brands provide consumers with a way to contest globalization, particularly among lower-income groups, also suggesting that global brands were being positioned as a threat to the ideal Islamic society. Global organizations such as Nestlé, McDonald's and Coca-Cola were seen by many of the study's participants as infidel brands. As you can probably tell, Izberk-Bilgin's study gave an overwhelmingly negative view of global brands as seen by the study's participants. There were some particularly interesting points made by the participants which could be grouped thematically into the notions of modesty, morality and tyranny. We'll go on to consider these now.

Modesty

Many of the quotations from participants centred around consumers' issues with the pervasiveness of Westernized culture and the extent to which it is imposed on other parts of the globe. They brought the strength of feeling against global Western brands to life and suggested that they could attempt to become more modest in their operations in the global arena. One participant commented: 'Consumption is a trap meant to addict us to European and American culture and their products. It's a trap that would swallow you if you were to fall prey to temptations.' Another participant suggested: 'What we need to do is think about how a real Muslim would live. If we lived to the principles like a true Muslim, we, as a society, wouldn't be in this mess' (Izberk-Bilgin, 2012).

These sentiments suggest that, from a consumer perspective, brands should bear in mind social equality and the potential for social rivalry which could be caused by the arrival of a global brand in any given country. However, in contrast, we might also consider modesty as a social glue which helps to prevent social fragmentation. If the threat of global brands overwhelming a particular culture were to be removed, that society may be less likely to become fragmented.

Morality

In discussing morality, Izberk-Bilgin's study again brought to life some interesting perspectives. For example: 'The first letter our son wrote down was "M" and it looked a lot like [the] McDonald's logo. I was really upset. We try to educate him, teach him that it isn't halal, but he's too young to understand.' A further quote suggests: 'There's nothing for us in those fast-food restaurants. We can't trust them to uphold our Islamic values.'

These quotations could be seen to cement the view that global brands embody Western lifestyles and try to instil Western values into the global arena. In the study, this was seen as threatening Islamic morality. As Izberk-Bilgin suggests, 'embracing those market offerings that are amicable to Islamic ideology while pushing back those that are not' can be seen as essential in consumers' understanding and use of global brands in a local context.

Tyranny

On the topic of tyranny, a participant commented: 'I stay away from anything that is going to offend my faith. My criterion, when I shop, is not the brand name but where its proceeds go, what kind of causes they use their profiles [for].' This quote suggests that global brands can often be seen as a threat to the Muslim faith and as a way of oppressing Muslim identity. In this scenario, Muslim consumers are painted as the victims of infidel Western brands.

How can Western brands respond to this level of criticism? Is there anything they can do to dissuade this way of thinking and feeling? One answer is to develop products that are sensitive to different cultures. Let's consider perfume. For Muslims, wearing fragrance goes beyond smelling nice. It symbolizes purity and spirituality. And yet many Western brands of perfume contain alcohol, which Islamic teaching forbids due to its intoxicating effects and potential to cause harm (Riwaya, 2024). There is therefore a clear market for alcohol-free perfume, which would not risk offending people's faith. Introducing products like alcohol-free perfume may be useful in further connecting global organizations and brands to consumers with different backgrounds, particularly those who find the all-pervasiveness of Western brands to be problematic.

Aikido brands

Aikido is a Japanese martial art which focuses on attacking your opponent by kicking or pounding them using their own energy or strength against them. The idea is to gain control of your opponent and throw them away.

How can we apply this to branding? Could a global brand's own fame, image or strength be used against them? Let's again return to cola, and specifically to the case of Mecca Cola, a French brand launched in 2002 with the aim of exploiting anti-American sentiment. On its website, its founder Tawfik Mathlouthi writes about how he founded the company 'to shake the conscience of Americans' (Mecca Cola, 2024a). At its launch, the company claimed that 10 per cent of its profits would go to a Palestinian charity and a further 10 per cent to charities in the United Kingdom (Mecca Cola, 2003). This could be an attempt to align with views such as those displayed by one of Izberk-Bilgin's study participants, that they make purchasing decisions based on where the proceeds of the brand go and the causes they support. While Mecca Cola has nothing like the global brand dominance of Coca-Cola, it is nevertheless still going strong after over 20 years. Its website homepage states: 'Out of 100 people surveyed in Pakistan, France, the United Arab Emirates, Malaysia or Senegal, everyone without exception has heard of Mecca Cola and can identify the brand' (Mecca Cola, 2024b).

Visually, Mecca Cola is very similar to Coca-Cola. The drink is presented in a red can with a very similar font. But, as we have seen, Mecca Cola is far from the highly visual symbol of globalization that we might determine Coca-Cola to be. Mecca Cola's visual association with Coca-Cola is an example of how brands can become associated with negative aspects of globalization when others use the fame, image and strengths of the brand against itself, particularly in relation to the aesthetics of the product.

CHAPTER SUMMARY

This chapter has explored the concept and role of brands and branding in a globalized world. In doing so, we have linked back to the notion of Kaplinsky and Morris's value chain to help us to gain perspective as to why the role of branding is key in contemporary global markets. Indeed, we might place significant emphasis on the role of branding, and to a certain extent on the design phases of the value chain, due to the loss of focus with regard to manufacturing given the potential for outsourcing production, leading to lower resource demands and responsibilities for global organizations.

We have also examined the role of brands as they pertain to customers and consumers, along with how they can both impact purchasing decisions and help to establish long-term relationships between organizations and consumers. Equally, as noted in the chapter, brands can also be useful in terms of consumers' portrayal of their identity, with individuals using brands to 'speak' (Lévi-Strauss, 1991), communicating, for example, elements of the identity they desire to portray. However, as also discussed in the chapter, things can and do go wrong for global brands. For instance, consider the case of Mecca Cola and Coca-Cola in light of the Aikido brand concept.

Readers might also draw parallels here to concepts discussed earlier on in this book, such as Chapter 2's history of marketing and the rise of its importance. Might we say the same thing here in relation to brands and branding?

We now turn to Chapter 7, where we explore half of the debate about whether the global marketplace is converging or diverging. (We cover the rest of the debate in Chapter 8.) In essence, this means that we will question whether the global marketplace is becoming more similar or more different. In doing so, we introduce a new key term, grobalization, and spend time exploring its subprocesses and potential consequences.

CHAPTER REVIEW QUESTIONS

- Why is organizational focus often placed on the design and marketing elements of Kaplinsky and Morris's value chain, rather than on the production of products?

- How would you define the concept of a 'brand'?

- Do you agree with the assertion that 'perception is more important than reality' (Duncan and Moriarty, 1998) when considering brands? Explain your answer using supporting examples.

- Do you think that you could taste the difference between your favourite food and a substitute offering? To what extent do you think that the branding controls your purchasing decisions in the supermarket?

- Consider brands that were in frequent use in your household as a child. Do you still use the same brands now? Why, or why not?
- Aside from the cola brands noted in the chapter, can you think of any other examples of Aikido brands?

KEY TERMS

Brand-based experiences: A way of creating ongoing exposure to a brand by designing events or experiences that consumers can participate in.

Greenwashing: The process of misleading consumers by claiming that your organization's processes and operations are more environmentally friendly than they actually are.

Mergers and acquisitions: When two companies merge together or a larger company buys a smaller company and absorbs it into its operations.

Value chain: The set of activities organizations undertake to bring their offering to market and create value. These can include product design, production and manufacturing, and marketing and branding.

References

AFP (2012) Living in the town that Disney built, www.youtube.com/watch?v=2zaMq8ZapR4 (archived at https://perma.cc/6A68-WYFA)

Atkins, B (2023) Manufacturing moving out of China for friendlier shores, *Forbes*, www.forbes.com/sites/betsyatkins/2023/08/07/manufacturing-moving-out-of-china-for-friendlier-shores/ (archived at https://perma.cc/EP59-YEU5)

Brewerton, D (2010) Lord Laing of Dunphail obituary, *The Guardian*, www.theguardian.com/business/2010/jul/12/lord-laing-of-dunphail-obituary (archived at https://perma.cc/E5CW-VFUR)

Britannica (2024) 20th Century Studios, www.britannica.com/money/20th-Century-Studios (archived at https://perma.cc/E8EW-MVU7)

Camper (2024) Camper history: IV – Camper communication campaigns, www.camper.com/sites/default/files/pdf/EN_04_com-campaigns_en.pdf (archived at https://perma.cc/9SM4-8R46)

CNN Money (1996) Time, TBS deal sealed, money.cnn.com/1996/07/17/companies/time_warner/ (archived at https://perma.cc/SS2Q-76RJ)

Crimmins, T (2012) Nike: Find your greatness, www.youtube.com/watch?v=WYP9AGtLvRg (archived at https://perma.cc/23YZ-9VLU)

Duncan, T and Moriarty, S E (1998) A communication-based marketing model for managing relationships, *Journal of Marketing*, 62 (2), 1–13

Food Active (2023) Location, location, location: Exploring the impact and implementation of the promotion of high in fat, sugar and salt products by location legislation in England, foodactive.org.uk/wp-content/uploads/2023/11/Location_Location_Location_Winter2023_FINAL.pdf (archived at https://perma.cc/NG2C-BZPS)

Fulleylove, R (2015) Great graphics in Design Museum's Camper 40th anniversary celebration, www.itsnicethat.com/articles/camper (archived at https://perma.cc/MDQ4-BPTV)

Hall & Partners (2021) Conscious brands 100: A new way to measure world-leading brands, hallandpartners.com/perspectives/conscious-brands-100 (archived at https://perma.cc/55C8-SLJ2)

Hancox, D (2019) *No Logo* at 20: Have we lost the battle against the total branding or our lives? *The Guardian*, www.theguardian.com/books/2019/aug/11/no-logo-naomi-klein-20-years-on-interview (archived at https://perma.cc/ZMN8-KEJ8)

Harvard Business School (2024) Key concepts: The value chain, www.isc.hbs.edu/strategy/business-strategy/Pages/the-value-chain.aspx (archived at https://perma.cc/234M-CKEF)

Hennepin History Museum (2018) Two peas in a pod: The Jolly Green Giant and the Little Green Sprout, hennepinhistory.org/two-peas-in-a-pod-the-jolly-green-giant-and-the-little-green-sprout/ (archived at https://perma.cc/4URT-5ZZ4)

Hirst, D and Burn, G (2002) *On the Way to Work*, Faber & Faber

Hochschild, A (1983) *The Managed Heart: Commercialization of human feeling*, University of California Press

Holt, D, Quelch, J and Taylor, E L (2004) How global brands compete, *Harvard Business Review*, hbr.org/2004/09/how-global-brands-compete (archived at https://perma.cc/CD4V-3RN7)

Izberk-Bilgin, E (2012) Infidel brands: Unveiling alternative meanings of global brands at the nexus of globalization, consumer culture, and Islamism, *Journal of Consumer Research*, 39 (4), 663–87

Kaplinsky, R and Morris, M (2001) A handbook for value chain research, www.researchgate.net/publication/42791981_A_Handbook_for_Value_Chain_Research (archived at https://perma.cc/CG26-ZVNK)

Klein, N (2000) *No Logo*, Flamingo

Lévi-Strauss, C (1991) *Totemism*, Merlin Press

Mecca Cola (2003) Mecca-Cola claim 10% of profits will go to a Palestinian Charity and a further 10% will go to UK charities, meccacolagroup.com/2003/01/21/western-mail/ (archived at https://perma.cc/93HX-FXYR)

Mecca Cola (2024a) The founder and you, meccacolagroup.com/the-founer-and-you/ (archived at https://perma.cc/8AKM-MRJS)

Mecca Cola (2024b) We are different, meccacolagroup.com (archived at https://perma.cc/P6V8-VF9V)

MEF (2003) No Logo: Brands. Globalization. Resistance, www.youtube.com/watch?v=oeTgLKNb5R0 (archived at https://perma.cc/9J3Q-7JHV)

MyArtBroker (2024a) Spots, www.myartbroker.com/artist-damien-hirst/collection-spots (archived at https://perma.cc/5D63-QQWF)

MyArtBroker (2024b) Damien Hirst value: Top prices paid at auction, www.myartbroker.com/artist-damien-hirst/record-prices/damien-hirst-record-prices (archived at https://perma.cc/2YZD-ZBCC)

Oswald, L R (2020) What do affluent Chinese consumers want?: A semiotic approach to building brand literacy in developing markets, in *Marketing Management: A cultural perspective* (2nd ed), Routledge, www.marketingsemiotics.com/wp-content/uploads/2012/03/LuxuryAdvertisingChina.pdf (archived at https://perma.cc/45P6-6768)

Porter, M E (1985) *Competitive Advantage: Creating and sustaining superior performance*, Free Press

Radiological Society of North America (2006) MRI shows brains respond better to name brands, *ScienceDaily*, www.sciencedaily.com/releases/2006/11/061128083022.htm (archived at https://perma.cc/57TZ-6VU7)

Riwaya (2024) Why are alcohol-free fragrances important in Islam? riwaya.co.uk/riwaya-blog/importance-of-alcohol-free-fragrances-in-islam/ (archived at https://perma.cc/CVF6-L2JM)

Schwartz, M S (2019) Disney officially owns 21st Century Fox, NPR, www.npr.org/2019/03/20/705009029/disney-officially-owns-21st-century-fox (archived at https://perma.cc/89Q4-PD25)

Tate (2024) Young British Artists (YBAs), www.tate.org.uk/art/art-terms/y/young-british-artists-ybas (archived at https://perma.cc/8PYV-HFGX)

Tracxn (2024) Acquisitions by The Walt Disney Company, tracxn.com/d/acquisitions/acquisitions-by-the-walt-disney-company/__o0wanQHNSabE09VL3X0guQVuS4O4aAkCHmNxQNB87MQ (archived at https://perma.cc/MV9B-672L)

Wieden, D (2024) Nike (1987) – Just Do It, *Creative Review*, www.creativereview.co.uk/just-do-it-slogan/ (archived at https://perma.cc/K5KG-AATM)

Willigan, G E (1992) High-performance marketing: An interview with Nike's Phil Knight, *Harvard Business Review*, hbr.org/1992/07/high-performance-marketing-an-interview-with-nikes-phil-knight (archived at https://perma.cc/SG46-ZANM)

7 | Cultural convergence: Consumption in the global marketplace

LEARNING OBJECTIVES

By the end of this chapter, you should be able to:

- clearly define and differentiate between globalization, glocalization and grobalization

- explain the three subprocesses of grobalization: capitalism, McDonaldization and Americanisms

- understand the difference between 'something' and 'nothing' as consequences of grobalization, and apply this knowledge to different offerings, scenarios, locations and so on

- discuss the various categories of the 'something'–'nothing' continuum

- critically discuss the notion of convergence in marketing efforts and, more broadly, in contemporary global markets

Introduction

This chapter is concerned with the concept of cultural convergence. Importantly, the arguments, theories and examples discussed in this chapter should be considered in addition to those presented in Chapter 8, as the latter provides some counterarguments that will likely broaden your understanding and thoughts around the complex topic of consumption in the global marketplace.

This chapter, however, is primarily focused on the role of grobalization in consumerism, and the consequences of this for organizations and consumers. Namely, the chapter discusses the distinction between globalization, glocalization and grobalization, along with grobalization's three subprocesses, consisting of capitalism, McDonaldization and Americanisms, before exploring the potential outcomes of 'something' and 'nothing'. The chapter further explores the 'something' and 'nothing' continuum, which consists of non-places, non-things, non-people and non-services, suggesting that 'something' and 'nothing' are highly present in contemporary retail and marketing environments.

To provide some initial content for our discussions of grobalization, the chapter begins with an introduction to the concept of the global village, as coined by McLuhan (1964). Links to Disneyization (Bryman, 2007) are also presented, facilitating a consideration of the similarities and differences in the principles proposed by Disneyization and McDonaldization, under the broader umbrella headings of grobalization and globalization. The chapter concludes with a case study looking at the uptake of cosmetic surgery among young Chinese women and men, providing further insight into the spread of grobalization from the West to the East, but with offerings that are perhaps higher stakes than might be seen with a typical offering.

The global village

Before delving into the theories as discussed during this chapter, it is important to discuss some context in which to ground our knowledge. In particular, the concept of the global village provides some key background to our understanding of organizations and consumers, and the ways in which they may behave as players in the global marketplace.

Coined by McLuhan in 1964, the term 'global village' places emphasis on the use and proliferation of media across geographical boundaries. Media, in this instance, might refer to a multitude of communications technologies, such as television, the telephone and the internet. This, McLuhan suggests, promotes interconnection, with consumers and organizations across the globe having the capacity to exchange and gather information, to make purchases, and so forth. We might also connect our thinking here to Dicken's Shrinking World concept (2015; see Chapter 2), as the global village also suggests that time and space compression is possible, however, in this case, with media specifically defying such dimensions.

On the surface, the global village concept may seem like a win-win situation for both organizations and consumers. It provides organizations and consumers across the globe with opportunities to engage with content, people and offerings that would not otherwise be available to them in their local area. However, de Mooij (2004) argues, 'If you assume people are the same everywhere, global media extend homogeneity.' This suggests that the global village – and, by its nature, the global communications media of which it is comprised – will lead to homogeneity. In other words, if consumers across the globe have access to the same media, information, offerings, and so on, we can expect the global marketplace to become the same for all consumers.

An extension of this thinking might be seen with the adoption of 'consumption symbols from people in other parts of the world; the assumption being that other behaviours also change. International news organizations in particular imply that American values are becoming universal' (de Mooij, 2004). Such considerations will become key in our discussions later in this chapter, with regard to grobalization.

However, we must also recognize that consumers are not all the same. Indeed, de Mooij notes that '[w]hat people do with their possessions does not converge'. Similarities might be drawn here to the earlier chapter covering consumer behaviour. While consumers across the globe may have access to a homogenized range of communications and offerings, organizations – as much as they may wish they could – cannot control how a consumer processes information received (think back to the encoding and decoding processes discussed in Chapter 5), nor what they do with an offering following a purchase.

This is where our reflections surrounding the global marketplace become more complex: although we as consumers can access everything and anything following the global village mentality, do we?

The three Gs: Globalization, glocalization and grobalization

In previous chapters, we have explored **globalization** and **glocalization**. To recap, globalization might be defined as a 'multidimensional set of social processes that create, multiply, stretch, and intensify worldwide social interdependencies and exchanges while at the same time fostering in people a growing awareness of deepening connections between the local and distant' (Steger, 2003). Glocalization, on the other hand, might be defined as 'the integration of the global and the local, producing a unique outcome wherever in the world it occurs' (Ritzer, 2007).

Grobalization, however, is a concept that Ritzer describes as the '[i]mperialistic ambitions of corporations, states, and others and their imposition of their ways of doing things, products, and so forth on the local'. To further unpack Ritzer's definition, we might suggest that nation-states, organizations and corporations have a need to impose themselves on various geographical areas around the world. The purpose of such an imposition is generally to increase their power, influence, and in some cases profits (Ritzer, 2007).

For readers conscious of the very similar sounds of globalization, glocalization and grobalization, who may wish to find some distinction by which to remember the meanings, a simple way to remember the meaning of grobalization is to consider the term as a combination of 'grow' and 'globalization'. In other words, the purpose of grobalization is to grow in power, influence, and sometimes profits, but in a global context.

Grobalization's three subprocesses

Grobalization can be seen as comprised of three subprocesses: capitalism, McDonaldization and Americanisms.

Capitalism

Grobalization suggests a rise in capitalism as organizations or other entities typically seek to grow in profit through their grobalized activities. This is accomplished by seeking to gain profits from nations other than, and often in addition to, those acquired in the organization's home country. Globalization can be a useful background for grobalized activities in this sense, as the removal of geographical constraints provides a rich and fluid environment in which an organization can look to enter and prosper in a range of geographical locations. Furthermore, organizations will often see that there is no viable alternative to capitalism, and as such to grobalization. This may be due to a range of environmental and market factors such as increased competition in an organization's home country, or the need to gain access to larger consumer markets to seek profit and thus sustained levels of economic viability.

McDonaldization

McDonaldization, the second of our grobalization subprocesses, is underpinned by rational bureaucracy and standardization, and is characterized by four key concepts: efficiency, calculability, predictability and control. McDonaldization, and McDonald's itself, has become so successful that a Big Mac Index tool has been developed to compare the price of McDonald's Big Mac burgers in different countries across the globe, and is characterized by the term 'Burgernomics' (The Economist, 2024).

ACTIVITY

The Big Mac Index

The Big Mac Index is a tool that compares the price of a Big Mac in a number of different countries across the globe. Explore the index and note the price of a Big Mac in your home country in comparison to a different destination. What does this tell you about both countries explored?

To access the Big Mac Index, visit: www.economist.com/big-mac-index.

Efficiency is concerned with the 'discovery and implementation of the best way to do virtually everything' (Ritzer, 2002). We might see this from a consumer perspective, with individuals and families purchasing fast food itself rather than opting to make a meal at home, and in using a drive-thru rather than entering the fast-food restaurant in order to save further time in the process. Equally, we might argue that additional time might be saved even in the ordering process, for example by ordering food via the McDonald's app which can then be picked up at the restaurant.

While these elements arguably aid the efficiency of the process for organizations in addition to consumers, there are also some specific organizational processes that might be seen as contributing to efficiency. For example, in its early days, McDonald's used a tennis court to sketch out and visualize where the numerous machines and workstations might be situated in their kitchens (Channel 5, 2019). The point of this was to determine the best flow to implement in the kitchen area of the restaurant, in order to improve efficiency and, as a result, productivity and profits.

Calculability, on the other hand, places value on quantification rather than quality. For example, if we take the infamous McDonald's French fries, emphasis is placed on standardization and being able to make enough product to satisfy demand, rather than on ensuring that the quality of the French fries is perfect each and every time they are produced.

Predictability considers a range of elements associated with an organization. If we once again take McDonald's as an example, we might be concerned with factors such as the layout of restaurants, aesthetics of the location and food, the meal itself, the ordering process and so on. Predictability, however, can go further than just our expectations when we enter a local restaurant. For example, consider the following scenario: you have just arrived at your holiday destination and made your way from the airport to the centre of the resort. The plane journey was delayed and the cabin crew did not have any meals or snacks for sale on your flight. You didn't have time to get any food at the airport, as, due to your flight delay, you had to run to make your transfer.

It is now lunchtime, and you are very hungry, but you do not speak the local language at your holiday destination. You see a McDonald's restaurant and a local restaurant in the resort centre. Which do you choose?

Chances are, you will choose to visit the McDonald's restaurant in this situation, as you are familiar with the processes and ordering system (typically digital, with the ability to translate the menu), and you know what the meal you order is likely to be like, along with being able to predict the quality of the meal that you will receive. This is where predictability comes into play: we know what to expect, so often will take the 'safest' or most familiar course of action.

Our final construct in McDonaldization is that of control. Control suggests the deskilling of workers in McDonaldized organizations as machines can undertake roles typically done by their human counterparts. For a simplified example, imagine needing to manually monitor the amount of time McDonald's French fries are cooked for, versus a programmed machine beeping to let you know when the item has finished cooking.

Arguably, control can also lead to dehumanization for both employees and consumers. Employees know what is expected of their performance at work, covering tasks such as a scripted welcome and order-taking process, whereas consumers, upon entering a McDonald's restaurant, know exactly how to order, along with the remainder of the processes to be followed during the visit. Here, we might link back to this chapter's earlier arguments in line with the discussion from de Mooij (2004) that we are becoming more similar: as in the case of a McDonaldized restaurant, many consumers may be consuming the items and experience in a very similar way.

Indeed, we might view McDonaldization as a world paradigm, a way in which to see the world where organization, standardization and control are king. As Ritzer (2002) notes, McDonaldization might be seen as 'the process by which the principles of the fast-food restaurant are coming to dominate more and more of American society as well as the rest of the world'.

While the above introduction to McDonaldization has used McDonald's itself as the obvious example, we can also see McDonaldization spreading much further and to a more varied set of organizations and institutions across the globe. For instance, Drane (2002) applies the principles of McDonaldization to the church and religion. Drane suggests that efficiency might be realized via the welcome to the service provided, with religious bookstores offering many of the same titles regardless of location, or with similar or the same musical programmes being used. This, Drane suggests, leads to a 'prepackaged church'. Calculability may be viewed in the number of attendees at a service, or in the number of individuals converting to a particular religion, particularly in 1970s and 1980s America. Predictability might also be seen in the form of services and the worship performed.

However, Drane cautions that this can lead to a temptation to treat people like clones; the faith becomes predictable, and even personal experiences like conversion to a different religion are packaged to fit a notion of how a 'true' conversion should be. Indeed, even the notion of imitating a 'successful' church's approach might be viewed as prescriptive, with control being viewed as the provision of 'one type of spiritualist diet', formed of a specific dress code, language and staff demeanour.

Americanisms

The final subprocess of grobalization is Americanisms. Americanisms are elements of American culture, such as ideas, customs, values, images, sayings and so on, that tend to overwhelm or compete with alternatives in a particular country (although the use of 'iz' rather than 'is' spellings are in fairness the preferred spelling for some terms, for example, within the Oxford English Dictionary). This might be seen in two countries having different words for the same item. Let's take the UK as an example. In the UK the word 'pavement' might be used, whereas 'sidewalk' would be used in America. Equally, 'two weeks' may be used in the UK, whereas in America it may be more common to say 'fortnight'. In this case, we might suggest that an Americanism has taken root in the UK if a large number of people start to use the terms 'sidewalk' and 'fortnight' instead of the usual British alternatives.

In these brief hypothetical examples, we can see the Americanized version of the word competing and overtaking the traditional British words. This essentially demonstrates Americanisms as a subprocess of grobalization, as we see influence, in this case from America, being applied to the UK. We often see Americanisms coming to fruition due to media such as movies or films (an example in itself!) being viewed by consumers in other countries, who then may adopt the language that they have heard on the screen.

Such Americanisms can be pervasive – have you noticed, for instance, that while writing this book from my desk in the UK, I am using the Americanized spellings for terms such as globalization, glocalization, grobalization and so on, rather than the English versions of globalisation, glocalisation and grobalisation? This speaks not only to the pervasive nature of Americanisms in TV shows, films and the like, but also to institutions where we may not expect them, such as education and academia. Wherever we encounter Americanisms, they may be perceived as annoying to some consumers, who may feel that they have to fight to preserve their native language.

ACTIVITY

Americanisms

What examples of Americanisms can you think of? Where did you come across these terms? How often do you say them?

To what extent, if any, do you think mass media impacts your use of Americanisms? Are there any specific examples of media that have influenced your speech patterns?

ACTIVITY

At the American 'intersection' (vs English 'crossroads') of language

Readers interested in learning more about Americanisms, including some further words that differ between American English and UK English language, may wish to listen to the episode of Michael Rosen's Word of Mouth podcast titled 'Like totally awesome: The Americanization of English' (2017).

Discerning readers may take some hints as to Rosen's stance on the intersection between American English and UK English language from the podcast's title. See if you can spot the clues!

Grobalization and consumerism

When considering the sum of grobalization's subprocesses, we might also call into question the 'means of consumption' (Ritzer, 2002) available to us as consumers. Often, the easiest solution is to make our purchases online or to visit a shopping centre/mall or shopping park (in other words, contemporary retail environments), rather than our local high street.

There has been much speculation in recent years surrounding the decline of local stores and high streets (Simpson, 2021), in favour of large, branded shopping areas such as centres, malls and retail parks. Ritzer deems these types of shopping locations 'cathedrals of consumption', noting the 'quasi-religious' acts of consumers inhabiting such spaces.

As Ritzer explains, shopping centres and similar settings allow access to an array of goods and services, not just allowing people to consume but encouraging consumption. In other words, Ritzer is suggesting that through centres of consumption such as the contemporary retail environments previously mentioned, we, as consumers, have easy access to a multitude of offerings and brands, allowing us to purchase from multiple product categories during one visit. While the steadfast consumer may visit a shopping centre to specifically purchase one item and then leave, often, consumers will decide to explore further stores and purchase additional offerings.

This is where Ritzer's suggestion that these settings encourage consumption becomes relevant, as contemporary retail environments facilitate, encourage and sometimes even push consumers towards making further purchases via availability, aesthetics and experiences. In doing so, a shopping centre or its American counterpart, the mall, might be deemed 'an extremely efficient and effective selling machine' (Ritzer, 2002) from the perspective of the consumer. For example, consider the last time that you visited such a place. Did you purchase only the item(s) that you went there for, or did you come away with multiple items that you did not originally intend to buy?

Shopping centres and the like are not all doom and gloom, however. As Ritzer notes, they provide consumers with the chance to spend time with their family and friends, and to 'consume together'. Indeed, we might draw links here to some of the more basic concepts in marketing, such as reference groups, with which we aim to gain acceptance and to reduce the risk associated with the purchases that we make. This, Waters (2002) equates to consumer identities being 'conflated to culture'. In essence, if consumers cannot afford a particular brand or offering seen as desirable by their reference group, individuals and their identities are being devalued as they cannot afford to make the same purchases as others.

Such concerns might be raised further still if we consider consumers in developing countries with typically much lower disposable income. Indeed, 'globalizing flows that fan out from economically advanced sectors to penetrate previously encapsulated cultures' (Waters, 2002) can become an issue. This is not only in relation to consumers having disposable income with which to purchase the offerings of the West, but also in that a standardized approach to consumerism becomes pervasive, seeking to remove elements of local consumption practices as individuals seek to purchase global rather than local offerings.

Grobalization and Disneyization

Disneyization is the process by which the principles of the Disney theme parks start to dominate more aspects of American and global society (Bryman, 2007), and might also be linked closely to grobalization. In particular, we might draw links between Disneyization and McDonaldization, as both seek to impart the principles of operations and ways of being across the globe.

However, we must also draw some distinctions here between the two concepts. While McDonaldization is categorized by predictability, calculability, control and efficiency, eliciting notions of a quick, cheap meal characterized by processes that might be anticipated by consumers in advance of their entering a McDonald's restaurant, Disneyization instead denotes expectations of higher price points, interactions and experiences.

That is not to say that we should be encouraged to view Disneyization as separate to grobalization. For example, if we consider the act of eating at a Disney restaurant, consumers will be likely accosted by themes, the temptation to purchase 'on-trend' items (much as relates to those promoted by prevalent social media users), and souvenirs to remind them of the experience. All of these, of course, come at a cost to the consumer, aligning with the grobalizing notion of profit creation. Such 'optional' extras (when viewed, for example, in comparison to a relatively simple meal in McDonald's) help Disney to create destinations.

Consider both a Disney theme park and a McDonald's restaurant: which would you be more likely to think of as a 'destination'? Chances are, you would consider a Disney theme park to be a destination, whereas a McDonald's restaurant is simply a location to be visited to get food. The creation of a destination encourages consumers to stay longer (in contrast to the McDonald's mentality of speed and efficiency) and ultimately to purchase more as we spend time during the visit and may wish to commemorate our experience via the purchase of merchandise.

Merchandizing in itself can be a useful tool. As Bryman (2007) explains, merchandizing might be viewed 'as a means of building on and extending an image and people's enjoyment of it', with such offerings also serving as a reminder of the visit, and perhaps as a lasting form of encouragement to revisit the destination.

Disneyization also encourages consumers to view shopping as play, a useful technique, given that consumers at theme parks (and other locations, such as cruise ships and airports) are essentially captive shoppers. In such instances, we may see a form of hybrid consumption, 'whereby the forms of consumption associated with different institutional spheres become interlocked with each other and increasingly difficult to distinguish' from other forms of consumption (think restaurants, theme parks, zoos, hotels and more), which 'are brought together in new and often imaginative ways' (Bryman, 2007), much as we see with Disney's use of themes throughout its parks.

The consequences of grobalization: 'Something' and 'nothing'

According to Ritzer (2007), there are two clear consequences of grobalization: 'something' and 'nothing'. Ritzer defines 'nothing' as 'a social form that is generally centrally conceived, controlled, and comparatively devoid of substantive content', whereas 'something' is defined as 'a social form that is generally indigenously conceived, controlled, and is comparatively rich in distinctive substantive content'.

ACTIVITY

'Something' or 'nothing'

In Figure 7.1, we can see two wooden spoons.

Spoon 1 – the image on the left is a wooden spoon purchased by the author in Kobe, Japan, from a small, family-run business which produces its own products in-house. Each spoon available for sale was slightly different aesthetically.

Figure 7.1   Wooden spoons

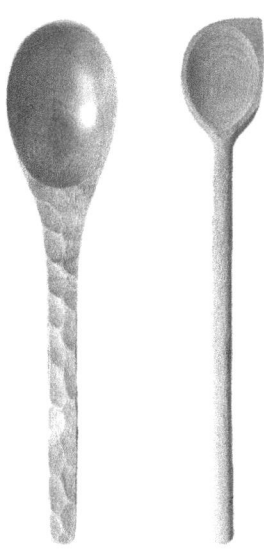

Spoon 2 – the image on the right is a mass-produced wooden spoon, with similar offerings being available from a number of stores across the globe. There are unlikely to be very few, if any, aesthetic differences between the offerings available for purchase. Can you tell which spoon is 'something' and which is 'nothing'?

To further unpack these definitions, 'nothing' is often generic, having nothing different or distinctive about it. In the context of contemporary marketing environments, 'nothing' might relate to a global organization practising a standardized approach to its offerings, communications, and so on. 'Something' is essentially the opposite of 'nothing'. We might expect 'something' to have a substantial amount of significantly different content to an alternative that we might purchase or engage with elsewhere. 'Something' is not centrally conceived or controlled, meaning that local rather than global interpretations and interventions in the construct of an offering are likely to be seen. Indeed, Ritzer draws clear links between grobalization and 'nothing', while 'something', he suggests, relates more closely to glocalization, with all concepts sitting under the umbrella heading of globalization.

Let's now put this into perspective via the use of some examples. If we consider a large global coffee chain such as Starbucks, we might expect to find the same drinks, merchandise and aesthetics when visiting the chain, regardless of the location that we choose to visit. This would suggest that Starbucks would be classed as 'nothing', given Ritzer's definitions.

Next, let's consider 'Blends', an independent coffee shop located in the West Midlands, UK. The coffee shop is not part of a chain and as such its aesthetics, marketing communication messages, products and so on are determined by the individuals who own the store, rather than being centrally determined by a large organization (such as with our Starbucks example). This means that Blends has a significant amount of local content and, if we were to visit another independent coffee shop in a different location, it is highly unlikely to be significantly similar to Blends. This, according to Ritzer's definitions, would suggest that Blends, and the other independent coffee shop, would be classed as 'something'.

'Something' and 'nothing' do not, however, have to relate only to brands or even products. Locations themselves can also be classed as 'something' or 'nothing'. For example, consider a typical mall in America. Regardless of which mall location you choose to visit, you would likely find the same brands or types of stores, restaurants and products, and even how offerings are displayed in the various stores would be the same. However, if you were then to visit an outdoor shopping street in, for example, Japan or France, you would be likely to find a rich cultural experience which would be different to one you may have in another location in the same country. This scenario would be our 'something', as we see much unique and distinctive content in comparison to the American mall, which sees very little in terms of differentiation between various locations.

Indeed, there are many entities that we might describe as 'something' or 'nothing'. Ritzer suggests, for example, non-places, non-things, non-people and non-services. Non-places refers to locations lacking in differentiating content, non-things to objects lacking in differentiating content, non-people to those who through their job role hold positions that require them to lack any distinctive content while at work, and non-services to services lacking any significant differentiating factors or elements.

ACTIVITY

'Something' and 'nothing'

For both 'something' and 'nothing', describe the following:

- a location that you have visited
- a product that you have purchased
- a service that you have used

Which did you prefer? 'Something' or 'nothing'? Why?

Customers as non-people?

While our above examples to a certain extent cover non-places, non-things and non-services, 'non-people' perhaps warrants additional explanation. Ritzer's (2007) impression is that during the performance of their roles in non-places ('nothing'), employees will take on 'nothing' characteristics. We might see this in visiting a fast-food chain or in contacting a call centre, where employees must stick to a script during their conversations with customers, and act or even dress in a particular way.

One might argue that consumers themselves become non-people when choosing to purchase from a non-place, as they become part of the expected process or interaction that is required for the offering to be successfully purchased and consumed. How does this idea make you feel as a customer?

ACTIVITY

'Something' or 'nothing': Your consumption practices?

Consider your own purchasing practices as a consumer. Which do you often prefer, 'something' or 'nothing'? Why? Does the offering you intend to purchase change your answer?

Figure 7.2   A visualization of the 'something'–'nothing' continuum

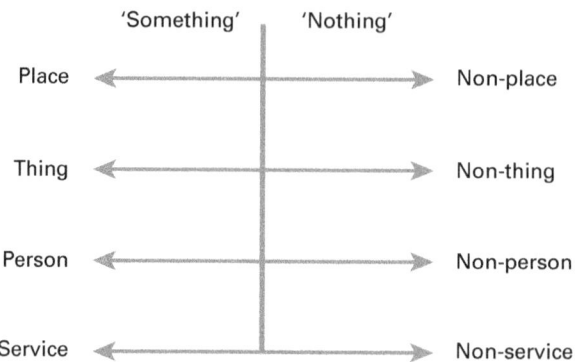

The 'something'–'nothing' continuum

The 'something'–'nothing' continuum (Ritzer, 2013) further allows us to categorize elements as 'something' and 'nothing', and to see their respective counterparts. We might take the categories in Figure 7.2 with which to explore this.

Let's now take as an example trying to book a holiday, and then apply this to the 'something'–'nothing' continuum.

REAL-WORLD EXAMPLE   The 'something' or 'nothing' holiday

- **Place:** Going in person to our local travel agency for advice and booking our trip would be classed as a place. Here, we will be able to ask specific questions about our planned destination and the booking, and to receive individualized responses to our questions. This means that visiting our local travel agency is filled with distinctive content.

- **Non-place:** If we instead decided to visit a travel agent's website to find advice and to book our trip, we would likely be met with the generic advice available to anyone who visited that webpage. This means that visiting the online version of the travel agency could be classed as a non-place as it lacks distinctive content.

- **Thing:** In our holiday booking example, a thing might be seen as an in-person agreement to pay for our holiday. This might, for example, involve us entering the travel agency in person once a month to interact with staff in order to make a scheduled payment.

- **Non-thing:** Rather than entering the travel agency to pay for our holiday, we might instead decide to make payments online or have certain amounts taken from our bank accounts at set periods of time by direct debit to cover the cost. Here, there is no interaction or personalization.

- **Person:** For example, we might visit our local travel agency and discuss our proposed holiday with a member of staff. This individual will likely be able to give advice about the chosen destination, alternatives, and even be able to share their own experience from visiting the destination.

- **Non-person:** If we take the online approach to booking our trip, we may have the option to pose any questions to a chatbot. However, answers are likely to be scripted based on the information we enter and may not always answer our questions properly or to the extent that we need. A Frequently Asked Questions (FAQs) section may also exist on the website, but again, this does not specifically answer any questions we might have, nor does it allow for any distinctive content for different users.

- **Service:** We might see service in a number of ways when booking our holiday, ranging from the initial advice given to us by colleagues in our local travel agency to having a travel agency representative on site when we arrive at our destination, to answer any questions that we might have.

- **Non-service:** Again, we might consider the usefulness of a chatbot in answering any questions that we might have, rather than having a colleague available to discuss queries with us. Another example of a non-service might be seen when we arrive at our destination. Instead of being welcomed by a travel agency representative, we might be directed to use an app or website to help us with issues.

Convergence in practice

Cathedrals of consumption themselves, in whatever form they may take, might be viewed as 'revolutionary' not only due to their own nature, but also in that they play a key role in 'the development and sustenance of contemporary hyperconsumption' (Ritzer, 2005). This, we might suggest, aligns closely with the global consumer who may access an almost infinite number of possible offerings via physical or online stores as and when they so wish it.

From the perspective of the stores (whether physical or digital) located in cathedrals of consumption, or indeed the cathedrals themselves, the objective is typically, as one might expect in line with the principles of grobalization, to grow profits and to retain economic viability. To accomplish this a heavy reliance on rationalization is required, again, as is to be expected when considering grobalization and its subprocesses. However, Ritzer argues that such rationalized and efficient ways of engaging with consumers do not appeal in the traditional sense, but rather that rationalization has its own 'limited kind of magic' (Ritzer, 2005), which, for example, might be seen via efficiency efforts in making offerings available to consumers or in the range of offerings provided.

While our discussions so far in this chapter have focused on what one might deem to be traditional (if still somewhat contemporary, in the case of the digital) locations of consumption (shopping malls/centres and the internet), contemporary marketing environments and consumption habits compel us to explore further avenues of consumption. Indeed, Ritzer discusses the blurring of such boundaries, noting other settings such as 'high schools, universities, museums, athletic stadiums, airports, television… and the home' as avenues for consumption. This speaks to the notion of global consumer culture as all-pervasive – is there anywhere where we are 'safe' from the temptation to engage with consumerist activities?

We often see such opportunities for consumption in unexpected places in our daily lives, and may well not even recognize them as contributing to the cathedrals of consumption that contemporary consumers have become so accustomed to. For example, the health-conscious among us may purchase a gym membership (an act of service consumption in itself). However, rather than the traditionally expected assumption of free water refills, we may be encouraged to instead add water to our gym subscription.

We can see an example of this with PureGym, which offers its members the option to add 'unlimited sports water' as an additional 'bolt on' to their membership from £4 a month (PureGym, 2024). PureGym users have the further option to purchase a padlock from one of the gym's vending machines – again, rather than the traditional mechanism of using a 'to be returned to the consumer' coin – to secure the locker during gym visits. This we might add to the somewhat-expected snacks vending machines in gym locations, but also to the offering of PureGym-branded goods like towels and headphones, along with a dedicated online shop. Thus, as Ritzer (2005) notes, more places start emulating shopping malls and cathedrals of consumption.

While the increased emphasis on arguably the consumption of 'nothing', as with our gym example above, certainly contributes to the imposition of brands via many touchpoints throughout our lives, there are perhaps some benefits to be had from the consumer perspective. While we may not expect the differentiation that comes with a 'something' offering, we may find it comforting to know that certain 'nothing' products will be available for purchase in many locations. For example, the prospect of an hour's gym workout without our forgotten headphones may seem daunting, thus making the few pounds spent for a replacement pair from a vending machine seem a bargain price indeed.

Equally, global consumers have come to expect a certain quality with regard to the 'nothing' goods that they purchase. To continue with our headphones example, we likely know that purchasing headphones from a gym vending machine is not likely to provide us with the highest quality of offering, but it is perhaps better than not having the product, or it may be better quality than we might have previously expected to find in a similar product in the same location.

REAL-WORLD EXAMPLE   Grobalization and cosmetic surgery

Cosmetic surgery is big business in China, often known as 'man-made beauty' or 'knifecut beauty' (Lindridge and Wang, 2008). Common cosmetic procedures might include editing the eyes, nose, lips or face, or the removal of excess fat. Such popularity can be seen with the rise of several social media apps like Gengmei, meaning 'more beautiful' in Chinese, which is dedicated to 'all things plastic surgery' in China. Launched in 2013, Gengmei had grown to 35 million users by 2021, with more than half of the app's users being young women in their twenties (Yip, 2021).

For example, the BBC tells the story of 23-year-old Ruxin, who scrolls through social media content related to plastic surgery every day. She hopes to undertake a double eyelid surgery to make her eyes appear larger, a procedure typically costing around $300–1,200.

However, it is not only young Chinese women seeking to undertake cosmetic surgery to improve their appearance. Young Chinese men, typically professionals, are also keen to enhance their appearance. Indeed, millions of young educated Chinese men are undergoing cosmetic surgery to tackle issues such as low confidence, a dislike of their appearance and feelings of inferiority. For these consumers of cosmetic surgery, there is a real hope that undergoing procedures will significantly change their lives for the better (France24, 2021). This hypothetical improvement via the undertaking of cosmetic surgery may be seen via a number of avenues, such as improvements in an individual's love life, but also through self-improvement and being able to gain additional opportunities, for example in the job market. Indeed, being seen as 'ordinary' is perhaps no longer enough to be able to compete in contemporary China.

Lindridge and Wang conducted a 2008 study of cosmetic surgery users in Shanghai, China, featuring 12 young women covering undergraduate, postgraduate, senior high school and junior high school level participants. These participants had undergone a range of cosmetic surgery procedures, such as 'growth surgery – leg breaking', 'face narrowing, jaw line rebuilding', 'liposuction' and more.

Participants in the study felt physical perfection alone would enable them to achieve career success and 'enhance their family's sense of face', while also noting that pre-requisites for jobs often mentioned height and/or physical appearance as did, perhaps surprisingly for consumers of a Western persuasion, university entrance interviews (Lindridge and Wang, 2008). Indeed, Chinese job applicants are often required to submit a photograph along with their application (Yip, 2021).

After undergoing cosmetic surgery, individuals typically appear happy to share stories of their procedures, although not when it comes to any pain that may have been endured during the process. This, according to Lindridge and Wang, allows participants to 'publicly demonstrate their commitment to personal change and willingness to engage with a modernizing China'. Such stories may even be told to potential employers, rather than just to family members and friends, hinting at their cosmetic surgery being seen as a badge of honour and commitment to personal 'growth'. But, if we delve deeper into the contextual debates surrounding cosmetic surgery in China, we uncover a complex and multifaceted structure in which young Chinese consumers are influenced by family, tradition and modern ways of consumption in China, and by Western media.

Cosmetic surgery in China is often proposed and supported by the parents of those who undergo it, typically more on the part of the mother than the father. This emphasis often means that parents will pay for cosmetic surgeries for their children. While Chinese mothers may see cosmetic surgery as an investment in their children's futures, this also helps with the need to gain and retain 'face' for the family through success. Face, in this instance, might be taken to mean the status of the family in society, often being retained or improved via the achievements of the children.

Furthermore, Western media and consumption practices arguably have a role in the increased Chinese interest in cosmetic procedures. Indeed, from a Western perspective, it might be argued that consumption leads to happiness. Western media such as magazines and television may also be deemed a key influence in terms of beauty standards in China. However, we might then question whether 'Chinese culture will become a poor imitation and misinterpretation of Western culture as one that pursues physical perfection and consumption from a self-indulgent individualistic perspective' (Lindridge and Wang, 2008).

In another stream, we might consider global consumerism more broadly, however, in the context of a modernized China. Indeed, according to Lindridge and Wang, individuals often purchase products that they perceive as 'congruent with their own self-image', suggesting a clash between modernization, in which consumption is rife, versus more traditional forms of collectivist being. This brings challenges for the individualistic modern Chinese consumer, in that they desire to have both family status as well as the perceived freedom of modernization. Therefore, changing an individual's body is loaded with cultural meaning and symbolic consumption to achieve an identity. Embodied capital might then be converted to 'cultural, economic, and social capital' (Lindridge and Wang, 2008), as per hopes for a better love life, opportunities and job role via the consumption of plastic surgery.

Questions

- Young Chinese consumers' decisions to undertake plastic surgery appear, at least in part, to be connected with the idea of progressing and succeeding with their lives. Can you explain why you think this is?

- To what extent do you think that Ritzer's (2007) concepts of grobalization and 'something' and 'nothing' are useful in understanding the case study?

- For the participants noted in the case study, how does undertaking cosmetic surgery link to the notion of saving 'face'?

CHAPTER SUMMARY

This chapter has covered the notion of cultural convergence, recapping the key theories of globalization and glocalization and adding a third 'G', grobalization, to the mix.

As we know from the chapter, grobalization is concerned with the growth of power, influence, and sometimes profits in areas aside from an organization's home country. Comprised of its three subprocesses (capitalism, McDonaldization and Americanisms), grobalization, according to Ritzer (2007), leads to the consequences of either 'something' or 'nothing', often dependent upon the depth of distinctive content present.

We have gone further than this to also explore the 'something'–'nothing' continuum, which demonstrates that not only physical offerings or services can be 'something' or 'nothing', but that many of the component parts of such entities might also be categorized as 'something' or 'nothing' (as with our earlier example of booking a holiday).

The chapter has also explored links to and similarities between McDonaldization, as one of grobalization's subprocesses, and Disneyization, with both concepts establishing principles of practice and operation that might be applied elsewhere across the globe.

The following chapter provides counterarguments to those contained in the current chapter. That is to say, rather than focusing on questions of convergence in the global market, we next turn our attention to the notion of divergence. In doing so, we lend focus to postmodernism and the postmodern consumer, considering implications of contemporary retail environments and their links to consumer identity, consumption habits, symbolic value and individualism.

CHAPTER REVIEW QUESTIONS

The three Gs

- Without looking at your previous notes, try to define the following terms:
  - globalization
  - glocalization
  - grobalization

The 'something'–'nothing' continuum

- From the chapter, we know that the 'something'–'nothing' continuum contains the following categories:
  - place vs non-place
  - thing vs non-thing
  - person vs non-person
  - service vs non-service

- To practise your understanding of the 'something'–'nothing' continuum, try to fill in the various categories in relation to the banking industry. Following this, select another industry of your own choice and try to complete the continuum.

'Something' or 'nothing': Your consumption practices

- Consider your own purchasing practices as a consumer. Which do you often prefer, 'something' or 'nothing'? Why? Does the offering you intend to purchase change your answer?

'Something' or 'nothing': Pervasiveness

- The chapter has explored the notions of 'something' and 'nothing' as the consequences of grobalization, including exploration of the 'something'–'nothing' continuum. Consider the following statement:
  - 'Something' is being replaced by 'nothing' in contemporary retail environments.
- Do you agree or disagree with this statement? Explain the reasoning behind your answer.

The destruction of the local

- Consider the following statement: Grobalization leads to the destruction of the local. Critically explore arguments both for and against this assertion and come to a solid stance as to your perspective.

Homogenization

- Critically discuss the assertion that 'grobalization is leading to a homogeneous culture'. Explain the reasons behind your answer.

Consumption at home

- Would you agree that your home might be classed as a 'cathedral of consumption' (Ritzer, 2005)? Explain your answer, and if you agree with the statement, provide examples as to why this might be the case.

Consumer engagement

- To what extent would you agree that '[t]he attraction is often the cathedral itself'?

Consumption-free zones

- In discussing the blurred boundaries that define contemporary global consumer environments, Ritzer (2005) notes locations such as 'high schools, universities, museums, athletic stadiums, airports, television... and the home' as potential avenues for consumption. Would you suggest any other 'unlikely' locations in which consumption is possible, and do you consider any locations to be free of the temptation to consume?

KEY TERMS

Americanisms: Elements of American culture, such as ideas, customs, values, images or sayings, that overwhelm or compete with alternative norms in a particular country or geographic region outside of America.

Capitalism: Relates to the private ownership of the means of production, with profit generation as a key concern. Prices and distribution systems are typically closely linked with competition in the market of interest.

Globalization: Briefly, interconnectivity, exchanges and communication across the globe.

Glocalization: The interaction between the local and the global, as often characterized by global organizations making small changes to better fit with local areas.

Grobalization: Efforts from organizations and other entities to grow in power, influence and sometimes profit in locations aside from their country of origin.

McDonaldization: An organizational process via which efficiency, calculability, predictability and control are emphasized in operations.

Nothing: An offering or other entity which has little to differentiate it from substitute offerings in alternative locations. Consumers are able to purchase 'nothing products' or to visit 'nothing' locations across the globe and reasonably expect to find the same or very similar contents.

Something: The opposite of 'nothing'. Offerings or other entities have much to differentiate them from substitute offerings in alternative locations. Consumers are not generally able to visit 'something' locations or to purchase 'something' products from multiple locations. If the offering is available in multiple locations, consumers should expect a significant amount of difference.

References

Bryman, A (2007) *The Disneyization of Society*, Sage Publications

Channel 5 (2019) Inside McDonald's: The 300 billion dollar burger business

de Mooij, M (2004) *Consumer Behaviour and Culture: Consequences for global marketing and advertising*, Sage Publications

Dicken, P (2015) *Global Shift: Mapping the changing contours of the world economy* (7th ed), Guilford Press

Drane, J (2002) The church and the iron cage, in G Ritzer, *McDonaldization: The reader*, Sage Publications

France24 (2021) 'Plastic surgery changed my life': The young Chinese men going under the knife, www.france24.com/en/video/20210909-plastic-surgery-changed-my-life-the-young-chinese-men-going-under-the-knife (archived at https://perma.cc/VGK8-WFFW)

Lindridge, A M and Wang, C (2008) Saving 'face' in China: Modernization, parental pressure, and plastic surgery, *Journal of Consumer Behaviour*, 7, 496–508

McLuhan, M (1964) *Understanding Media: The extensions of man*, McGraw-Hill

PureGym (2024) Unlimited sports water, www.puregym.com/membership-options/bolt-ons/sports-water/ (archived at https://perma.cc/M77M-GWWL)

Ritzer, G (2002) *McDonaldization: The reader*, Sage Publications

Ritzer, G (2005) *Enchanting a Disenchanted World: Revolutionizing the means of consumption* (2nd ed), Pine Forge Press

Ritzer, G (2007) *The Globalization of Nothing 2*, Sage Publications

Ritzer, G (2013) *Sociology of Globalization* (1st ed), Routledge

Rosen, M (2017) Like, totally awesome: The Americanisation of English, *Word of Mouth*, www.bbc.co.uk/programmes/b08g5533 (archived at https://perma.cc/HJ7M-4XD6)

Simpson, E (2021) Almost 50 shops a day disappear from high streets, BBC News, www.bbc.co.uk/news/business-58433461 (archived at https://perma.cc/9LTC-UN9U)

Steger, M B (2003) *Globalization: A very short introduction* (2nd ed), Oxford University Press

The Economist (2024) Our Big Mac Index shows how burger prices differ across borders, www.economist.com/big-mac-index (archived at https://perma.cc/9MJA-HTWN)

Waters, M (2002) McDonaldization and the global culture, in G Ritzer, *McDonaldization: The reader*, Sage Publications

Yip, W (2021) Plastic surgery booming in China despite the dangers, BBC News, www.bbc.co.uk/news/world-asia-china-57691525 (archived at https://perma.cc/5QW5-M3VJ)

8 | Cultural divergence: Consumption in the global marketplace

LEARNING OBJECTIVES

By the end of this chapter, you should be able to:

- explain the concept of postmodernism and describe key characteristics that might be assigned to postmodern consumers

- critically discuss the notion of consumer identity, with reference to the role of symbolic value as assigned to the offerings that customers purchase

- critically evaluate the notion of individualism as extant in contemporary global marketing environments

- explain and support your viewpoint as to whether divergence or convergence is prevalent in the contemporary global marketplace

Introduction

The companion to Chapter 7, this chapter seeks to explore the other perspective to consumption in the global marketplace, that of cultural divergence. While Chapter 7 was primarily concerned with the consequence of 'nothing' (Ritzer, 2007), the present chapter looks to explore and question the opposing view, that 'something' is still indeed possible in contemporary global consumption practices and arenas.

The chapter begins with a discussion of postmodernism and the postmodern consumer, setting the stage for later discussions involving the creative and playful characteristics that represent the 'typical' postmodern consumer. In doing so, we delve into global consumption habits, exploring why, although consumers across the globe often have the ability and option to purchase the same offerings, differentiation arguably still exists. Here, we link to elements such as the symbolic meanings behind the purchases made by consumers, which speak to Ritzer's arguments, in which we might see 'nothing' turned into 'something' via the input of the postmodern consumer.

While cultural diversity as linked to the postmodern consumer and their consumption habits will play a central role in this chapter, counterarguments with regard to consumers only being able to purchase what is available to them (i.e. offerings that are made available to consumer markets by marketers and global organizations, in this instance) will also be explored. This leads us to a discussion of individualism, and whether this can indeed even exist for consumers in contemporary globalized and grobalized consumption environments.

The chapter further questions whether the local is influencing the global, or whether it is the global ultimately influencing the local. Here, you may wish to revisit discussions earlier in this text in relation to glocalization, in order to further cement or to refresh your understanding of the term. In such discussions, we will lend specific focus to the role played by the internet and online shopping, and also to recommendation engines such as Netflix and Amazon and their use of algorithms to inform the content recommended to users. Such discussions further add to the debate surrounding whether individualism might be achieved in the contemporary global marketplace or if, again, consumers view and purchase content according to the whims and predictions of marketers and global organizations.

Postmodernism

To set the scene, we must first try to define the multifaceted and complex concept of **postmodernism**. To start with a standard dictionary definition, Oxford Learner's Dictionaries (2024) describes it as a late 20th-century movement that reacted against modern styles. However, depending on the discipline, we might find a range of varied definitions for postmodernism, including reference to its links to elements and disciplines such as music, film, architecture, anthropology, geography and more (Featherstone, 2007), while also being described as having 'playful, iconoclastic, irreverent and, all too often, pretentious emphasis on non-traditional approaches to explication (poems, prayers, sketches, etc.)' (Brown, 1994).

Despite such definitions, we might still suggest that postmodernism 'does not contain a precise meaning and refers to many fragmented cultural phenomena' (Germirli, 2024). For the purposes of linking together postmodernism and marketing, however, Brown's 1993 discussion perhaps provides the best basis for our subsequent discussions.

Postmodern characteristics and consumers

Brown (1993a) discussed a number of characteristics in relation to the links between consumption, marketing and postmodernism, going so far as to suggest that 'the urge to consume is a characteristic symptom, perhaps the characteristic symptom, of the postmodern condition' (Brown, 1993b). When applied to consumers themselves, we might discern several key characteristics:

- **Fragmentation:** Fragmentation suggest that everything is disconnected, that individualized rather than mass marketing approaches are key, and that smaller segments in a target market are the ideal focus for organizations.

- **De-differentiation:** Here, we refer to the blurring of established boundaries and the like, but in particular for the purposes of this text to the blurred boundaries between the local and the global. We might also include other elements in such smudgings, such as culture, education and politics (Germirli, 2024).

- **Hyper-reality:** Hyper-reality speaks to the notion of simulation becoming real, to a breakdown of the distinction between fantasy and reality, and to a loss of authenticity. Here, we might reference examples such as theme parks and video games which blur the expectations of daily life with almost magical experiences and expectations.

- **Pastiche:** Pastiche simply refers to a mixture of styles, whether they be past or present. Such a collage might be applied across a range of offerings and disciplines, from the offerings we purchase to architecture, film and other media, and so on.

- **Anti-foundationalism:** The purpose of anti-foundationalism is to avoid the mainstream and/or traditional approaches. A key characteristic relates to anti-establishment views and beliefs.

Further to the above, the more general characteristics of pluralism, in other words 'anything goes', and chronology, a form of nostalgia for the past (by anyone, not just the older generations), might also be seen as abundant in postmodernism and as such in the characteristics that we might use to define the postmodern consumer.

The postmodern consumer arising from postmodernism

So, how do such characteristics translate into marketing? Ultimately, via postmodernism, we see a heightened level of suspicion towards the global cultural and marketing narratives, the notion of marketing being able to react and to be altered to change with customers and consumers, and advertising as required to be presented in a format that customers will find appropriate – a difficult task perhaps, given that under postmodernism individualism is key.

Such flexibility in the realm of the **postmodern consumer** can certainly be useful in supporting the consumer identity that an individual may wish to don at any given time.

For example, Brown (1993b) explains that shopping centres provide stages for postmodern consumers to act out fantasies and acquire props for their consumption in different roles they perform (e.g. wife, sports enthusiast, bargain hunter). This relates to not only the offerings that we consume, but also to the multitude of 'faces' any one consumer might possess and choose to inhabit at any given time depending on our feelings or requirements during our shopping trip. We might draw parallels here to Goffman's (1971) notions of altering our performance in line with an audience's expectations.

In this case, however, we, as postmodern consumers, are choosing the consumer identity with which to adorn ourselves in entering the shopping mall/centre, retail park, online store and so on, with the brands and stores our audience. For interested readers, plenty of further discussions on identity can be found in the literature, for example in the works of Linstead and Thomas (2002), who view identities as 'masks that are actively used, manipulated and created' (also see Goffman's (1971) discussion of masks and identity), and Brown and Lewis (2011), who note that 'identities are fabricated, but within webs of meaning that individuals have themselves helped to spin'.

Postmodernism, then, results in consumers who might be seen as creative, playful and imaginative. They are emancipated via their disregard for established practice and traditional roles and constraints, often via their consumption of offerings and cultural resources that may have previously been unavailable to the modernist consumers who came before them. For this, we might arguably thank the concepts of globalization and grobalization, despite this chapter's intended purpose of arguments against the latter's prevalence.

Postmodern consumers might also be characterized as being market savvy: in other words, sceptical of brands and related marketing activities. Certainly, for contemporary consumers, there is perhaps an expectation that they will undertake research on any significant offerings to be purchased, whether that is in relation to the offering itself or to the brand from which it originates. (By 'significant', in this instance, I mean planned purchases, those requiring a higher level of involvement or those that might come with a particularly high price tag, rather than low involvement, cheap or impulse purchases.) Often such concerns may be viewed as related to factors such as quality or sustainability.

ACTIVITY

Postmodernism

Postmodernism

- What evidence (if any) have you seen of postmodernism in the contemporary global consumer landscape? You may wish to consider your own experiences as a consumer to help your thinking around this question.

Postmodernism and globalization

- To what extent do Brown's (1993a, 1993b) characteristics of postmodernism conflict with or support Ritzer's (2007) grobalization consequences of 'something' and 'nothing'?

The postmodern consumer

- Would you class yourself as a postmodern consumer? Why, or why not? Provide examples in support of your answer.

Sources of identity and consumption habits

While the discussed characteristics of postmodernism provide some insight into the postmodern consumer and how they might behave in the global marketplace, we must go further still to fully understand how consumption connects with the postmodern consumer. In particular, postmodern consumers will often (whether consciously or unconsciously) use their consumption habits as a way to create meaningful lives. This is because, to a certain extent, postmodern consumers might be seen to create the 'self' through the consumption of particular offerings.

While we might suggest that this goes further than in consumption of the offerings we might find at a retail destination or online store, such as with museums, entertainment, education and so forth, consumption of physical offerings can provide others (the audience, as Goffman (1971) would state) with the cues to understand at least to a certain extent the identity that an individual wishes to portray. To provide a brief, simple example, an individual wearing all black clothing and heavy black and white makeup may wish to convey their identity as part of the goth subculture, while an individual wearing trainers and a tracksuit may wish to be perceived as sporty or athletic. Through these examples, we see the creation of the self, and that self as being shown to others: our audience.

In such instances, we may find that consumers develop strong attachments to particular brands and objects, in that they help an individual's identity to be perceived in the desired way by the intended audience. They may also serve in providing meaning to the individual's life (for example, via opening doors to acceptance in certain subcultures and so on), and in outwardly confirming the identity choices made by an individual.

ACTIVITY

Sources of identity

If a postmodern world is fragmented and consumers play the role of creative hero, what is important about the products that we choose to purchase? Provide an example of an offering that you have purchased to illustrate your answer further.

Symbolic value

Such discussions might be linked to symbolic value, a concept which is enshrined in contemporary consumption practices, and in the global marketplace. While post-modern consumers have the potential to rebel against marketing campaigns through the subversion of an offering's or advertisement's intended meaning, symbolic value offers a further avenue via which consumers might find differentiation in the gro-balized and standardized offerings which have come to dominate our beloved cathe-drals of consumption (Levitt, 1983; Ritzer, 2002, 2007).

Importantly, we refer here to the symbolic rather than the functional value of of-ferings. For instance, one might find a generic offering such as a plain black t-shirt in many clothing stores, with each t-shirt designed to perform the same basic function. However, without some distinction between offerings, for example a brand logo, consumers may struggle to use the item to construct their identity in a meaningful way due to a lack of alignment with their desired identity. This, we might argue, is due to brands being aligned with an individual's quest for symbolic value.

When considering symbolic value, we are not just discussing the availability of offerings around the world with which postmodern consumers might build and sus-tain their desired identities. Rather, we are referring to the need for the images and symbols associated with these offerings to also be spread to a range of geographical locations. Without such efforts, the intended audience (Goffman, 1971) of identities built and performed via the consumption of such offerings is unlikely to be properly understood as intended by the individual hosting the identity.

With such considerations in mind, we can view the global marketplace as provid-ing a range of factors that may contribute to an individual's identity, or to the crea-tion of a desired identity, via that individual's consumption practices. For instance, elements such as offerings themselves, images and symbols might be used in the construction and maintenance of an identity. The beauty of the global marketplace is that it provides consumers with increasing numbers of offerings with which to do this, but with the caveat that the offerings provided are likely to be available to con-sumers across the entirety of the global marketplace. In other words, while we may seek to construct our identities using offerings, symbols, images and so forth, others have the same access to the same components.

This links to Ritzer's (2007) arguments in line with homogenization, in that, re-gardless of location, consumers around the world might access the same offerings. Opposed to this, however, is the notion that identity is a rather personal construct. Although others may have the same access to these elements and offerings, they are unlikely to consume and use them for identity formation in exactly the same ways as another consumer. This is due, in part, to consumer backgrounds, experiences and the like, all of which will colour how an offering is used in identity formation. Indeed, as Elliott and Wattanasuwan (1998) suggest, while consumers learn through socialization and exposure to mass media, not everyone who buys the same product does so for the same symbolic meaning.

Via such efforts, our reasons, therefore, will differ from consumer to consumer even in purchasing the same offerings as one another. This leads to greater diversity, again, despite the consumption of the same offerings across the globe. As such, we might suggest that while the availability of a standardized offering across the globe should be seen as 'nothing', it is in fact transformed to 'something' (Ritzer, 2007) through the differentiation provided by the individual consumer when used in concert with their local understandings, background, experiences and so on in the construction of identity.

Increasing cultural diversity

So, as we now know, increasing the availability of cultural resources and offerings via globalization and the global marketplace, when added to the identity construction performed by postmodern consumers, leads us to feelings of increased cultural diversity. We might also link here to the concept of glocalization and the grobalization consequence of 'something' (Ritzer, 2007), as we see the global being assimilated into the local via a number of different mechanisms and interpretations.

To visualize how this might work in practice, let's consider the consumer (as in other marketing theories and approaches) as a black box. We can know what the consumer tells us, but we cannot know what is going on inside the black box, just therefore marketers cannot know what happens inside the minds of consumers. This process, or thinking, feeling and so forth about, in this case, an offering, is internal and is therefore private to the individual consumer in question. However, we can start to see difference being produced if we consider any given number of consumers with their black boxes. If we have the same product going into the black box (or in other words, being offered to a number of different consumers), consumers' interpretations will differ due to their backgrounds, experiences, memories, product and brand associations, and so forth.

This results in a rainbow of varied possibilities emanating from the same offering, as each consumer processes and interacts with the offering in a slightly or significantly different way. Through such processes, we start to see that local cultures and the people within them adapt and reinterpret global influences and offerings available via the global marketplace in a local context.

ACTIVITY

Cultural diversity

Why might we expect to see a variety of different outcomes if a number of consumers in the global marketplace purchase the same product?

ACTIVITY

Global or local yoga?

Reinterpretations between the global and the local might be seen, for example, in the case of glocal yoga, as reported by Askegaard and Eckhardt (2012), who discuss the origins of yoga in India and how its introduction to a global stage resulted in a number of changes of meaning being associated with the practice. The authors further discuss how a reappropriation of yoga into India following global developments to the practice impacted how local Indian consumers felt a change in feeling and meaning towards the practice of yoga.

Such examples call into question whether the local might be influencing the global (in this case, through the introduction of yoga in the first instance), or whether the global should be seen as influencing the local (as in the changes brought to the practice and meanings of yoga as determined by a global audience). Such considerations become increasingly complex when we then consider the reappropriation of yoga to India.

However, despite the potential for differentiation in taking a 'nothing' offering and transforming it into 'something' via its interpretation and use by the individual consumer, there is still a key caveat to consider. This comes in the form of such opportunities for self-expression being determined and indeed dominated by the marketing segmentation strategies of global organizations. Despite our desire as postmodern consumers to seek individualism and expression via our consumption practices, these practices are still at the whim of the global organizations that decide to manufacture and market the offerings that we purchase. In other words, if an organization does not deem a potential offering to be profitable enough to warrant the expenditure of production and promotion required to bring the offering to market, it will be unlikely to ever reach the physical and digital shelves which consumers might access and, thus, it will be unavailable as a device via which we might construct and sustain our identities.

That is not to say that those among us who prefer alternative offerings to those provided by the mainstream are to be without hope. Subcultures can also mean big business for organizations, and, as such, we still see the production and marketing of alternative products via which we might construct our identities, albeit typically on a smaller scale. This variation will, however, still typically be around common themes that are likely to see a reasonable level of sales – after all, as a global or even grobal organization, is it not the point to make profits?

Take for example, lip balm – a fairly standard product available across the globe in a variety of flavours. However, to accommodate varied consumer tastes some perhaps surprising flavours have also been introduced, such as a Cheetos cheese flavour lip balm, a Reese's chocolate peanut butter cup flavoured lip balm, a Mentos mint flavoured lip balm, and a grape Fanta flavoured lip balm, to name but a few, all available thanks to the grobalizing efforts of Amazon. While it is unlikely that a Cheetos cheese flavoured lip balm would appeal to the majority of consumers (or perhaps just not to this author?), the example helps us to see that subcultures may have varied local expressions in exploring a global phenomenon.

Individualism

Our discussions around cultural diversity have to this point contended that, simply, individualism is possible via the identity construction of consumers, even if they are constructing their identity via the use of global or grobal offerings available to all in the global marketplace. However, Morgan (2009) offers a different view in this context, stating that 'ultimately there is no individualism per se achieved through the act of consumption, rather than a making up of the self within categories pre-defined by others as the basis for personal identity'. Indeed, this is a view that perhaps makes sense given our earlier discussions as to the offering made available by global and grobal organizations in their quest for profits.

Discussions of this ilk also give rise to the notion of opportunities for local consumption being judged against established global standards and brands. For one such example, we often associate global or standard products with a higher quality, and as such judge them to be a less risky purchase than an alternative offering that we might procure from our own locale.

Divergence or convergence?

Much of our discussion in the chapter so far has hinted at the proclivity for consumption via the internet. It is perhaps the quickest and often the cheapest way for consumers to gain access to offerings from the global marketplace. Indeed, the internet plays a vital role in contemporary consumption practice, notable as one way in which cultural resources and offerings become more widely available and accessible to consumers across the globe.

REAL-WORLD EXAMPLE   Temu and the American Super Bowl

One relative newcomer to the online shopping scene is the internet shopping platform Temu, which was founded in Boston, Massachusetts in 2022 (Temu, 2024a) as the US offshoot of Chinese online retailer Pinduoduo (Chow, 2022). Available in almost 50 countries (Kennedy, 2024), the platform has enjoyed mass popularity in a number of geographical locations. For example, upon entering the US market, Temu became the most downloaded app in the US within four months of its launch (Chow, 2022).

Temu, meaning 'team up, price down' (Temu, 2024a) according to the organization, boasts a huge range of offerings across varied categories, retailing items from home, kitchen, sports and pet supplies to clothing, stationery, toys, tools and more. Temu sells heavily discounted products, mostly shipped directly from factories or warehouses in China, while also using gamification, free gifts, vouchers and other promotional tools to encourage customers to make purchases and to share information about the brand and its offerings with their personal networks. Low pricing appears to be the shopping platform's hook for consumers, with the site likened to having the aesthetics of 'a virtual dollar store' (Chow, 2022).

Such discounted prices are made possible not only by production in China, where wage costs are typically far lower than those of the West, but also by the organization's focus on using next-gen manufacturing processes. In essence, next-gen manufacturing assumes that consumers will initiate demand for offerings, and manufacturers will then produce them in accordance with customer orders and intelligence gained from the shopping platform's analytics. As Temu (2024b) itself suggests, this type of approach can result in 'lower costs for both consumers and merchandise partners due to economies of scale from better product fit, increased revenue, and less waste from mismatched production'.

Furthermore, Temu boasts that it helps to establish connections between millions of manufacturers and consumers directly, with the mission to empower them to 'live a better life' and to 'fulfil their dreams in an inclusive environment' (Temu, 2024a).

While not its first foray into mass advertising (Temu also bought advertisement time during the 2023 Super Bowl, the National Football League's annual championship game), Temu's 2024 Super Bowl adverts appear to have caused quite the stir. The three 30-second commercials that ran are reported to have cost about $7 million each and promote the notion of 'living a Champagne lifestyle on a beer budget' (Faithfull, 2024).

While on the surface Temu may seem too good to be true, and it certainly appears to have been portrayed that way in its Super Bowl adverts, there are of course some negative implications of business on such a large scale. First, we might question the environmental and human implications of high-volume and low-price selling models, as often can be seen in attempting to gain economies of scale. More specifically, in 2023 reports suggested that Temu had been 'hit with a personal data security class action lawsuit and accusations of using slave labor' (Danziger, 2024; also see Hadero, 2023).

From the consumer perspective, we might also question the model employed by Temu in terms of its shipping approach. While arguably somewhat faster than other online shopping platforms of a similar type where goods are manufactured in countries outside the West, consumers are still required to wait for goods to arrive with no next-day delivery option. This presents an issue when much of Temu's approach is concerned with novelty and driving consumers towards impulse purchases. However, when delivery is relatively slow, we as consumers are being denied the instant gratification that we would gain from making such a purchase, for example, in a physical store, or the reasonably quick gratification we might expect if next-day delivery options are available when shopping online.

Questions

- What factors lie behind Temu's success to date, and what challenges does the organization face?

- If an individual purchases an item from Temu, are they buying 'something' or 'nothing' (Ritzer, 2007)?

- Temu (2024a) describes itself as helping customers to 'live a better life' and to 'fulfil their dreams' through the products that it sells. To what extent do you believe this to be true? Why? Would your answer remain the same when considering other stakeholders such as manufacturers and their workers?

- Which, if any, problems might be associated with Western consumers 'living a Champagne lifestyle on a beer budget'?

- To what extent is the shopping experience that Temu attempts to provide applicable to all consumers, not just those living in the West?

The caveat here is that when we visit the internet in whichever way, shape or form (think websites, mobile, social media, television and so on) and for whatever purpose (to watch a film or TV series, to make a purchase, to read articles that may be of interest, to scroll through social media, etc.), we leave ourselves open to internet cookies and spy pixels. These entities register our interests from our online activities, often logging them with advertising agencies and other organizations, which ultimately allows them to better target us. After all, if an organization already knows what we have explored online previously, why wouldn't we want to return to the same or similar content?

There are other benefits to be gained by consumers when shopping online, particularly if we explore the case of recommendation engines in the guise of shopping platforms. Take, for example, online giant Amazon. Amazon has a far wider range of products than any consumer could reasonably ever expect to find in a physical store, or perhaps even in a whole mall or shopping centre. This means that consumers can find almost any product that they may desire while shopping online, rather than just those offerings deemed to be worthy of shelf space in a traditional bricks and mortar store.

The downside, however, of shopping in such a way online is that we can see a dehumanization of culture taking place. This is not least as it relates to working culture, where Amazon have been accused of a lack of safety in their workplaces, alongside requiring workers to fulfil an unrealistic number of packing goals during shifts (Sainato, 2023). For consumers, we might argue that having so much availability actually removes choice. If, for example, we were to enter a bricks and mortar store in search of a new hat, we would need to select our hat from those available in the store. This gives us a fairly limited choice, and only allows us to choose from those offerings deemed worthy of shop floor space. However, we may see and ultimately choose to purchase items that differ from our normal style of choice.

If we were to search online for our new hat, the choices appear endless. But do those choices show all of the options available to us? Chances are that many of the items that you would see presented in an online shopping platform such as Amazon would be fairly similar to one another. This is because through your previous use of online shopping and the internet and subsequent monitoring via cookies and spy pixels, organizations can gain an idea of the products that you might like to buy, and as such will show those offerings to you. While this might be a useful function for those who are time-poor and/or do not wish to visit a physical store or to scroll through multiple pages of content to find a suitable hat, it does remove the option of seeing alternatives that may be different to our normal choice of offering.

With this in mind, such online retailers predict what we are likely to like and will show us different versions of this, rather than allowing us to see the full (if limited) range of offerings, some of which we may dislike, as would be available to us in a physical store.

In other words, recommendation engines such as Amazon are very good at predicting what we want before we know we want it, whether that relates to products themselves, or just to the styles, colouring, patterns and so on that we might find attractive. Such online stores also continue to personalize our landing pages when we 'enter' the digital store. Arguably, this piques our interest as consumers as we see new products that are being specifically recommended for us as individuals, and often these will be things that we like or will be closely related to items that we have previously searched for.

While the above example centred around the notion of shopping online, we also see recommendations in other areas, such as with home entertainment. Take, for example, Netflix. Using similar mechanisms, Netflix is able to establish the type of content that we might like to watch, based on what we have watched previously.

This gives us, as consumers, relevant recommendations based on topics and programmes that we have previously enjoyed, but it often removes any suggestion of content types that we have not watched previously. In other words, if we have not previously watched it, Netflix does not know that this would be content enjoyable to the consumer, and does not suggest it. How do we then as consumers find new content that is not just more of the same? A wicked problem in itself…

However, when we do find, and in this case watch, content that is of interest, the internet can help to broaden our horizons further. This is via access to entertainment offerings that would not have previously been available in our locale. This, however, brings discussions of grobalization and Americanisms back to the fore, as although we have an increased number of resources via which we can construct and express our identities, these resources are still available for others to use for the same purpose.

So, then, the market homogenizes via the internet. Or does it…? Just because there is a wide range of offerings available to consumers via the internet does not mean that consumers will purchase them. Indeed, when faced with overwhelming choice, consumers will often buy the same thing or may purchase from the first page of search results, rather than digging deeper into the wealth of offerings available to them. What at first glance may have held the potential to lead to diversity, arguably often fails to do so.

Universal application

The second critique of diversity with which we must concern ourselves is that of universal application. Ideas of freedom and playfulness as expressed by definitions of the postmodern consumer in their consumption practices are supposed to lead to salvation and entertainment. However, we must question for whom is this notion relevant, and is this a standardized opportunity across the entirety of the globe?

The short answer to the latter question is a resounding 'no'. Consumers need money and other resources such as infrastructure in their home countries to be able to participate in consumerism, particularly if we view the style of consumption as promoted by the West and characterized by the view of global consumerism as 'a widespread and unquenchable desire for material possessions' (Ger and Belk, 1999). While Western consumers may be able to afford to consume in such a manner, in some cases but certainly not in all, such conceptions of consumerism are not in line with a world where much of the population struggles to purchase the most basic of offerings. This brings to the fore questions surrounding whether consumption and consumer freedom to engage in global consumerism might be viewed as an elitist privilege.

Furthermore, such conceptions might be seen as contrasting with Ritzer's (2007) view that 'the local is still needed as an alternative to grobalization. For example,

Varman and Vikas (2007) explicitly discuss the relationship between postmodern consumption practices and consumer freedom. While many of the arguments raised by Varman and Vikas seek to support the notion that not all consumers are free to, or have equal freedom to, consume as they might wish in the global marketplace (a notion that we will cover more fully in Chapters 9 and 10 of this book), the authors do support the view that access to resources remains critical for consumers to exercise this freedom.

REAL-WORLD EXAMPLE   Inca Kola

Inca Kola, characterized by 'its yellow-gold colour, sweet flavour and secret formula' (Knowledge at Wharton, 2012), is a rare case in that it is one of a small number of select local brands that have been successful in beating Coca-Cola on its home turf.

The Peruvian brand was first brought to market in 1935 thanks to a British family who moved to Peru and founded the organization in 1910 (Knowledge at Wharton, 2012). Inca Kola's entry to market in 1935 might be seen as further linking with the local arena, in that it coincided with the 400th anniversary of the founding of Lima, Peru's capital city (Arca Continental, 2024).

Fast forward to 1936 and we see Coca-Cola's entry to the Peruvian market. With rivalry with Coca-Cola stretching back almost to the organization's creation, Inca Kola leverages its local connections rather than pandering to global trends, being seen as the 'go-to' soft drink choice for Peruvians both in their home country and abroad to accompany any traditional Peruvian meal. Alcalde (2009) suggests that Peruvian restaurants will include Inca Kola on their menus, not just as a refreshing drink option but as a 'sign of authenticity'. In doing so, the brand's identity is being shown as closely linked to the Peruvian national identity, with symbolism being used on its products' packaging along with brand slogans which heavily emphasize the national identity of Peru.

As of 2012, Inca Kola held a 26 per cent share in its local market and Coca-Cola held the slightly lower share of 25.5 per cent, with around 50 brands competing in Peru's soft drinks market in total (Knowledge at Wharton, 2012). This success might be judged as due to a combination of two key ingredients: the use of heritage and modernity, but 'via the exclusion of contemporary indigenous people' (Alcalde, 2009). In supporting this viewpoint, Alcalde suggests that we might look to the composition of Inca Kola's adverts (particularly to the stereotypical assumptions of job roles and status, and to the people portraying Inca Kola consumers in the commercials) and the notion of Inca Kola being seen by some, particularly poorer Peruvian consumers as a more expensive offering in comparison to other local alternatives where a lower price might be paid for more product.

Due to Inca Kola's success in the Peruvian market, Coca-Cola subsequently purchased 50 per cent of the organization's shares in 1999 (Knowledge at Wharton, 2012) opting to deploy a defensive strategy in adding Inca Kola to the Coca-Cola brand portfolio. The purpose of purchasing such a significant amount of Inca Kola's shares, rather than destroying the brand and thus a major competitor, is at least in part, due to the threat of cannibalization. There was also no guarantee that, if unable to purchase Inca Kola, Peruvian cola consumers would make the switch to Coca-Cola products. Instead, they may have switched their loyalty to one of the other competitor offerings in the market.

Indeed, Coca-Cola might be viewed 'as a symbol of American colonization and hegemony' with more local, Peruvian soft drinks being seen as an 'ethical alternative' (Alcalde, 2009). However, is this truly the case? If we consider the points raised with regards to Inca Kola's commercials, can we not see Inca Kola as still homogenizing, but rather than on an American or even global scale, does this hegemony not play out in the Peruvian context?

To explore this perspective further, we might look to the notion of global offerings becoming indigenized in some form as the perspective of the local is imbued within them – in other words, resulting in a new combination of the global which also includes the local.

Regardless of the complexities between the local and the global, the case of Inca Kola demonstrates that it is indeed important to bridge the gap (at least to a certain extent) between the two. Equally, bridges between the traditional and modern are also required in order to capture the attention of consumers from different generations. As such, throughout the case study we see a Peruvian-global modernity being presented rather than an American-global modernity (Alcalde, 2009), with the former being seen to embrace globalization alongside Peru's heritage, culture and pride.

Questions

- To what extent does the Peruvian love of Inca Kola suggest that consumers located in Peru are resisting globalization? Explain your answer.

- Why did Coca-Cola decide to purchase a 50 per cent share of Inca Kola? As a marketer, would you have recommended the same action? Why, or why not?

- Alcalde suggests that Inca Kola's approach to advertising includes the 'exclusion of contemporary indigenous people'. To what extent does this contribute to the brand's success in the local and global arenas?

CHAPTER SUMMARY

To conclude, in this chapter we have explored a range of factors and debates surrounding cultural divergence, as opposed to the ideas covered in the previous chapter on cultural convergence.

Postmodernism and the postmodern consumer as a base from which to begin this chapter's discussions served to deepen our understanding of the interplay between 'something' and 'nothing' (Ritzer, 2007), and in so doing to uncover the notion that it may not be as easy as we first think to decide whether something is indeed 'something' or 'nothing'. In particular, differentiation, identity and symbolic meanings which might initially be seen as 'nothing' can be transformed into 'something' via the input of the postmodern consumer.

However, if we then focus on the notion of the market as providing the same offerings to consumers across much of the globe, does 'something' once again return to 'nothing'? It is these twists and turns that this chapter has sought to highlight, not with the purpose of determining whether 'something' or 'nothing' is most prevalent in the contemporary marketing arena, but rather to broaden our understanding of the complexities involved in determining, for example, an offering's status.

We might also question whether an item might be both 'something' and 'nothing'. If one consumer purchases a generic item that holds no particular meaning for them, it may be deemed 'nothing', whereas for another consumer that same item might have a host of meanings, resulting in it being labelled 'something'. Thus, what initially may have seemed simple to determine based on Ritzer's (2007) definitions of 'something' and 'nothing' actually becomes far more complex when we delve under the surface.

Aside from discussions of postmodernism and its connections to Ritzer's theory, the chapter also explored the interplay between the local and the global. In doing so, questions surrounding whether the local is influencing the global or whether the global is dominating the local were brought to the fore. In connection to such arguments, a further section of significance in the chapter related to recommendation engines, such as Amazon and Netflix. Again, what might once have seemed straightforward when considering individualism and consumer choice becomes more complicated when we begin to understand how the recommendations we receive are determined. From the music that we stream to the products that we purchase, the TV series and films that we watch and the social media advertisements that we view, all are suggested with us, the individual consumer, in mind. So, is this individualism, or is this a case of the market determining what we, as individuals, would like based purely on what we have already said that we like, disregarding the potential for any change or difference in our tastes?

Keeping debates surrounding convergence and divergence in the global marketplace in mind, the next chapter lends focus to the notion of ethics. This comes in the form of discussion as to why ethics is, or should be, an important consideration in marketing activities, along with the inclusion of a range of key ethical theories.

Furthermore, the chapter seeks to engage readers with debates surrounding the potential outcomes of a dislocation of production and consumption practices across the globe, outlining a range of potential outcomes for a variety of stakeholders, and what those same stakeholders might do in efforts to enact change.

CHAPTER REVIEW QUESTIONS

- Explain Brown's (1993b) conceptions of postmodernism.

- What does Brown suggest as key characteristics linked to the postmodern consumer?

- Would you class yourself as a postmodern consumer? Why, or why not? If you class yourself as a postmodern consumer, explain a past consumer experience to illustrate your claim.

- To what extent does symbolic value impact your own consumer behaviour? Provide an example to further your answer.

- To what extent do you feel that the use of internet cookies and spy pixels is unethical? Consider your answer from the perspectives of an individual customer and a marketer.

KEY TERMS

Individualism: Individualism is concerned with the individual and their right to practice (with a marketing perspective in mind) consumption, identity and so forth in a way of their choosing. Individualism is often discussed in comparison to a more collective way of being and consuming. Individualism is a key element of postmodernism and the postmodern consumer (see the entries below).

Internet cookies: Internet cookies hold similarities to recommendation engines (see entry below) in that they track user behaviour and actions in an online environment. Common uses for internet cookies are to identify users and to enhance the personalization of users' online experiences.

Postmodern consumers: Postmodern consumers are typically suspicious of marketing activities, have a dislike of established practice and institutions, are market-savvy and are creative and imaginative in their consumption practices.

Postmodernism: Postmodernism might be characterized as a mixture of features, styles, disciplines and approaches, often linked, for instance, to the arts and architecture. Further key characteristics of postmodernism centre around elements such as scepticism and mistrust.

Recommendation engines: Recommendation engines, for example Amazon's shopping platform or Netflix, rely on data and analytics to predict consumer behaviour. From this analysis, it is then possible to make suggestions for products and other offerings that might appeal to individual consumers.

Spy pixels: Spy pixels are typically incredibly small images included in marketing communications such as emails. They allow an organization to see an individual's interaction with the marketing communication's content. However, there are a number of critiques of spy pixels with regards to marketing communication as there is typically a lack of explicit consent required from recipients for such information to be gathered.

Symbolic value: Symbolic value relates to the importance, significance or meaning attributed to an object, typically by an object's owner. Symbolic value might be comprised of several elements such as cultural or social meaning.

References

Alcalde, C M (2009) Between Incas and Indians: Inca Kola and the construction of a Peruvian-global modernity, *Journal of Consumer Culture*, 9 (1) 31–54

Arca Continental (2024) We are Continental Arca Lindley, www.arcacontinentallindley.pe/nosotros/ (archived at https://perma.cc/7WLY-VW8Q)

Askegaard, S and Eckhardt, G M (2012) Glocal Yoga: Re-appropriation in the Indian consumptionscape, *Marketing Theory*, 12 (1), 45–60

Brown, A D and Lewis, M A (2011) Identities, discipline and routines, *Organization Studies,* 15 (1), 5–28

Brown, S (1993a) Postmodern marketing? *European Journal of Marketing*, 27 (4), 19–34

Brown, S (1993b) Postmodern marketing: Principles, practice and premises, *Irish Marketing Review*, 6, 91–100

Brown, S (1994) Marketing as multiplex: Screening postmodernism, *European Journal of Marketing*, 28 (8/9), 27–51

Chow, A R (2022) The truth about Temu, the most downloaded new app in America, *Time*, www.time.com/6243738/temu-app-complaints/ (archived at https://perma.cc/VWA9-YLDR)

Danziger, P (2024) Behind the curtain: The Temu Superbowl ad, *The Robin Report*, www.therobinreport.com/behind-the-curtain-the-temu-superbowl-ad/ (archived at https://perma.cc/787N-XVX5)

Elliott, R and Wattanasuwan, K (1998) Brands as symbolic resources for the construction of identity, *International Journal of Advertising*, 17, 131–44

Faithfull, M (2024) 7 things to know about Temu before you 'Shop like a billionaire', Forbes, www.forbes.com/sites/markfaithfull/2024/02/13/7-things-to-know-about-temu-before-you-shop-like-a-billionaire/ (archived at https://perma.cc/RW6S-89YP)

Featherstone, M (2007) *Consumer Culture and Postmodernism* (2nd ed), Sage Publications

Ger, G and Belk, R W (1996) I'd like to buy the world a Coke: Consumptionscapes of the 'less affluent world', *Journal of Consumer Policy*, 19 (3), 271–304

Germirli, S (2024) Postmodern marketing and its impact on traditional marketing approaches: Is Kotler dead? *American Journal of Humanities and Social Sciences Research*, 8 (4), 135–39

Goffman, E (1971) *The Presentation of the Self in Everyday Life*, Allen Lane

Hadero, H (2023) Congressional report says there's an extremely high risk Temu's supply chains have forced labor, AP News, www.apnews.com/article/temu-shein-forced-labor-china-de7b5398c76fda58404abc6ec5684972 (archived at https://perma.cc/7PPH-MHS3)

Kennedy, L (2024) Temu explained: Is this online shopping platform worth using?, Choice, www.choice.com.au/shopping/online-shopping/buying-online/articles/what-is-temu (archived at https://perma.cc/TEJ8-A7NZ)

Knowledge at Wharton (2012) Branding lessons from Inca Kola, the Peruvian soda that bested Cola-Cola, knowledge.wharton.upenn.edu/article/branding-lessons-from-inca-kola-the-peruvian-soda-that-bested-coca-cola/ (archived at https://perma.cc/7FUH-PU99)

Levitt, T (1983) The globalization of markets, *Harvard Business Review*, 61 (3), 92–102

Linstead, A and Thomas, R (2002), 'What do you want from me?': A poststructuralist feminist reading of middle managers' identities, *Culture & Organization*, 8 (1), 1–20

Morgan, G (2009) Globalization, in *Understanding Corporate Life*, Sage Publications

Oxford Learner's Dictionaries (2024) Postmodernism, www.oxfordlearnersdictionaries.com/definition/english/postmodernism?q=postmodernism (archived at https://perma.cc/8KYG-7HBG)

Ritzer, G (2002) *McDonaldization: The reader*, Sage Publications

Ritzer, G (2007) *The Globalization of Nothing 2*, Sage Publications

Sainato, M (2023) 'They're more concerned about profit': Osha, DoJ take on Amazon's gruelling working conditions, *The Guardian*, www.theguardian.com/technology/2023/mar/02/amazon-safety-citations-osha-department-of-justice (archived at https://perma.cc/3PAJ-GFB8)

Temu (2024a) What is Temu? www.temu.com/about-temu.html (archived at https://perma.cc/2ALX-DJ7G)

Temu (2024b) What does Temu sell? www.temu.com/what-is-temu.html (archived at https://perma.cc/PA89-8L6U)

Varman, R and Vikas, R (2007) Freedom and consumption: Toward conceptualising systematic constraints for subaltern consumers in a capitalist society, *Consumption, Markets and Culture*, 10 (2), 117–31

9 | Ethics in the global marketplace

LEARNING OBJECTIVES

By the end of this chapter, you should be able to:

- explain why ethics is a key concept for consideration in marketing activities
- discuss and apply a range of ethical theories to marketing scenarios
- critically evaluate the dislocation of production and consumption, commenting on impacts for stakeholders such as workers and consumers
- debate key environmental implications and organizational tactics with respect to production and consumption in the global marketplace
- discuss the role of varied stakeholders as agents for change, commenting on the notion of transformation as achieved via consumption practices

Introduction

Ethics. You might sigh and think of how bored you are going to be reading this chapter. However, ethics doesn't have to be boring, long-winded, or any host of other negative descriptors that have been applied by students in previous years. It can, however, be multifaceted and complex. It is also an arguably a subjective notion, in which different parties may hold differing views of the same situations, actions and so forth, resulting in several ways of alternative thinking and action. While at times frustrating for some in trying to understand (or even change!) another's viewpoint, this differentiation can be due to a host of reasons, such as our own backgrounds, experiences, perspectives and the interests we represent as the stakeholder of a particular entity (for example, as a student, a consumer, an organization, a shareholder, etc.).

As you might by now expect, we begin the chapter with a discussion of prevalent ethical theories. That is not to say that the chapter is only concerned with introducing you to ethical theory. Rather, the chapter is intended as a brief introduction to a small number of the many ethical theories that are portrayed in the extant literature, with our primary focus instead being to explore how ethics plays out when applied to marketing and broader societal issues in a global context.

The ethical theories with which we will concern ourselves at the outset of the chapter include deontological ethics, teleological ethics, descriptive and normative realism and constructive pluralism. Following this, the chapter seeks to explore ethical issues as related to the global marketplace, such the exploitation of labour forces and the environmental impacts of production and consumption.

We then move to discuss some of the unethical tactics used by organizations in order to appear more ethically friendly than they perhaps are. For example, approaches such as greenwashing and false and/or misleading claims.

While the above context may seem to promote feelings of 'doom and gloom', the latter part of the chapter takes a more positive stance on ethics by looking at the potential for change. This comes in the form of exploring the actions various stakeholders (think organizations, governments, consumers and more) may take in order to be seen as agents of change, as those who act and think positively – and not only in where they spend their money. Here, the chapter delves into the notion of positive transformation via consumption, linking to entities and concepts such as Fairtrade, education, information and consumer rights.

Let's begin with some context and our discussion of ethical theories. As you read through the remainder of the chapter, do keep these theories in mind to help you to frame your thinking around the varied ethical issues and examples included in the text. You may also wish to think about identity (think of Goffman's (1971) identity masks as discussed in Chapter 8) and the varied perspectives that any one individual may hold. For example, while reading through the chapter, consider your own identities and how each of them might respond to the information and examples portrayed. For instance, do you have the same viewpoint on the chapter's contents as a student, as a consumer, as an employee, as a community member, and so on?

Marketing and ethics

As a contemporary global society, we are used to seeing marketing all around us, all the time. In fact, we are so used to it, we might not even recognize its prevalence. From the huge flashing and video adverts stereotypical of locations such as Osaka's Dotonbori River in Japan and New York's Times Square, to the infamous *Crazy Taxi* computer game in which users could previously 'drive' around a virtual location filled with famous brands, to product placement in films and TV series – advertising is everywhere. Even often in those places which we, the unsuspecting consumer, might not expect, much as with Ritzer's (2007) discussions of the lack of consumption-free zones.

Is it any wonder, then, that our lives are filled with brands. For instance, Kotler et al (2019) provide some perspective in imagining the scenario of a typical consumer's morning: search online for the description. Does this sound familiar? If so, chances are that you have fallen 'victim' to numerous advertising campaigns, as arguably so do the majority of consumers. Examples such as that provided by Kotler et al demonstrate the influence and impact that marketing can have on consumers' purchases and their daily lives, which might in turn lead us to discussions of organizational ethics and of our consumption habits.

It is important to remember that marketing activities are not neutral. Simply put, the arguably primary function of marketing is to persuade the target audience to make a purchase, to think in a certain way or to take an action of some sort. As such, while Kotler et al's description of the branded morning might sound familiar to Western consumers, is this the case for consumers uniformly across the globe? Specifically, do you think it is the likely branded morning scenario for consumers in a developing country?

ACTIVITY

A branded morning

How many brands do you interact with before leaving your home on a typical morning?

Ethics vs morality

In order to further frame the questions raised in this discussion and those which we are yet to cover in the chapter, we first need to consider the ethical theories and understand the parameters of the ethical dilemmas of marketing ethics in a global context. Aside from various ethical theories themselves, we might also interest ourselves with the concept of morality. **Morality** defines right and wrong through social practices, customs, etc. and is transmitted across generations. **Ethics**, on the other hand, might be broadly defined as pertaining to 'reflection on the nature and justification of right actions' (Arnold et al, 2019).

The distinction then between ethics and morality appears to lie with morality pertaining to a social lens, while ethics may be seen as more concerned with an individual's reflection (although shared ethics are certainly possible) on the correctness of actions and, at times, the outcomes of those actions.

Ethical theories and the global marketplace

There are a number of ethical theories to which we might lend our focus in this chapter. However, as previously stated, the intent of this chapter lies more in helping you to apply ethical theories to real-world issues and scenarios. That being said, we will cover a small number of prevalent ethical theories. Do feel free to read further around the concept of ethical theory should you wish to uncover additional viewpoints and approaches to ethics and the global marketplace.

Deontological ethics

In essence, **deontological ethics** suggests that we should not intentionally harm another individual, 'even in the pursuit of good ends' (McNaughton and Rawling, 2005). This means that deontologists are typically more concerned with their actions, rather than the consequences of those actions. For example, let's say you purchased a new mobile phone for your friend who was worried about their car breaking down while on a long-distance trip. The purchase and gift would be your action – which is inherently a nice gesture, in this case. But let's say your friend then decides to use the phone that you have gifted them while driving and receives six penalty points on their driving licence. This consequence is clearly not desirable (nor an arguably ethical action on the part of the driver), but it is also not the fault of the gift giver.

In this scenario, then, the action is inherently good and therefore no problem with the action might be seen by the gift giver, even when the consequence of the action is bad (although it does not have to be). This provides us with an explanation of how a deontologist may view ethics. Essentially, deontologists look for and use rules for a moral life, acting towards others as they would ideally hope others would act towards them.

Teleological/consequentialist ethics

Teleological and consequentialist ethics prioritize the opposite considerations to those of deontological ethical approaches. That is to say that while deontologists are concerned with action rather than consequence, teleological or consequentialist ethics are concerned with the end result, rather than the actions taken to produce it. To reprise our previous example in relation to the travelling friend and the gifted mobile phone, under teleological/consequentialist ethical theories, the initial gift of the phone would not be ethical, as the end result was not positive. The most good that might be achieved for the most people is generally the goal of teleological and consequentialist ethics.

Ethical realism

Here, we might split our discussion of ethical realism into two distinct camps: descriptive ethical realism and normative ethical realism.

Descriptive ethical realism notes that what a particular culture deems to be morally right or wrong is in fact right or wrong for any individuals in that culture, even if those rules, actions and so on would be viewed differently when applied to a different culture. To use a somewhat extreme example, countries such as Canada, Mexico, Argentina and the UK have abolished the death penalty, which for inhabitants is generally seen to be the morally right decision as per the ethics of those living in these locations.

However, the same logic might be applied to ethics and morality in locations such as Belarus, Libya, Cuba and China in which the death penalty is still legal (World Population Review, 2024). This type of ethics relates to 'what *should* be the case or what *ought* to be believed' in a particular geographical location or culture (Arnold et al, 2019).

Normative ethical realism, on the other hand, is concerned with attempts to 'formulate and defend basic moral norms', aiming to determine 'what *ought* to be done, which needs to be distinguished from what *is*, in fact, practised' (Arnold et al, 2019).

Constructive pluralism

The final of our ethical theories to which we will turn our attention in this chapter (although, as previously mentioned, there are many more that you may wish to pursue via further reading) is constructive pluralism. **Constructive pluralism** promotes diversity and difference, along with the notion that humans can exist together while holding differing and potentially conflicting viewpoints. Constructive pluralism, by its pluralistic nature, allows for a multitude of perspectives, as well as acknowledging that further learning about morality and ethics, and how they might be adopted and intertwined with human nature and action, is still very much possible. However, as with all things ethics, there are likely to be those who are in opposition to constructive pluralism and who instead prefer to stick to the more traditional ways of thinking, being and acting.

The ethics of ethics

So, while the ethical theories that we have discussed in the chapter present some interesting potential avenues via which we might seek to govern our own conduct, there are, of course, some pitfalls that we should also be aware of.

For instance, Barnett et al (2007) note that ethical theories are generally separated into those that privilege the right, and those that privilege the good. Ethics, however, is not always so straightforward, particularly if we add issues of individual versus collective morality into the mix.

Furthermore, ethical models might be viewed as too restrictive and demanding on people, imagining a situation where it's possible to collate and calculate information and consequences before an action. Equally, potential issues exist with regard to deontological approaches to ethics, as they may appear to 'present an implausible picture of actors rationally judging the degree to which each of their actions conforms to a very abstract principle of universalisation' (Barnett et al, 2007).

Ultimately, Barnett et al suggest that such ethical theories can be 'inflexible, leaving little room for the complexities and ambivalences of ethical decision making'. So, to return to the heading of this section, we might question: is it indeed ethical for ethical theories to place such responsibilities on the shoulders of individual stakeholders, and is it reasonable or even practical to imagine that those stakeholders might have the forethought to consider the implications of their actions and the consequences of those actions several steps ahead of time? Or is this a bar set too high for the majority of individuals?

REAL-WORLD EXAMPLE   Taylor Swift: The 'ethical billionaire'?

When considering the big hitters of the music industry, ethics might be the farthest thing from your mind. However, in between the private jets, limousines, extravagant fashion choices, parties and so on, some celebrities also make efforts to pay their success forward to communities, via their donations to various charities and funds.

One such music heavy hitter is global powerhouse Taylor Swift. Regardless of whether you love or hate her music, '[i]t is hard to find someone who has not heard of Taylor Swift' (Bland, 2024). Swift started out as a 'small town singer', signing her first record deal at just 16 years old and releasing her first single *Tim McGraw* in 2006.

Hailed by many as one of the greatest stars of all time, Swift gained her billionaire status in 2023 (Dailey and Aniftos, 2024). Aside from performing for her 'Swiftie' fans and producing a wealth of immensely popular music, Swift is no stranger to using her platform to speak on political and social justice issues such as LGBTQ+ rights (Madarang, 2023) and to back political candidates who align with her views. For example, Swift openly backed American Democratic presidential candidate Joe Biden against rival Donald Trump during the 2020 presidential election cycle (Otte, 2024).

Swift is also fairly well known for her charitable donations, of which there are numerous examples. For instance, past donations from Swift have included books to her home town's library and financial donations to schools in New York, to animal foundations, to flood relief efforts, to hurricane and tornado relief funds, to food banks, to cancer causes, and in support of struggling fans during the Covid-19 pandemic. Swift has also thrown her support behind issues of a legal nature, including with singer Kesha's legal issues back in 2016 (Geraghty, 2024).

While Swift frequently donates to charities and good causes, her generosity has perhaps been most publicized during her recent Eras Tour, which saw Swift making a number of relatively large financial donations to food banks in the cities in which she performed (Geraghty, 2024). The Chief Executive of Cardiff food bank, for example, suggested that Swift's donation has given the food bank 'the "breathing space" to try something different', noting that the food bank plans to 'buy an articulated lorry full of food and other most-needed items to supplement our emergency food parcels' (Hill, 2024). Echoes of a similar sentiment might be heard around the UK, as with Liverpool's St Andrew's Community Network Chief Executive stating that Swift had provided 'the most incredible gift' by 'essentially [having] paid our food bill for 12 months' (Hill, 2024).

There can be little doubt that Swift's generosity and openness in her views on key societal issues has made an impact on fans and local communities. However, her ownership of a number of properties and a private jet, along with a penchant for expensive designer items, has also been illuminated in recent online forums (Dailey and Aniftos, 2024). For example, reports suggest that the Roberto Cavalli black and red one-legged jumpsuit donned by Swift during her Reputation set of the Eras Tour may have cost around $1,700, while another outfit worn by Swift during the Eras Tour, an Oscar de la Renta sequin and crystal bodysuit, is reported to have cost over $2,800 (Padia, 2024).

The purchase and use of such expensive items may lead us to some key questions regarding the ethics of Swift's consumption. For instance, we may question whether Swift is doing enough for society given her current influence. Or, alternatively, are we simply expecting too much from an individual who requires the trappings of private jets and designer gear to uphold her superstar image and thus be able to continually contribute in a charitable manner?

Such considerations have been noted by some of Swift's fans, who are reported to be deliberating over the 'ethicality of her wealth' (Slabbekoorn, 2024). Before we delve into such discussions in further detail, let's put the amount of money in question into perspective. *The Pitt News* (Liez, 2022), for example, notes that it can be difficult to conceptualize the amount of money under consideration, but that if you had a billion dollars and spent $1,000 each day, it would take you 2,740 years to spend it all.

So, given her public donations and openness in terms of views of societal issues, 'is it possible that Swift can redefine the narrative of mass wealth'? (Slabbekoorn, 2024). Or might the more cynical among us take the view that such donations are better described as efforts to maintain her generous public image? After all, private, anonymous donations are also, no doubt, possible. This draws to the fore the notion that the amounts billionaires donate to charitable causes constitute small sums in comparison to their overall wealth. Indeed, can there ever be such a thing as an 'ethical billionaire'? (Liez, 2022).

So, Swiftie or not, perhaps it's time to jump in your *Getaway Car* and *Speak Now* with your friends to see if the actions of *Miss Americana* herself are living up to their *Wildest Dreams*, or if the notion of an ethical billionaire is simply *Folklore* better resembling *The Last Great American Dynasty*.

Questions

- Is Taylor Swift an 'ethical billionaire'? Explain your answer.

- Who, if anyone, would you suggest is an ethical billionaire? Why?

- To what extent, in your opinion, do Taylor Swift's charitable efforts equate to efforts to promote her own brand image?

- Should we have higher expectations of celebrities in challenging and tackling societal issues than a 'normal' individual? Why?

Ethical issues and the global marketplace

Now that we have a grasp of some of the key ethical theories that we might use to frame actions (and their consequences) in the global marketplace, let's next turn to some of the ethical issues to which they might be applied. In doing so, the chapter introduces a number of potential ethical issues, several of which we will pick up and cover in further detail in the following chapters.

Dislocation of production and consumption

The dislocation of production and consumption essentially relates to producers (in other words, workers) who cannot consume, and to consumers who do not produce. This presents an interesting issue in that we might question whether it is ethically or even morally right for an individual to be manufacturing an offering that they could not possibly hope to afford to purchase. Equally, we might link here to questions surrounding the ethics and morality of the ways in which wealth, and particularly disposable income, is generated and distributed across the globe. For example, if you were producing a beautiful item of clothing in a factory, how would you then feel if you couldn't afford to purchase the item that you, yourself, had made? How do you as a consumer feel knowing that you can (hypothetically) afford to purchase this same offering, but the person who made it cannot?

We might discuss a number of stakeholder perspectives here, including as they relate to the ethicality of the organization's own actions. The dislocation of production and consumption speaks to a wide host of ethical issues, such as the power of organizations and inherent lack of power that some workers may possess. For example, you may wish to consider workers in developing countries here, but to complicate matters further, arguably poor ethical practices towards workers can also be seen in other locations across the globe, such as with poor working conditions and practices being uncovered in Leicester (UK) in 2022 and again in Manchester (UK) in 2023, in relation to garment manufacturing processes (Butler, 2022; Panorama, 2023).

Exploitation of labour forces

The exploitation of labour forces will draw many parallels with the issues already raised in relation to the dislocation of production and consumption, in that it might most frequently be seen as raised by the media in regard to the treatment and conditions of sweatshop workers. However, we might also look to other issues here, such as unionization. In writing about workers in developing countries, Klein (2000) suggests that workers may resist attempts to improve working conditions and pay by unionizing, due to worries that factories will be closed down, resulting in a loss of jobs.

This, of course, presents a moral dilemma in itself: to speak up about poor conditions in a working environment and to risk the loss of your job, or to endure the poor conditions for the sake of retaining that same job. Neither of these, this author would imagine, present an enviable position from the perspective of most individuals.

Again, this is not just an issue to be faced by those in developing countries. For example, workers have recently been involved in what has been described as a 'David vs Goliath battle' (Conway and Masud, 2024) with regard to a historic bid for union recognition at the Amazon warehouse in Coventry (UK). A close result was achieved as 49.5 per cent of balloted workers voted in favour of unionization, while 50.5 per cent voted against. To date, Amazon does not recognize any union in its UK operations, arguably leaving workers with little bargaining power to change the terms of their employment.

ACTIVITY

Unionization

To what extent do you think that all workers, regardless of geographical location or industry, should have the right to join a trade union? In constructing your answer, consider varied viewpoints such as those of workers and organizations.

Serving the poorest consumers first

Our next ethical concern relates primarily to consumers at the bottom of the pyramid (which we will explore in further detail in Chapter 11), typically described as those in developing countries. However, that is not to say that such issues are not transferrable to other consumers to a certain extent, in other locations across the globe.

In brief, imagine the image of a three-dimensional pyramid. The bottom of the pyramid is low (equating to the amount of disposable income that consumers may have at this level of the pyramid), yet it is also wide (equating to the large number of individuals who exist at this level). In comparison, if we were to view the top of the pyramid, we would see a small number of consumers with a large amount of disposable income. Essentially, the higher up the pyramid a consumer sits, the more disposable income they are likely to have, with fewer individuals sitting towards the top of the pyramid as dictated by wealth distribution systems.

To return to the ethical concerns at hand, marketers should, ideally, carefully consider their approach to serving customers at the bottom of the pyramid. There are a number of debates surrounding whether it is even ethical, for example, for Western marketers, organizations and brands to be targeting such consumers, where any income might arguably be better spent on items such as food, clothing or education. We also see brands offering smaller versions of offerings (think, for example, of shampoo and conditioner sachets designed to provide a trial of the offering) for a reduced price, but, ethically, we might question whether this actually provides any benefits for poorer consumers, or whether it just tempts them to spend the small amount of disposable income that they do have on a product that they don't really need. Such themes will be further explored in Chapters 10 and 11.

The spread of consumerism and cultural homogenization

A wider ethical issue, the spread of consumerism, requires thought from two distinct perspectives. First, the contemporary global marketplace tends to focus on the spread of consumerism, trends, brands and so on, from the West to the rest of the world. While one might argue that this provides consumers with additional options in relation to the offerings that might be purchased, we could alternatively link back to Ritzer's (2007) notion of 'nothing', in that we see the potential for a multitude of cultures and geographical locations across the globe becoming homogenized via their consumption patterns and the implementation of infrastructure required and designed to support the consumption cathedrals (Ritzer, 2005) to which we have become accustomed.

Second, we might also concern ourselves with the spread of global consumerism in itself, via continuous desires to purchase the latest devices, fashions and so on, basically resulting in a never-ending demand for new offerings. While good news for brands and organizations, the implications for the finite resources of the earth via increased consumption on a global scale are perhaps not so positive.

Vulnerable consumers and questionable practices

In considering vulnerable consumers, we might concern ourselves with those consumers at the bottom of the pyramid, as discussed in the section above. However, 'vulnerable consumers' does not just have to relate to consumers who have a low amount of disposable income. Here, we might also contemplate consumers who might be considered as unable to make informed decisions as to the offerings that they purchase. For example, this might include consumers dealing with illness or addiction, consumers from older generations, children, and so on.

Taking a different perspective, we might also question the tracking practices of organizations while consumers browse online. As Dahl (2015) explains, all activities online transmit traceable data, whether it's browsing, making payments or streaming a TV programme. This brings to the fore questions of consumer anonymity in the global marketplace and whether the monitoring of consumer behaviour in such a way is ethical. Indeed, it is entirely possible for organizations to create a thorough profile of an individual consumer's behaviour via such tracking processes, leading to questions as to whether consumer privacy is being violated.

Environmental impacts

As we know, with the spread of global consumerism, we see individuals purchasing an increased number of offerings regardless of their geographical location. However, we must also consider the other side of the consumption equation: what happens when we no longer want or need the products that we have purchased?

REAL-WORLD EXAMPLE   Fast fashion, e-waste and the Great Pacific Garbage Patch

Fast fashion is a well-publicized and much critiqued industry, in which a large number of items with a (theoretically) short lifespan due to the fast-moving nature of global fashion trends are generated. As of 2023, fast fashion waste accounted for nearly 10 per cent of global carbon emissions, with 1.92 million tonnes of textile waste being created each year. For example, the majority of fashion items returned by consumers to retailers end up in landfill because it costs the company more to put them back in circulation than to get rid of them. To provide some further perspective, of the 100 billion garments produced each year, 92 million tonnes end up in landfill (Earth.org, 2023).

However, it is not just the garments themselves that we must be concerned with, but the resources that are used during their creation. For example, according to Earth.org, the fashion industry is suggested to be responsible for 20 per cent of global waste water. Furthermore, our discussion so far does not account for CO_2 emissions released during the process of dyeing garments, which contribute to the pollution of water sources, along with the microplastics released when materials such as nylon or polyester are washed. As such, even the most conscientious of fashion consumers may unwittingly contribute to the environmental damage caused by the fashion industry.

It is, of course, not just the fast fashion industry that creates harmful and excessive waste. Small electronic items such as cables, lights, mini fans and disposable vapes and so on are also a notable issue, particularly as each item contains valuable raw materials such as copper and lithium, which could be recovered through recycling. Indeed, according to the Waste Electrical and Electronic Equipment Forum, on a global scale, each year consumers throw away 9 billion kilograms of 'cables, toys, vapes, novelty clothes and similar devices which they often don't recognize as e-waste' (King, 2023).

While not only arguably wasteful given that many components of e-waste might otherwise be recycled, improper disposal to dump sites can also cause serious side effects for both humans and the earth. To name but a few such examples, consequences may include 'reduced lung and respiratory function and adverse outcomes for neurodevelopment' (World Health Organization, 2023). A rather scary thought, considering the pace at which we consume and discard such items on a global scale.

The use and disposal of plastic is another key issue. While steps have been taken in recent years, such as with the UK's restrictions on the provision of free plastic bags in stores and bans of plastic straws in pubs and restaurants to try to limit plastic waste, there is arguably much more to be done. As evidence for the need to further tackle plastic production and waste, we might consider the damage being done to the world's oceans.

One specific example of such damage can be seen with the Great Pacific Garbage Patch. Primarily consisting of microplastics and fishing waste, the introduction of such items into the water can have devastating impacts for the animals who live there. For instance, 'animals may confuse materials for food or get trapped in plastic nets' (National Geographic, 2024). Added to this are impacts on ocean food networks and, much like with our earlier discussion of fast fashion, pollution via the release of harmful chemicals into the world's waters.

Greenwashing

Greenwashing is perhaps the most commonly known tactic used by organizations. In essence, greenwashing is a practice designed to make an organization appear more environmentally friendly than it actually is. Here, we might link to wider ethical debates such as whether organizational efforts surrounding sustainability are actually genuine, or whether they are simply an act designed to gain positive public relations in the media. While the following section of false and/or misleading claims might also be considered under the heading of greenwashing, further considerations can be made in relation to presenting consumers (and other stakeholders) with irrelevant information, or in efforts to be seen as the lesser of two evils.

ACTIVITY

Greenwashing

Does it matter if organizational sustainability efforts are genuine or simply just acts designed to garner positive public relations if they achieve the same good ends? Why?

Which examples of greenwashing can you think of? What were the implications for the organization in question, and what might have been done differently by the organization?

False and/or misleading claims

Much as with greenwashing, organizations may decide to use false or misleading claims in efforts to promote and sell their offerings to consumers. Let's, for example, consider the cosmetics industry. Organizations may suggest that their products are not tested on animals, that they do not carry out animal testing, and that their offerings are cruelty free. Sounds great, right? Well, while the above claims might technically be true, there is still some room for organizations to be creative. For example, if an organization says its products are not tested on animals, this may be true as the final product is not tested on animals but there is nothing to say that individual ingredients have not been tested in this way. Equally, an organization may profess that they do not carry out animal testing, but they are not telling the consumer whether another organization is completing this on their behalf.

Thus, while our hypothetical cosmetic organization's claims may be technically true, they are in fact rather deceitful towards the consumer, being designed to present a greener image than might in truth be deserved.

Voluntary vs compulsory codes of conduct

With so many potential ways in which organizations might act unethically, we might suggest that the introduction of codes of conduct via which organizational behaviour might be governed are required. However, whether such codes of conduct should be voluntary or compulsory are still up for debate in many areas. A key question we might ask ourselves here is whether, if codes of conduct are to be voluntary, what would stop only the organizations who are already making good efforts to act in ethical and sustainably responsible ways from using them. Equally, if codes of conduct are to become compulsory, which parties should be in charge of monitoring and enforcement?

Agents of change

While the chapter up to this point has painted a somewhat negative picture of organizations and their use of ethics in regard to a number of issues, there is perhaps hope for better in the form of agents of change. As we will see in the following sections, agents of change can encompass a number of different stakeholders, such as individuals, governments and organizations themselves.

While you read through the remainder of the chapter, consider your own identity (as a student, consumer, etc.) and whether your own actions, or those you might take in the future, could potentially help to create positive change.

Governments

One key actor to which we might look for change in relation to ethics and sustainability is government. Whether local or national, governments and the laws they set can have a huge impact on our lives and on the offerings that we are able to purchase. For instance, governments can take certain actions in relation to the marketplace, such as setting minimum and maximum prices for products and services, prohibiting certain competitive pricing strategies, passing protective legislation and even banning certain products.

REAL-WORLD EXAMPLE   The US Government bans Kinder Eggs

Kinder Eggs, a hollow chocolate egg with an inner plastic capsule containing a small toy inside, were introduced to the market in 1974 (Ferrero, 2024). Interestingly, however, Kinder Eggs have been banned in America since before they were even created! This is due to the 1938 Food, Drug, and Cosmetic Act which raised 'safety concerns related to having a "non-nutritive object" like a plastic capsule inside a confectionery product' (Carroll, 2023).

Thus, while we might enjoy a Kinder Egg in countries such as the UK or even Mexico, American chocolate lovers remain unable to get their Kinder Egg fix on their home turf.

Organizations

Given the discussion of a range of unethical organizational actions and approaches earlier on in this chapter, the perhaps obvious place for change to occur is within organizations themselves. Whether voluntary or compulsory codes of conduct are in place (if they exist at all), contemporary organizations with a focus on sustainability will often make efforts to focus on meeting the **triple bottom line**.

The triple bottom line essentially requires organizations to measure success by more than profits alone. This is encapsulated by the 3Ps of people, planet and profit. With the triple bottom line, the trick is to also effect positive change for people and the planet, all while still making a profit. Profit, as you might expect, speaks to keeping an organization's shareholders happy, along with maintaining the financial viability of the organization. In terms of people, organizations may look to introduce some form of positive societal impact, often expanding their focus to include the creation of benefits (which are not necessarily financially based) for stakeholders, as well as those already created for shareholders.

Finally, a positive impact on the planet under the triple bottom line approach is important and might, for example, be seen via efforts to reduce the impacts of climate change created during the organization's operations, in using only ethically sourced materials and in making changes to logistics to improve efficiency and sustainability.

Organizations must also operate in line with the expectations of stakeholders such as their current and potential customers and consumers. As discussed earlier on in the chapter, whether efforts are perceived by stakeholders as genuine rather than purely a public relations tool designed to improve or combat negative perceptions of the organization can be important. But so can whether an organization meets the expectations of stakeholders in relation to the ways in which it operates. These expectations are likely to differ depending on factors such as the size of the organization, the industry in which it sits, how well known the organization is, and so forth.

For example, would you have the same expectations in relation to ethics and sustainability in considering your local dentist, a chain supermarket, a local window-cleaning business, and a chain garden centre? Chances are, you would perhaps expect more effort from the larger chain organizations, as they are better known on a larger scale and likely have more financial resources and influence in their own supply chains via which change might be created.

Customers and consumers

Our final stakeholder group to be explored in this section is that of customers and consumers. At the most basic level, customers show their support for organizations and their practices via the purchases that they make. For instance, if a consumer doesn't support testing on animals they may buy cruelty-free cosmetics; if they don't agree with the consumption of animals, they will purchase vegetarian or vegan meals; or if the customer dislikes reported employee working practices at large chain online retailers, they may choose to support their local high street instead.

The list goes on, with many alternative ways in which our purchases can help to support the organizations and causes that we deem important to us as customers and consumers. This we might deem ethical consumption, choosing to spend our hard-earned money on offerings which support the principles we hold dear, with the choice being freely made by the individual customer.

REAL-WORLD EXAMPLE   Fairtrade

The Fairtrade movement was introduced in 1992 to enable farmers to take more control over their lives and futures (Fairtrade Foundation, 2024; Fairtrade, 2024a). In doing so, Fairtrade connects producers with the people who buy their products, demonstrating to consumers that they can create change through their purchase choices. In other words, when customers purchase a Fairtrade product, they can be assured that 'producers and businesses have met internationally agreed standards which have been independently certified' (Fairtrade, 2024a).

Added to this, such standards mean that workers receive a fair pay for their labour, that good working conditions are in place and that workers have the right to form trade unions should they wish to do so. Within the Fairtrade movement, we also see an emphasis on equality between men and women, and that production is environmentally sustainable.

Fairtrade products include staple items which you may expect, such as bananas, chocolate, coffee, cotton, tea and wine, but also some products that you may not expect to find under the Fairtrade label, like beauty products, flowers and even gold (Fairtrade, 2024b).

Consumer education

While customers and consumers can and do act as agents of change, information is often required in order for them to realize that such behaviour is possible, or even necessary. Indeed, here we relate our discussion not only to the protection of workers producing offerings, but also to customers and consumers themselves.

With this in mind, consumer education is key, and there is a variety of independent sources via which consumers might learn about organizations and their offerings. One such example comes in the form of Which?, an organization that describes itself as 'the UK's consumer champion', dedicated not to making profits but rather for the protection of consumers as 'a powerful force for good, here to make life simpler, fairer and safer for everyone' (Which?, 2024a).

The organization provides consumers with information about alternative products and brands that they may purchase when looking for a specific item, along with advice about how to save money in a range of scenarios. For instance, in a comparison article in relation to air fryer brands, Which? provides key information succinctly to help customers to make a good choice based on their needs. The information provided spans elements such as price, warranty information, any extra features that the product might have and any limitations. Which? also offers a range of reviews which tell consumers how the air fryers performed during lab tests, before presenting a table comparing the brands and products under review and ultimately suggesting the top products recommended for purchase consideration (Which?, 2024b).

The concept of consumer education is not new. For instance, in the US, President John F Kennedy first introduced the Consumer Bill of Rights in 1962, which was later expanded with endorsement by the United Nations, to further reflect modern consumerism at the time. According to Mass.gov (2024), the Bill originally included the right to safety, the right to be informed, the right to choose, the right to be heard, the right to education and the right to redress. These 'rights' suggest protection for customers and consumers on a range of topics, such as the marketing of potentially dangerous products, the competitive pricing of products and the availability of information to better inform purchase decision making.

A further, and arguably fairly popular, source of consumer education came in the form of Vance Packard's book *The Hidden Persuaders*, first published in 1957. In a nutshell, Packard's text contributed to a renewed interest in consumer education via its discussions of media manipulation in the 1950s. While he focused on the US market, Packard includes a specific note to British readers, stating that 'Americans have become the most manipulated people outside the Iron Curtain', and warning that '[m]anipulation by playing on the public's subconscious is clearly spreading'. The author goes on to imply that similar patterns of manipulation from advertising and marketing activities would inevitably be heading for British shores, if it had not already made it there…

Consumer choice

So, if consumers have access to a wealth of information and are invested in supporting ethical and sustainable business practices, why do we all not support organizations that meet our ideals in terms of these criteria all of the time? The perhaps obvious answer is price. Simply put, when organizations pay workers a fair wage and install decent working conditions, when logistics become more ethically and sustainably efficient, and so on, it costs organizations money. Even when following the triple bottom line approach, an organization must still make a certain amount of profit in order to achieve financial sustainability, which in turn allows it to continue to make progress towards the people and planet elements of the triple bottom line. This necessity, therefore, often requires customers to pay a higher price point in comparison to a less sustainable, less ethical substitute offering.

Let's take a women's jumper as an example. A quick internet search reveals the cheapest jumper at fast fashion retailer Boohoo to be priced at £3 (Boohoo, 2024) while the more sustainability-focused Sugarhill Brighton store's cheapest offering comes in at £40.60 (Sugarhill Brighton, 2024). While both jumpers are currently on sale at the time of writing, the price difference of £37.60 perhaps seems somewhat large considering both offerings perform the same function. This may make a big difference to the number of offerings customers can afford to purchase and to the frequency with which they do so, due to personal finance and budget restrictions.

Price, however, is not the only reason why customers may not always choose the sustainable or ethical option. Have you ever heard of Sugarhill Brighton? Chances are, unless you have been specifically looking for sustainable clothing, you may not have come across the organization or others like it. This is often the case when we compare well-known organizational giants and lesser-known independent organizations with, arguably, advertising and public relations budgets often at the heart of our consumer knowledge. After all, if you don't know that something exists, how would you know to look for it?

Equally, we might look to the availability of offerings to explain the reasons behind our purchases. For many items (again, often budget-dependent), we may simply look to purchase the cheapest item from a range of alternatives, and often none of those alternatives are particularly sustainable. Thus, product availability also plays a role in our selections, much as with the earlier discussed notion of only being able to select what is marketed and made available to us by marketers, brands and organizations.

Furthermore, we might consider the impact and effectiveness of an individual consumer taking action with regard to the ethical and sustainable associations of any purchases they make. Do one person's actions make a difference, or is there no point if consumers as a collective do not champion the same causes and organizations via their spending patterns? We might also mention here the concept of the **knowing–doing gap**, which suggests that there is a disconnect between what a person knows, and what they ultimately choose to do. For example, as a consumer, we might know that we should ideally be purchasing clothing made from ethically sourced and sustainable materials and our ideal self may indeed desire to do so. However, as we have already discussed, such items may not be easily accessible, or may prove to be too expensive, and thus in actuality we may choose a cheaper and less ethical and/or sustainable option.

So, what can I do?

Despite this discussion in relation to the power of the individual versus the collective, many consumers do choose to take action on an individual scale in concert with their ethical and sustainable beliefs and values. This may be through a number of different actions. For example:

- Individuals might choose to vote for political parties and politicians who hold similar values to themselves in relation to ethics and sustainability.
- Customers and consumers might take more conscious decisions to reduce their carbon footprint via their consumption habits, such as eating less or no meat, using public transport or carpooling instead of using a single occupancy vehicle, recycling, purchasing slow fashion items rather than fast fashion or reducing the purchase of single use (often plastic) products.
- Individuals could support and/or participate in peaceful climate action campaigns designed to demand changes in legislation and policy.
- Customers might boycott organizations and brands that they believe to be acting unethically or unsustainably, or even make efforts to protest or shame those same entities into doing the 'right' thing.
- Customers might make deliberate choices about the ways in which they spend their money, and where they choose to shop, whether that is in an online or physical store.

Transformation via consumption

Low and Davenport (2005) posit that '[e]thical consumerism is a seductive concept because it suggests the transformative power of individual choice and action. It is also a message of inclusion – all consumers can, through the simple act of choosing one good in preference to another, create positive social and environmental change'. However, we must also return here to earlier notions of the power of the individual consumer to achieve real substantive change via their spending habits.

For example, consider the last time that you went food shopping. Did you consider the ethical and sustainable implications associated with the items that you purchased, or were you simply more concerned with what you planned to eat for your evening meal? Chances are you probably did not really consider where each of the products that you purchased had come from, or that the offerings you selected might be seen as political engagement (achieved via your supermarket selections).

So, what do you think? Can transformation be achieved via consumption? Or is this simply a case of pitting individuals against global organizations, with no hope of change due to the individual consumer's actions?

CHAPTER SUMMARY

This chapter began by introducing you to some of the key links between marketing, the global marketplace and ethics. In particular, the distinction between ethics and morality was discussed and several key ethical theories were introduced, thus setting the scene for the remainder of the chapter. If you recall, the introduction to this chapter encouraged you to consider the various ethical theories discussed as you moved through the remainder of the chapter. Now, here at our conclusion, you are further encouraged to take these theories with you and apply them as appropriate throughout the rest of this book and beyond. This will, the author hopes, shed further light on some of the debates and challenges to be explored in the book's remaining chapters.

Further to exploring core ethical theories with which stakeholder behaviour might be examined and to some extent measured, the chapter has also concerned itself with the discussion of a range of ethical issues that present themselves in the global marketplace. This exploration ranged from issues such as the dislocation of production and consumption to the exploitation of labour forces, the spread of consumerism and cultural homogenization, the ethics surrounding offerings being available to the world's poorest consumers, questionable practices and advertising to vulnerable consumers, and the environmental impacts associated with increased consumption and production.

Taking a more positive turn, the latter part of this chapter has sought to introduce some mechanisms for change, with a variety of stakeholders such as organizations, consumers, customers and governments being included in the discussion. As you are hopefully now aware (if you were not already informed on such points), consumer education can be a vital tool in ensuring the protection of consumers against a host of marketing techniques and poor-quality organizational offerings and approaches. From such discussions, we can see that there is the potential for agents of change, and that consumers can play a significant role in making such changes happen. As such, I leave it to you, readers, with the information presented in this book's earlier chapters in mind, to decide whether transformation via consumption is indeed possible.

While keeping discussions of ethics in focus, the following chapter seeks to expand our application via consideration of production in the global marketplace.

In doing so, we will recap the notion of the value chain and how this relates to contemporary organizational focus, along with the role of export processing zones in contemporary retail and manufacturing landscapes. Here, we will lend focus to the potential consequences of outsourcing production, along with exploring such consequences from the perspectives of various stakeholders. Specifically linking back to discussions of ethics in the current chapter, Chapter 10 provokes consideration of the links between ethics, choice and sweatshop work, along with exploring the consequences of offshoring service work.

CHAPTER REVIEW QUESTIONS

Unexpected advertising

- Where is the most unexpected place that you have seen an advert? Did you find its placement in the noted location intrusive, inappropriate or annoying?

The ethics of ethics

- To what extent would you agree that consumers, rather than organizations, should consider the ethical implications associated with offerings available for purchase?

Production and consumption inequalities

- How do you feel as a consumer who can, in theory, afford to purchase an item which could not be purchased due to financial constraints by the individual who made it?

- How would you feel as a worker producing products that you could not hope to afford?

Sample-sized products

- To what extent is it ethical for organizations to offer smaller-sized products for reduced prices (in comparison to higher prices charged for full-sized versions of a product) to consumers at the bottom of the pyramid? Why?

Environmental implications

- To what extent do you consider the environmental implications of the purchases you make when shopping?

- What could consumers do to help to tackle textile waste, carbon emissions, landfill usage, water waste and the release of microplastics associated with the fast fashion industry?
- How might various stakeholders (think consumers, organizations, governments, charities and so on) seek to better tackle the use and disposal of plastic items in the future?
- Which stakeholder(s) should be charged with cleaning up the Great Pacific Garbage Patch? Why?

Codes of conduct

- Do you think that organizations should follow voluntary or compulsory codes of conduct? Why? Does your answer change if you consider organizations in a number of different industries?

The knowing–doing gap

- Can you think of an instance in your own patterns of consumption where the knowing–doing gap has, or might be, applied? Why do you think this was the case, or might be the case in future?

Ethical consumerism

- To what extent do you agree with the assertion from Low and Davenport (2005) that '[e]thical consumerism is a seductive concept'? Explain the reasons behind your answer.

KEY TERMS

Boycotting: Typically, where an individual or group of customers refuses to purchase the offerings of a specific organization or brand, due to a disagreement in principles, values, or over concerns regarding the organization or brand's actions or procedures.

Constructive pluralism: A branch of ethics which lends focus to diversity and difference, with the central notion that humans may have conflicting viewpoints and have much to learn still. However, constructive pluralism, despite these challenges, still asserts that humans should be able to coexist peacefully.

Deontological ethics: Deontological ethical theory lends focus to the actions taken by individuals, rather than the outcomes that those same actions might produce.

Descriptive ethical realism: Descriptive ethical realism is a branch of ethical theory which suggests that what a particular culture deems to be morally right or wrong is in fact right or wrong for any individuals inhabiting that culture. This branch of ethical theory suggests that there is no universal right or wrong, as things that are right and wrong in one culture may be viewed entirely differently by another.

Ethics: Simply put, ethics is the consideration and efforts to define right and wrong, ultimately governing the behaviour of individuals and groups.

Greenwashing: Greenwashing occurs when an organization or other entity makes an effort to appear more environmentally friendly than it actually is. This can also be seen as trying to dupe consumers.

Knowing–doing gap: The knowing–doing gap suggests that while stakeholders such as customers may have knowledge about what they 'should' do (for example, which offerings are more sustainable than other alternatives), they will still choose to do something different (such as purchasing a lesser sustainable offering due to, for example, a lower price point or availability). The 'gap' relates to the difference between what the consumers know and the action(s) that they ultimately take.

Morality: Morality relates to the social practice of doing something 'right' or 'wrong', and is closely linked to other elements such as an individual's culture and heritage.

Normative ethical realism: A normative ethical realism approach would advocate for base moral norms from which a society or culture might operate. The emphasis here is on progress, in determining what should be done, rather than remaining committed to what is already done.

Teleological and consequentialist ethics: Ethical approaches which are concerned with the end result, rather than any actions taken to achieve that end result.

Triple bottom line: The triple bottom line is an approach taken by some organizations that places importance on the 3Ps: profit, people and planet. Organizations using the triple bottom line approach will still work to make profits to secure their future financial viability, but will also make efforts to do wider good for society and the environment.

References

Arnold, D G, Beauchamp, T L and Bowie, N E (2019) *Ethical Theory and Business* (10th ed), Cambridge University Press

Barnett, C, Cafaro, P and Newholm, T (2007) Philosophy and ethical consumption, in R Harrison, T Newholm and D Shaw (eds), *The Ethical Consumer*, Sage Publications

Bland, G (2024) Taylor Swift's huge impact on the world, Story Maps, www.storymaps.com/stories/e4f1bd731bfe410288f46add0cfa6cf5 (archived at https://perma.cc/M2HJ-6F9F)

Boohoo (2024) Search results for jumper, www.boohoo.com/search?q=jumper&srule=price-low-to-high&sz=40&start=0 (archived at https://perma.cc/WPD4-EUFF)

Butler, S (2022) Poor working conditions persist in Leicester garment factories, finds survey, *The Guardian*, www.theguardian.com/uk-news/2022/jun/13/poor-working-conditions-persist-in-leicester-garment-factories-finds-survey (archived at https://perma.cc/W7S9-H2RT)

Carroll, P (2023) Why these popular chocolate easter eggs are banned in the US, despite being legal almost everywhere else, Foundation for Economic Education, www.fee.org/articles/why-these-popular-chocolate-easter-eggs-are-banned-in-the-us-despite-being-legal-almost-everywhere-else (archived at https://perma.cc/5PF8-A4V3)

Conway, Z and Masud, F (2024) Amazon workers narrowly reject union in historic vote, BBC News, www.bbc.co.uk/news/articles/c8vd72zrpr1o (archived at https://perma.cc/GJQ5-8J7J)

Dahl, S (2015) Ethics in new media, in *Marketing Ethics and Society*, Sage Publications

Dailey, H and Aniftos, R (2024) A timeline of Taylor Swift's generosity, *Billboard*, www.billboard.com/lists/taylor-swifts-charity-donations-gifts-timeline/dec-2022-she-supports-pet-rescue-foundation/ (archived at https://perma.cc/5YG3-9KP5)

Earth.org (2023) 10 concerning fast fashion waste statistics, www.earth.org/statistics-about-fast-fashion-waste/ (archived at https://perma.cc/S6PJ-XJJL)

Fairtrade (2024a) What is Fairtrade? www.fairtrade.net/about/what-is-fairtrade (archived at https://perma.cc/GVD9-ADNJ)

Fairtrade (2024b) Buying Fairtrade, www.fairtrade.org.uk/Buying-Fairtrade/ (archived at https://perma.cc/K36V-SY5Q)

Fairtrade Foundation (2024) The history of Fairtrade timeline activity, https://schools.fairtrade.org.uk/teaching-resources/the-history-of-fairtrade/ (archived at https://perma.cc/3ZPK-CVCP)

Ferrero (2024) Kinder Surprise, www.kinder.com/uk/en/the-kinder-story/04 (archived at https://perma.cc/LH4V-8Z86)

Geraghty, H (2024) UK food banks open up about impact of Taylor Swift's donations during Eras tour, *Huffington Post*, www.huffingtonpost.co.uk/entry/uk-food-banks-reveal-taylor-swift-donations-during-eras-tour_uk_667bde86e4b07cb66c6c3700 (archived at https://perma.cc/895U-CAEG)

Goffman, E (1971) *The Presentation of the Self in Everyday Life*, Allen Lane

Hill, A (2024) Taylor Swift donation enables Cardiff food bank to buy lorry full of supplies, *The Guardian*, www.theguardian.com/music/article/2024/jun/25/taylor-swift-donation-enables-cardiff-food-bank-lorry-supplies (archived at https://perma.cc/6WMU-6TFG)

King, B (2023) Nearly half a billion small tech items thrown away, BBC News, www.bbc.co.uk/news/business-67082005 (archived at https://perma.cc/3YFH-C9TD)

Klein, N (2000) *No Logo* (10th ed), HarperCollins

Kotler, P, Keller, K L, Goodman, M and Hansen, T (2019) *Marketing Management* (4th ed), Pearson

Liez, S (2022) Opinion: There are no ethical billionaires, *The Pitt News*, www.pittnews.com/article/175763/opinions/opinion-there-are-no-ethical-billionaires/ (archived at https://perma.cc/8F7U-U5XX)

Low, W and Davenport, E (2005) Has the medium (roast) become the message? The ethics of marketing Fair Trade in the mainstream, *International Marketing Review*, 22 (5), 494–511

Madarang, C (2023) Taylor Swift delivers Pride month message on 'Eras Tour': 'This is a safe space for you', *Rolling Stone*, www.rollingstone.com/music/music-news/taylor-swift-pride-month-eras-tour-chicago-1234746863/ (archived at https://perma.cc/7D7H-9ZNG)

Mass.gov (2024) Consumer Bill of Rights, www.mass.gov/info-details/consumer-bill-of-rights (archived at https://perma.cc/UHG4-B4PT)

McNaughton, D and Rawling, P (2005) Deontology, in *The Oxford Handbook of Ethical Theory*, Oxford University Press

National Geographic (2024) Great Pacific Garbage Patch, https://education.nationalgeographic.org/resource/great-pacific-garbage-patch/ (archived at https://perma.cc/8GBZ-QKAL)

Otte, J (2024) 'She could absolutely change my mind': Readers on Taylor Swift's political influence, *The Guardian*, www.theguardian.com/music/2024/feb/06/taylor-swift-political-voting-election-influence (archived at https://perma.cc/MZ6J-EPWZ)

Packard, V (1957) *The Hidden Persuaders*, Penguin Books

Padia, V (2024) The most expensive outfits worn by Taylor Swift in her Eras tour, ranked, The Richest, www.therichest.com/taylor-swift-most-expensive-outfits-eras-tour/ (archived at https://perma.cc/5MBP-KPEQ)

Panorama (2023) Fast fashion: Boohoo breaks promises on ethical overhaul, BBC News, www.bbc.co.uk/news/uk-67218916 (archived at https://perma.cc/G2ST-QK8H)

Ritzer, G (2005) *Enchanting a Disenchanted World: Revolutionizing the means of consumption* (2nd ed), Pine Forge Press

Ritzer, G (2007) *The Globalization of Nothing 2*, Sage Publications

Slabbekoorn, Z (2024) Taylor Swift fans claim she's the first ethical billionaire and that's why so many people don't like her, Your Tango, www.yourtango.com/entertainment/taylor-swift-fans-claim-first-ethical-billionaire-people-dislike-her (archived at https://perma.cc/KLC4-LN27)

Sugarhill Brighton (2024) Search jumper, www.sugarhillbrighton.com/search?filter.v.price.gte=&filter.v.price.lte=&sort_by=price-ascending&type=product%2Cpage&options%5Bprefix%5D=last&q=jumper (archived at https://perma.cc/AEA9-4LCX)

Which? (2024a) About Which? www.which.co.uk/about-which (archived at https://perma.cc/F96L-SZFM)

Which? (2024b) Ninja Foodi vs Tower Air Fryer vs Tefal Actifry: Which one should you buy? www.which.co.uk/reviews/air-fryers/article/philips-airfryer-vs-tefal-actifry-which-one-should-you-buy-aLVyo0N2eBJv (archived at https://perma.cc/GSK6-R3WH)

World Health Organization (2023) Electronic waste (e-waste), www.who.int/news-room/fact-sheets/detail/electronic-waste-(e-waste) (archived at https://perma.cc/RJ7K-R6K9)

World Population Review (2024) Countries with death penalty, www.worldpopulationreview.com/country-rankings/countries-with-death-penalty (archived at https://perma.cc/2F6K-9H9S)

10 | Production and the global marketplace

LEARNING OBJECTIVES

By the end of this chapter, you should be able to:

- explain the purpose and usefulness of the value chain in a global marketing perspective
- critically discuss the role of export processing zones and their consequences for a range of stakeholders such as workers, contractors, subcontractors and global organizations
- critically evaluate the notion of choice as it pertains to discussions of sweatshops and ethics
- determine the various advantages and disadvantages of offshoring service work from a range of stakeholder perspectives

Introduction

This chapter sets the scene with a recap of Kaplinsky and Morris's value chain, as previously discussed in Chapter 6, before moving on to discuss the consequences of organizations lending focus to design and marketing rather than production in the value chain.

Following this, the chapter explores the concept of **outsourcing** manufacturing to developing countries, including discussion of Klein's well-regarded 2001 text *No Logo*. Here, our discussions will be concerned with exploration of the consequences of outsourcing, as it relates to tax breaks and holidays, a lack of responsibility, and cheap labour, for example, from the organizational perspective.

However, we will also explore alternative perspectives to that of the organization, such as those of workers. Often, as we will see in the chapter, workers get the raw end of the deal. Yes, there is the possibility of employment in manufacturing for global organizations, but the implications for workers and subcontractors more broadly can be dire. For example, these may include low pay, irregular working patterns and poor working conditions. We will place further emphasis on the lack of progress in this area, contrasting Klein's work with, for example, recent exposés regarding **fast fashion** and **ultra-fast fashion** organizations such as Shein in 2022 and Boohoo in 2023.

The pros and cons of exporting jobs from a range of stakeholder perspectives, including brands, customers, manufacturers, subcontractors and workers, will be covered, along with the role of **export processing zones** in global production. Additional comparison to the lack of progress made in this area can be evidenced, as we will explore in the chapter via the monthly wage for garment manufacturers in different countries in year-by-year comparisons.

Further debates provide comparison between the supposed 'benefits' of sweatshop employment (think back to the previous chapter on ethics here) vs sweatshop work as an economic necessity (Zwolinski, 2007).

Emphasis will also be placed on **offshoring** for the service industry, including a focus on language trafficking and location masking (Mirchandani, 2004). The discussion will again consider a variety of stakeholder perspectives, but in particular what brands themselves might seek to gain from employing such tactics. Linking again back to the notion of ethics, the chapter will consider whether such employment is better than the next best alternative, keeping in mind the arguments of producers who cannot afford to consume what they produce (or often, even the basic basket of staples such as food and clothing), disparity in disposable income across countries (Dicken, 2015), and whether organizations showcase production practices as per reality or as a public relations exercise.

The value chain and organizational focus

To begin our discussions in this chapter, it is perhaps relevant to first reiterate (or to perhaps cover for the first time, for those who were keen to read this chapter and may have skipped earlier sections of this book) some key elements in relation to production on a global scale.

Our recap begins with Kaplinsky and Morris's 2001 notion of the value chain, which is constructed from three elements: design, production and marketing. As the majority of global organizations (and, indeed, some smaller organizations too) would no doubt agree, profit is a central concern and, as such, organizations are likely to lend their focus to the areas and activities from which the highest amount of profit might be generated.

As previously discussed in Chapter 6, manufacturing (or production, to use Kaplinsky and Morris's term), is no longer the focus area for most global organizations. Indeed, manufacturing was arguably the key element in the value chain, with production often being specialized in specific geographical areas (think back to Chapter 6 and products like shoes, pottery, coal and steel being made in Staffordshire and Stoke-on-Trent, UK). We might also link back to the country-of-origin effect here (as initially discussed in Chapter 4), via which consumers assign certain characteristics to any offering due to the location of the brand's origins. Positive associations in relation to quality can, as we know, be key in determining the choice of one offering or brand over another, and thus production in specific countries or more local locations (for instance, pottery made in Stoke-on-Trent, UK) can have significant implications for popularity, perceptions of quality, sales and profit margins.

However, contemporary global organizations have, for the most part, moved away from this emphasis on production, instead focusing on the design and marketing elements of the value chain (Kaplinsky and Morris, 2001). This arguably is due in large part to changes in competition. To put it simply, it is now cheaper to produce items in locations classed as emerging and developing economies than it is to produce that same item in the country in which it was designed. For example, Apple products are well-known for being designed in the US, but are typically produced in locations such as Asia.

While the financial ramifications of production in geographical areas such as Asia are likely to be positive (via a number of potential savings, which we will explore in more depth throughout the chapter), global organizations are still typically determined to keep the design and marketing elements of the value chain in their home countries. This is because of the importance placed on brands within contemporary global consumerism. That is to say that individual products themselves will not last forever – they will inevitably break, wear out or become unwanted by consumers – whereas the brand itself might be classed as enduring (aside from any public relations or other mishaps…) along with being flexible and innovative enough to continue to be attractive to customers in the long term. In other words, while we could not expect the individual products that we purchase to remain in our lives indefinitely, brands themselves are another story entirely. This, Klein (2001) suggests, equates to the 'conceptual brilliance of the "brands, not products" strategy'.

To provide a brief example, let's consider the value chain in relation to a new pair of shoes. Let's also say that our shoes are being designed in the UK, produced in China and then sold in the UK and the US. In this instance, the reward (the financial remuneration when the shoes are purchased by a customer) will not go to the people who have made the shoes in China. Instead, that reward goes to the people who have designed the shoes, and to the marketers who have convinced customers to part with their hard-earned cash in exchange for the item – who, in other words, have convinced the customer that the brand, not just the product, is worth paying for.

To summarize, in terms of organizational focus, this means that value is now in the marketing, branding, design and innovation spheres of Kaplinsky and Morris's value chain, rather than in the production of offerings. This has led to many Western organizations disposing of the manufacturing facilities (along with their associated responsibilities) that they may have previously owned, with production instead being outsourced to other geographical areas around the globe.

ACTIVITY ⬚

Kaplinsky and Morris's value chain

What are the three stages of Kaplinsky and Morris's value chain? Why is it useful for marketers to have an understanding of this model?

Export processing zones

Examples of global organizations outsourcing their manufacturing can be seen with export processing zones. Export processing zones are described by Papadopoulos and Malhotra (2007) as 'geographically defined areas within developing countries, intended to attract export-oriented foreign direct investment (FDI) by offering barrier-free environments and special incentives to firms that operate in them'. For the host countries this can result in an increase in economic growth, while global organizations outsourcing their manufacturing to export processing zones can often expect significant financial savings in comparison to manufacturing at home. This may, for example, be seen through duty-free or reduced import and export charges, and in tax breaks.

Export processing zones can be used to create a wealth of different products, such as garments, shoes, electronics, machines and cars. In practice, this results in global organizations shipping in 'the pieces of cloth or computer parts – free of import tax – and the cheap, non-union workforce assembles it for them. The then finished garments or electronics are shipped back out, with no export tax' (Klein, 2001).

Klein discusses the specific case of the Cavite Export Processing Zone, in the Filipino town of Rosario, 90 miles south of Manila, which produces goods exclusively for the export market. Export processing zones are typically characterized by guards and gates, designed to keep workers in and everyone else out. Staff in export processing zones are typically young women, with Klein reporting 52 economic zones in the Philippines alone in 2001, offering employment to 495,000 workers. As such, from the perspective of global organizations, Klein suggests that export processing zones offer 'zero-risk globalization'.

The processes and consequences of outsourcing production

Klein (2001) discusses a number of consequences in relation to the outsourcing of production to developing countries. In particular, the author notes the potential for tax breaks or tax holidays for global organizations sending their manufacturing requirements to emerging countries. In such cases, emerging countries may decide to offer certain incentives in the form of lowered tax or even tax-free benefits to encourage global organizations to bring their production needs to them. This, Klein suggests, results in organizations becoming 'economic tourists rather than long-term investors'. Why, you may ask, would organizations be seen in this way?

Consider the perspective of a global organization looking to manufacture products for as little as possible financially. If a particular host country offers you a tax incentive to take your production there, you will likely do so. However, once that tax break or holiday ends, you will have to pay more. So, the perhaps obvious (if ethically dubious?) thing to do is to move manufacturing to a different country, perhaps also offering tax incentives to lure in global brands. While this may be great news for organizations wishing to dedicate the majority of their resources to the design and marketing elements (as per Kaplinsky and Morris's value chain), this is not such good news for other stakeholders.

Once the tax break or holiday period ends, the host country will often lose the business of the global organization, which, as discussed above, is likely to seek a better tax deal elsewhere. However, it is not just a case of the global organization winning and the host country losing when we consider the outsourcing of manufacturing. We must also consider those consequences as related to the individuals and organizations who will actually complete the manufacturing processes which result in global organizations having finished products to sell.

Contractors and subcontractors

While host countries may wish to attract foreign investment to export processing zones via the introduction of tax breaks, tax holidays and the like, this does not account for what happens once a global organization decides to send its manufacturing requirements to a particular country.

While orders for the manufacturing amounts of particular products can certainly vary (this is something that we will discuss in more depth later on in this chapter), we must also consider what happens when very large orders are received. While large orders in themselves may not be a problem for manufacturers, the timescales imposed by global organizations may well be, especially when a large quantity of a particular product is required in a very short turnaround time. This can result in manufacturers becoming overwhelmed, with no way that they can meet the demand within the timeframe specified. However, manufacturers do not typically wish to risk losing contracts from global organizations and as such must still find a way to complete any orders.

Let's take a hypothetical example. Let's say that a global organization decides to order 50,000 t-shirts from manufacturer A, which is located in an export processing zone, agreeing to pay £1 for each item produced. The global organization requires our hypothetical order to be completed and shipped within 24 hours. From this £1, manufacturer A will need to make a profit to ensure financial sustainability; however, they will also need to pay their workers. But here we hit an issue, as manufacturer A does not have enough workers to create the 50,000 t-shirts in 24 hours, even if those workers continued production during the full time period allowed by the global organization.

In this type of scenario, manufacturer A may decide that they need some help to produce the order and might ask manufacturer B to help with the production as a subcontractor. While this action may help manufacturer A to complete the global organization's order, it also has financial implications for both manufacturing organizations and their respective workers. Let's say that manufacturer A decides to take 50 pence and to pay their workers 10 pence per item. That leaves 40 pence per item that can be offered to manufacturer B for their help with completing the order. Of course, manufacturer B also wants to make a profit, so let's say they take 35 pence per item. This leaves only 5 pence per item to be paid to manufacturer B's workers.

While the example here is purely hypothetical and not intended as reflective of the amounts paid by global organizations, nor the financial amounts assigned to manufacturers or their workers, it does serve to show the implications for both organizations and workers in terms of profits and wages from the orders of global organizations. Indeed, we might suggest that we see the global organization squeezing manufacturing organizations, who in turn have little choice but to do the same to their workers and any subcontractors with whom they work to complete orders within the required time limits.

Extreme implications

Evidence shows that workers themselves are paid very little for their role in the manufacturing process. Again, consider Kaplinsky and Morris's value chain here, but this time in relation to ethics. Does it seem right to you that the people who work to create the items we purchase from global organizations receive the least remuneration from the process?

Aside from very low pay, such workers also face poor working conditions. In the above example, we saw a very large order being required for completion within 24 hours. Klein also reports very long working hours for those employed in export processing zones. But the opposite can also be true, in that if few orders are received there is little work to be done and, therefore, no pay cheque to collect. Furthermore, the lack of unionization in export processing zones due to fears surrounding job losses and factory closures may serve to reinforce poor working conditions due to a lack of resistance.

Equally, Klein suggests that a culture of fear runs through these zones, from governments afraid of losing the factories to the workers worrying about their job security. A worrying thought indeed, if even an export processing zone's host country's government is afraid of the ramifications of the loss of global organizations' patronage. This view might be reinforced by host country governments offering the services of their military to deal with unrest, and putting their own people forward to receive the lowest wages (Klein, 2001).

Garment manufacturer wages

Let's explore wages for garment workers across various countries over the past few years, with amounts measured in US dollars.

If we start our exploration in 2017, we can see that the minimum monthly wage expected for garment workers varies significantly between countries. We see US workers being paid the most at $1,864, with South Korean workers our second largest earners at $1,251. On the other side of the scale, we have our lowest earners in Sri Lanka with $194 per month, and workers in Bangladesh only just above them at $197 (Lu, 2018).

Now let's take a look at how those figures compare to a similar snapshot of garment workers' monthly wages in 2019. Here, we see additional data for more countries being included, along with some significant shifts in the top and bottom earners, along with the amount of financial remuneration awarded to garment manufacturer workers. Now, we see workers in Belgium achieving the highest salary at $1,764, with UK workers a close second at $1,734. Ethiopia comes in at the lowest end of the scale with $26, with Madagascan workers receiving the next highest amount of $54 per month (Lu, 2020).

This data presents some interesting (if somewhat worrying) statistics. The country in which the highest average monthly wages might be achieved by garment manufacturing workers has shifted, as has the country with the lowest wage. The highest amount paid has decreased by $100, with the US dropping to the seventh highest earning country with workers being paid $1,160 per month – a decrease of $704 per month. There is also a significant difference between the lowest paid countries as shown by the data for 2017 and 2019. While Sri Lankan workers previously received $194 per month for their efforts, there has been a $168 per month drop in the lowest rate of pay, that of workers in Ethiopia. Our previous lowest earner, Sri Lanka, however, is still not much better off, climbing two places with a reduced pay rate for workers of $55 per month.

Klein also shares the specific example of a garment factory seamstress in the Philippines, Carmelita Alonzo. Carmelita's story is a sad one. During a heavy order period she had been working many overnight shifts at the factory in which she was employed, with a two-hour commute to return home following her shifts. Added to this was the fact that she was ill with pneumonia. Carmelita asked for time off from work due to her illness, but, as Klein reports, this request was denied. Ultimately, Alonzo was hospitalized and died on 8 March 1997 – International Women's Day – with her colleagues suggesting that she died of overwork (Klein, 2001).

While there are clearly a number of benefits and limitations to export processing zones depending on which stakeholder view we explore, we might also link back here to the removal of responsibility for global organizations in owning and operating their own manufacturing spaces. Interestingly, a key requirement of the global brand is that it be highly visible to potential customers and consumers, with the idea generally being to build the brand's name recognition across the globe.

However, as Klein (2001) reports, export processing zones might be the only places where 'superbrands' keep their profile to a minimum. Their logos don't appear on the factories and different labels aren't segregated, but produced side by side by the same workers. In Cavite, Klein found an 'unswished' place that was actually a Nike shoe factory. (By 'unswished', Klein is of course referring to the Nike symbol, suggesting the irony of the production factory as the only place in which Nike and other organizations are not so keen to display their branding.)

Exporting jobs

As we know from earlier discussions in this chapter of Kaplinsky and Morris's value chain, production used to be an organizational focus, and yet now this is perhaps the area in which organizations pay the least attention. With this decreased emphasis comes the notion of exporting jobs. In other words, what we refer to here are jobs such as factory work being removed from one country (typically the brand's country of origin) and moved to another geographical location (usually in an emerging economy).

There are, of course, both benefits and limitations to exporting job roles. For instance, those who agree with exporting jobs might suggest that it is beneficial for developing countries through the necessary overseas investment required to move jobs from one place to another, in addition to the creation of jobs themselves in host countries. This, for example, might be seen via the introduction of infrastructure required to complete the work, or in the financial remuneration being awarded to workers in developing rather than developed countries. Furthermore, we might suggest that such efforts encourage long-term economic development in poorer countries via, for example, job creation. To top this off, the global organizations themselves can of course expect cheap labour and economies of scale.

However, the other side of the argument is that exporting jobs is not such a good thing. Arguments here might link to the poor working conditions and pay that we have already discussed during the chapter. Other issues such as racism may also become apparent and, of course, if a global organization is exporting job roles from developed to developing countries, we see job losses in those developed countries.

The worker perspective

So, much of the chapter so far has painted an arguably bleak impression of export processing zones and the conditions and pay that their workers might expect. However, let's now consider what the workers themselves say about their jobs. In 2016, *The Guardian* reported on 'The grim truth of Chinese factories producing the West's Christmas toys', sharing the perspective of various stakeholders (Chamberlain, 2016). One such stakeholder, worker Xiao Fang, reportedly claimed she was one of the 'luckier' ones, making Barbie dolls for the Christmas market – despite the 11-hour days, six days a week, and the living conditions that kept her from her family.

Whether you agree or disagree that Xiao Fang is one of the 'luckier' workers, there are some additional points that we must consider. For example, the article investigates several factories in China working to produce toys for the West's Christmas market, and found that individuals can be expected to work with hazardous chemicals such as banana oil and isopropyl alcohol, which 'can cause dizziness and even death in high concentrations' (Chamberlain, 2016). Equally, overtime can run to nearly three times the legal limit, with some workers reporting having to complete more than 100 hours of overtime a month with wages beginning at £1.08 an hour.

Sweatshops, choice and ethics

Sweatshops are a 'complicated phenomenon' (Zwolinski, 2007), attracting frequent criticism from numerous sources about issues including those already mentioned (poor working conditions, hours and pay). Despite such critiques, it is perhaps useful to dig a little further into the moral and ethical implications of sweatshop work and the potential impacts when the opportunities for such work are removed.

For instance, Zwolinski argues that an individual's choice to accept sweatshop work is an act of their autonomy and, importantly, 'an expression of their preference'. This relates to the preference for sweatshop labour over other alternative forms of employment that may be available, but it does not suggest that a worker may have any specific 'intrinsic desire' to engage in sweatshop work – rather, that an individual might simply prefer 'working there to anything else she [or they] might do'. That being said, sweatshop workers are likely to face a 'severely constrained set of options', with unemployment not being a viable option due to the need to pay for the basic necessities of life.

Often, such workers will also face additional challenges in that they do not have the funds required to relocate to other geographical areas in which higher-paid low-skilled work may be available, nor do they have the funds required to pursue educational qualifications which may eventually lead to a higher-paying job role.

Regardless of whether we (to take a Western perspective) may potentially view sweatshops as inherently wrong, Zwolinski argues that, while sweatshops are harmful to workers, they are so in the context of providing financial benefit, and the readiness of workers to consent to the work shows that they view that benefit as considerable. So, regardless of whether we (the generalized West) might consider sweatshops to be wrong, the individual's choice and willingness to take employment in a sweatshop still relate to their autonomy and choice, even if we disagree with that choice.

Zwolinski argues that we should respect the choices and autonomy of others, even where we may disagree with their choices. Thus, the respect that we hold for another's autonomy may stop us from acting in a way that we feel would serve their best interests (that is not to say whether our intervention would be right or wrong; indeed, you may wish to revisit Chapter 9 on ethics to further solidify your viewpoint here).

What we may wish to question further here, however, is the validity of the choices available to sweatshop workers. To put this into further perspective, Zwolinski provides the following example: 'An agent faced with the gunman's threat of "your money or your life".' This is still a choice, even if both options are restricted and harmful, and if the agent chooses to hand over their wallet, it shows that this is preferable to losing their life. While a somewhat extreme example, here we see the illustration of choice. Neither choice may be 'good' or preferable if we had a more extensive range of options, but this is the option set that we must, in this case, choose from. In the case of the sweatshop worker, we can apply the same principles. The choice to work in a sweatshop may not be ideal or even 'good', but it is arguably better than the other alternative forms of employment available.

Added to this, we might consider that sweatshop workers do not choose to complete their work to pass the time, for enjoyment in the activity of work itself, nor to make money to spend on life's luxuries. Instead, such work is completed largely due to the pressures of survival, both for the individual worker and for their family. This might be, for example, to provide an education for their own children, so that the next generation can escape the cycle of poverty. Indeed, as Zwolinski explains, even work such as in sweatshops 'which falls short of a living wage can still help a worker feed their family, educate their children, and generally make their lives better than they would have been without it'. So, with such concerns and pressures for workers in mind, we might question, much as Miller (in Zwolinski, 2007) does, whether the choice made to work in a sweatshop is only made due to the 'coercion of economic necessity'.

Here, we might argue that any attempts to remove sweatshops, 'while knowing that sweatshop labour is the most preferred option of many workers, is to knowingly act in a way which is likely to cause workers harm' (Zwolinski, 2007) via the removal of that choice. Kates (2023) introduces the concept of 'nonworseness', suggesting that 'it cannot be morally worse to exploit someone than not to interact with them at all when the interaction 1) is mutually beneficial, 2) is voluntary, and 3) has no negative effects on third parties'.

To explicitly apply the nonworseness principle as described by Kates to sweatshop work, we might suggest that 1) sweatshop work can be seen as mutually beneficial in that workers are paid for their efforts and the factories in which they work make profit via the fulfilment of contracts with global organizations, 2) sweatshop workers freely make the choice to work in these factories from the forms of employment available to them, and 3) third parties are not negatively impacted (for example, the sweatshop worker's family may benefit from the potentially higher wages provided from sweatshop work, compared to alternative forms of employment in which a lower wage might be paid).

The removal of choice

With such concerns in mind, Zwolinski suggests that actors such as host and home country governments, along with consumers, should make efforts 'to refrain from acting in ways which are likely to deprive sweatshop workers of their jobs'. This might, for example, be via governments banning the import and/or export of items produced by sweatshop workers, or by customers and consumers deciding not to purchase items made in sweatshops. Again, if such actions were to take place, we would be limiting the workers' choice as to whether to participate in sweatshop work, as it is likely that fewer (if any) sweatshop jobs would be available if such conditions were to be put in place.

While conditions and pay (particularly from a Western perspective) may not be ideal or even 'good', the introduction of bans and boycotts removes the individual worker's choice as to whether to engage in sweatshop work or not, and this is morally questionable, while also limiting access to the rewards of work for those individuals.

Such efforts to remove sweatshops as viable sources of employment, or even just efforts to improve the conditions or rate of pay to which workers are subjected (if 'subjected' is indeed the correct word choice here, given that we are, after all, discussing choice…), may still result in the loss of job roles due to factory closures or the movement of production to another country where cheaper labour is still available. Arguably, any efforts to improve conditions will cost global organizations and manufacturers money, and as we know from our earlier discussions in this chapter in relation to contractors and subcontractors, without the possibility of financial viability, there is no point in running a sweatshop.

That being said, Kates (2023) argues that people working in sweatshops, are morally owed a non-exploitative wage even though the work is 'optional'. However, Kates also concedes that the nonworseness claim tries to demonstrate that 'there cannot be something morally wrong about a mutually beneficial and voluntary transaction if neither party is obliged to enter into it'. A wicked problem, indeed.

A final point of relevance here might be seen in linking back to the global organizations and brands which place orders with sweatshops in the first place, and our perceptions of them as customers and consumers. As Zwolinski explains, we might criticize a particular organization that we view as not doing enough to help a certain group of individuals, while at the same time not faulting other organizations which fail to do anything at all to help the group in question.

We might link here to the notion of expectations on, for example, Western global organizations which send their manufacturing requirements to be completed in the sweatshop environment. We, the consumer, might expect that global organization to play some beneficiary role in attempting to improve working conditions and pay for the workers manufacturing the goods which it will later bring to the consumer market. But why? Why do we not also expect this organization to help other individuals in developing countries who may be in worse financial straits than those working in sweatshops? After all, sweatshop work is often touted as the best paid position from the alternatives available.

Equally, why do we expect such organizations to do so much, and yet have no expectations of other organizations who do not manufacture their items in sweatshops? Taking this view, we might question, like Kates, whether from the perspective of a developing country and its workers, it is more damaging for global organizations to keep manufacturing processes in their home or other developed countries, as this limits opportunities for employment and the wages that inevitably come with them, however small those wages might be.

ACTIVITY

Sweatshops and choice

What is meant by the 'nonworseness claim'. To what extent do you agree with this notion?

Explain your stance in relation to the following assertion from Kates: 'How can it be morally worse to exploit the global poor than not to transact with them at all, when exploitation is voluntary and makes them better off?'

REAL-WORLD EXAMPLE   The human implications of the garment manufacturing industry

The world is no stranger to arguments pertaining to the poor conditions faced by some individuals working in sweatshops in developing countries.

Historically, young women were lured to work in sweatshops from rural areas with the promise of income from which they might send money back home to their families. While for some, 'the garment industry has meant opportunity, [and] independence' (Newman, 2017), we might question whether in a globalized world with fierce competition between global brands, our consumption habits are really worth the human cost. However, it is not just the consumer who must consider such issues. As you might already expect, organizations often compete on price, and clothing manufacturers are no exception to this rule. This means that the easiest way to compete is often to support low prices via the use of cheap labour. But what do the implications of acting in such a way entail?

For instance, in 2012 a fire in the **Tazreen Fashions factory** in Bangladesh killed at least 112 workers. This was likely caused by a short circuit on the ground floor which spread up to the ninth floor where workers were trapped due to narrow or blocked fire escapes.

Move forwards a mere five months in time, and we see another disaster for Bangladesh's garment factory workers. A perhaps better publicized example, the **Rana Plaza factory disaster** in Bangladesh in 2013 claimed the lives of 1,134 and injured more than 2,500. The Rana Plaza building, located near Dhaka, housed a number of different factories manufacturing clothing for some of the West's biggest fashion brands, including United Colors of Benetton, Bonmarché, The Children's Place, El Corte Inglés, Monsoon Accessorize, Mango, Matalan, Primark and Walmart.

Cracks were spotted in the building's structure the day before the disaster, leading it to be evacuated and closed, but the building's owner is reported to have 'later stated that it was safe to return to and threatened to withhold pay from anyone who refused to return to work' (Jones, 2020). The next day, the building collapsed, leaving workers trapped under the remnants of the building and its machinery for hours and even, in some cases, for days. Aside from the deaths caused by the disaster, for survivors, this led to a devastating range of health concerns, such as amputation. According to *The Independent*, the building was not fit to bear the 'weight and vibrations of factory machinery', with its upper floors also being added without the required permit, making them structurally unsafe.

It is not, however, only threats of fire and unsound building structures and the like that cast a dark shadow over the world's garment industry, nor is it only the poor practices taking place in developing countries. To provide an example, let's explore the case of Rotchana Sussman, who moved from her home country of Thailand to the suburb of El Monte, in California, US, due to promises of work as a seamstress.

The El Monte housing complex, situated around 22 miles from the Hollywood Hills, was surrounded by barbed wire and had 24-hour armed security. On her arrival in the US, Sussman's passport was taken from her and along with 71 other Thai nationals she ended up working as a 'virtual slave', putting in 18-hour days in a converted home that was eventually raided by authorities in 1995.

The El Monte seamstresses worked and lived in the same building, with the structure's garage doors being opened every morning to get the bags of clothing out so they could be transported to brand-name retailers.

As if this lack of physical freedom, not only in daily life but also in the lack of ability to return home due to the confiscation of travel documents, was not enough, workers were paid only $400 per month. With low pay to start with, workers such as Sussman were also told that they must pay back the money used to travel to the US, along with being charged 'exorbitant prices' by their employer for essentials such as food and toiletry items (Crossan and Garsd, 2017).

Questions

- How might disasters such as the Rana Plaza building collapse and the Tazreen Fashions factory fire be avoided in the future?

- Consider the role played by different stakeholders such as consumers, factory owners, workers, governments and global brands, as outlined in the case study. What, if anything, might each stakeholder have done differently in efforts to avoid such outcomes?

- To what extent does the case study make you want to become an agent of change? Explain your answer, noting any actions that you may consider taking in the future in this regard.

Offshoring services

The production of physical goods such as clothes, electronics and the like is not the only area in which we see jobs being exported to developing countries. Services are also often exported, which provides an interesting case when much of the developed world might be classed as heavily involved in the knowledge work and tertiary industries.

This we might term 'offshoring', which means relocating service-related activities away from the organization's home country (Doh et al, in Klimek, 2020). Klimek notes that offshoring can improve productivity and profits for organizations, along with the opportunities for employment and the associated wages to be received for workers in host countries (by host countries, I refer to the countries in which the service work takes place under offshoring practices).

While there are, as discussed, some potential benefits of offshoring, there are of course also potential pitfalls. For instance, Klimek notes that offshoring is responsible for millions of jobs and a 'race to the bottom' in terms of wages; in addition, a 'shift of white-collar jobs towards emerging economies means also offshoring the prosperity of the middle class' of the organization's home country. This, Klimek suggests, results in offshoring host countries being seen as the 'winners' of the globalization of business processes as they are able to attract the business of global organizations and create thousands of jobs. In reality, though, these winners are often accused of 'stealing' jobs from the company's host country.

Call centres

For instance, Mirchandani (2004) conducted a study of call centre workers in New Delhi, India who were providing voice-to-voice services to clients dialling toll-free numbers in North America on issues such as insurance, banking, credit cards and more. Mirchandani's study explored this transnational call centre work from the perspectives of workers, managers and trainers, all situated in the Noida export processing zone in New Delhi.

Workers dealt with incoming calls from customers only (as opposed to cold calling customers), and all of the study's participants had undergraduate degrees, with a number of workers also holding postgraduate qualifications. Workers earned between Rs 550 and Rs 10,000 (US$120–220) per month (though one male worker who had seven years of work experience earned Rs 30,000 (US$650)). Each worker was also assigned a pseudonym to be used during their interactions with their American customers.

While being connected to a worker located in a different country to our own when contacting a call centre is something that many of us will have experienced, Taylor and Bain (in Mirchandani, 2004) note that it can be more difficult to offshore customer-facing call centres as opposed to behind-the-scenes activities, due to the direct interaction required between workers and customers. This is, perhaps in part, due to the voice-to-voice nature of interactions between staff and customers, but we might also refer here to the notion of sweatshops producing physical goods as discussed earlier in this chapter.

In the case of physical goods being made in sweatshops, we as consumers might see the 'made in X' label on the items that we purchase, but that is generally where our interaction ends. With this in mind, it is arguably easy for the consumer to ignore this information, as there is no direct contact with workers in other countries. When we consider the live and interactive nature of the call centre, this same distancing is not possible. Such arguments might also be applied to other types of service work, where it is not necessary for direct interaction between workers and customers to take place.

Mirchandani notes the use of scripts for use by workers as efforts to 'control the nature, timing, norms and structure of work in India', with the additional requirement of workers performing 'emotional labour as part of their jobs'. This, as we will see throughout the rest of this section, might be through the ways in which workers are expected to edit their own identities and locations as perceived by their customers and in how they deal with those customers in themselves. While in some cases scripts can support workers to stay on track with customers and handle disagreeable interactions, workers in this case found the use of scripts to be 'deskilling, repetitive and tedious'. In order to ensure that scripted work in call centres is completed to the organization's satisfaction, Mirchandani tells us of the 'monitoring and language training' used by organizations, which includes 'generic (such as accent, grammar, customer service) and process-specific (about the products) training before [workers] are allowed to take calls'.

While we might expect to undertake training for a new job role, especially if a script is to be followed during call centre work, it is perhaps somewhat out of the ordinary (in the West, at least) for training on elements such as worker accents and grammar to be provided before the role commences. This Mirchandani refers to as 'language trafficking', or as the 'spread of particular types of English throughout the world'. Such efforts, in this case, require workers to neutralize their Indian-English accents in favour of American-English accents.

A 24/7 mentality

The use of scripts and attempts to alter the accents of call centre workers in India are not, however, the only issue that we might raise here in relation to call centre work. As Mirchandani notes, there is an expectation that American customers will place calls to the Indian call centre during American daytime hours, rather than during the Indian traditional working day. As a result, with a time difference of up to 16 hours between the two countries, the Indian call centre is predominantly operating at night. Through such mechanisms, a 24/7 business mentality might be achieved; however, this comes at a cost to Indian workers. As the 'Western clock time is exported across the globe and used as the standard', Indian call centre workers are obligated to work during national holidays and at most weekends. This results in workers feeling cut off from family and friends and becoming distanced from daily social life and other infrastructure, which primarily takes place during the daytime.

Added to this is the requirement, often handed down by the global organizations offshoring their service work to locations such as India, to mask the geographical location of call centre workers, with workers also not being permitted to share details of their location with customers during calls. And what, you may ask, is the purpose of such efforts? The short answer, as Mirchandani explains, is to protect

American corporations' interests from the racism of their local customers, while efforts may also be centred around avoiding 'ignorance towards Indians, concern about local jobs, and assumptions about exploitative transnational corporate practices'. Indeed, the Indian call centre workers featured in Mirchandani's study referred to their American callers as 'stupid', with the view that 'highly educated Indian workers employed in middle class, white collar occupations are serving often lower class, poorly educated American callers'. This suggests the potential for discrimination to be performed by both parties.

So, then, why might Indian workers who are highly educated be willing to take on such work? Mirchandani provides some insight as to why: it is promoted as desirable and specialized work; they are often housed in clean structures (with emphasis on building entrances being comprised of glass and marble, for instance); worker transport services add to the prestige; the salary is often double what local organizations might offer. Thus, despite the multitude of drawbacks of call centre work in India, we do still see a number of distinct benefits for individuals undertaking this type of work.

However, we might still liken the offshored call centre to a sweatshop, in that conditions and pay are not as favourable as if the role were to be completed in an organization's home country. Equally, we might also link back here to the notion of ethics and morality via the nature of the conditions imposed on workers by the global organizations for which they work.

ACTIVITY

Exporting call centre work

Explain the term 'language trafficking'.
    How would you feel if language trafficking was a requirement at your place of work?
    Why might call centre work be seen as short term by workers at Indian transnational call centres?
    What are the benefits and limitations for Indian's employed in transnational call centres, according to Mirchandani? Can you think of any other benefits or limitations?

Relevance to global consumption

While much of this chapter has focused on those who make or deliver products and services, rather than those who consume them, arguments as to why concepts such as offshoring and outsourcing are relevant to contemporary global consumerism practices are still of significance.

For instance, we might link here to the concept of the 24/7 mentality with services; as customers, we want what we want, when we want it. The same thing might be said for products. When we decide that we want to purchase a specific item, we expect that supply will be able to keep up with our demand. To enable such consumeristic mechanisms on a global scale, however, we see the plethora of concerns and issues discussed throughout this chapter (the treatment, conditions and wages of workers). We also might note here the relevance of producers who are not consumers, along with the unequal distribution of wealth between developed and developing countries across the globe. While as consumers we can take actions (such as those outlined in Chapter 9's discussions of agents of change), feelings of guilt and discomfort as to the conditions of employment for those producing the products that we purchase, or those who man the phones of the service centres we call, may still prevail.

That being said, while there are mechanisms (for example, see Chapter 9's discussion of consumer education) in place to help consumers and other stakeholders gain information about the offerings that they buy, including in relation to their sustainability credentials and production approaches, is there perhaps still more to be done? If we, as consumers, do not know about nor have the ability to research the products we buy and the organizations we buy them from, how are we to proactively and responsibly act as agents for change?

Such considerations suggest that more still needs to be done at the organizational level, particularly in relation to organizational transparency as to the production methods used during manufacturing processes. In considering the global fashion industry, one entity attempting to shed further light on the levels of transparency that organizations share with stakeholders (along with other useful information) is Fashion Revolution.

Fashion Revolution

Fashion Revolution was founded in response to the 2013 Rana Plaza disaster and is the largest fashion activism movement in the world, using research, education and advocacy to mobilize society (Fashion Revolution, 2024a). Fashion Revolution publishes an annual transparency index report (available via the organization's website, if you would like to explore this in further detail). One special edition of the report 'What fuels fashion?' ranked 250 fashion brands on the transparency of their policies in relation to climate energy and supply chains (Fashion Revolution, 2024b).

The report lists a number of key findings in relation to the activities and transparency of many of our favourite global fashion brands. For instance, the report details that the majority of big fashion brands (89 per cent) do not disclose how many clothes they make annually, and 45 per cent of brands fail to disclose either how much they make or the raw material emissions footprint of what is produced.

However, perhaps more closely related to the contents of this chapter are statistics published by Fashion Revolution in their fashion transparency index. For example, the 2022 index provides a somewhat alarming range of information: only 12 per cent of brands publish a purchasing code of conduct, showing reluctance to be transparent about the impacts of their purchasing practices; though 48 per cent of brands are disclosing their first tier suppliers, half don't disclose anything at all (Fashion Revolution, 2022). The 2022 fashion transparency index also quotes Aruna Kashyap, Associate Director (Corporate Accountability), Economic Justice and Right Division, Human Rights Watch. Kashyap stated that transparency was essential to any serious efforts brands make to develop a supply chain free from human rights abuses.

While most would likely agree with such a notion, to what extent, two years on from the report, do you think that we have reached this, based on the earlier discussions in this chapter?

REAL-WORLD EXAMPLE   Transparency and ultra-fast fashion

Chances are, if you have ever visited social media platforms such as TikTok, Instagram, YouTube and so on, you will have come across content related to fast or ultra-fast fashion brands (brands that can release new items on a weekly or sometimes even daily basis), such as Shein and Boohoo. While these brands do of course advertise through the likes of celebrity endorsement and influencer marketing, much of the content popping up on our social media platforms is created by users themselves. Whether motivated by the promise of free items from the brands they discuss in their video reviews, or just from the excitement of sharing their latest haul, it is clear that user sharing of such videos has become a growing trend in recent years. For those yet to come across such videos, a 'haul' typically relates to a fashion customer opening and trying on the various items they have ordered to show the audience for their video the purchases, often also focusing on showing what was ordered versus what was received.

One such example comes with ultra-fast fashion brand Shein. With its headquarters in, and most products being dispatched from, China, Shein has introduced international warehouses based in Asia, America, Europe and the Middle East to make sure that orders are received as fast as possible (Shein, 2024a) by its customers in over 150 countries. The brand describes itself as a global e-retailer committed to making the beauty of fashion accessible to all. This, the brand suggests, is accomplished via the use of on-demand manufacturing technology and an agile supply chain, as well as software to track sales and communicate with factories in real time (Shein, 2024b). This approach, Shein notes, holds the dual benefits of allowing the brand to offer a wide range of styles without creating excessive inventory waste, in addition to allowing shorter time periods in which customers must wait for their orders.

Shein is also no stranger to the increased focus on sustainability and ethics that has swept across the world in recent years. For instance, its website provides links to the brand's statement on UK modern slavery (Shein, 2024c), along with a further webpage discussing the brand's impact, initiatives, statistics and more, all with sustainability in mind. Here, the brand lists some interesting statistics, ranging from its senior management being 40 per cent female to 100 per cent of Shein's premium MOTF brand's packaging being made from recycled plastics (Shein, 2024d).

While there can be no doubt that Shein's website hopes to promote the brand's green credentials and efforts towards sustainability, there are of course some issues of which we must still be aware. In 2021, the BBC reported that Shein had approximately 600,000 products for sale on its online platform, and relied on thousands of third-party suppliers and 200 contract manufacturers to fulfil its orders. This equates to a fast turnaround on products: 6 per cent of inventory remains in stock 90 days or more (Jones, 2021).

Open the Shein app or website, and the first thing that users are likely to see is a range of coupons or other promotions. While this may seem generous of the brand, it is, in fact, a marketing ploy designed to get us to spend more money. And, as of 2024, the BBC notes that the average cost of a Shein-branded clothing item is just £7.90, potentially making it easier for us to add just one more thing to our digital baskets (Thomas et al, 2024). While the cost may not be particularly high for us financially as customers and consumers, there are, of course, other potential costs that we must take into consideration. For instance, concerns surrounding the impact of mass-producing low-cost clothes along with labour challenges in manufacturing processes have been regularly reported by various news outlets. We see such challenges with reports that Chinese workers for some of Shein's suppliers are still working 75-hour weeks (Edwards, 2024).

Equally, fast fashion brand Boohoo has been under the spotlight in recent years due to concerns around its approach to sustainability, transparency and the ethical treatment of workers. Yet, much as with Shein's website, Boohoo makes attempts to push their (or the illusion of their) sustainability efforts. A quick online search, for instance, reveals Boohoo's 'UP.FRONT' sustainability plan, which details three core focus areas for the brand: to make clothing smarter, to improve relations with suppliers and to embed responsibility within the organization (Boohoo, 2024)

While we might typically expect concerns about Boohoo's supply chain to primarily relate to workers in developing countries, here we instead discuss the production of Boohoo garments in factories in Leicester, UK, where workers are 'taking home as little as £4 an hour' (Bracchi, 2020) for their labour, far below the UK's minimum wage. Workers also report their pay slips as suggesting higher rates of pay than they are actually receiving, along with pressures to attend work even when they are sick, in order not to lose their jobs.

In more recent news, Boohoo still appears to be in hot water, this time due to the use of labels suggesting that garments had been made in the UK, when they had actually been made in South Asia (Panorama, 2024). As the BBC reports, original labels were removed from items of clothing at the Thurmaston Lane factory in Leicester in 2023. The fact that such actions took place at this site is another kick in the teeth for sustainability-focused customers, as the hope was that Boohoo could demonstrate that sustainable production and operations are possible on home soil. Unfortunately, these efforts appear to have failed, with Boohoo having now confirmed the site's closure (Martin, 2024).

Perhaps even more disappointing is that the Thurmaston Lane factory closure comes on the back of previous well-documented failings from the brand in the sustainability and ethics spheres. For instance, a 2023 BBC Panorama investigation found that Boohoo had failed to live up to a 2020 promise to overhaul its practices (Panorama, 2023).

Questions

- After reading the case study, has your impression of fast and ultra-fast fashion companies changed? If so, in which ways?

- Would you shop with fast or ultra-fast fashion brands in the future? Why, or why not?

- To what extent do you think that fast and ultra-fast fashion brands should be doing more to protect the workers who make their clothes? What should this 'help' look like?

- To what extent do the coupons and gamification (for instance, in offering points for product reviews and the like) provided by such organizations contribute to the environmental and human costs as outlined within the case study?

- Do you consider the ethical and sustainability efforts of fast and ultra-fast fashion brands to be public relations exercises, or to be genuine efforts for change? Explain the reasons behind your answer.

CHAPTER SUMMARY

The chapter began by revising the discussions of Kaplinsky and Morris's value chain from Chapter 6, along with subsequent discussions of where organizational focus is likely to sit within the supply chain. With this in mind, we see the rise of elements such as the brand itself, innovation and design, with manufacturing taking a back seat in organizational priorities. This, as we know from the current chapter, is due to efforts to gain the highest level of financial return from organizational efforts.

Following this brief recap, we moved on to explore the concept of export processing zones, along with the consequences of global brands outsourcing their production. Here we covered the use and financial implications of using contractors and subcontractors, paying particular attention to the plight of export processing zone workers in developing countries. Here, our discussion turned to the concept of sweatshops, along with providing some debate as to choice, necessity and ethics in working locations. This, the chapter sought to show, is a multifaceted and complex phenomenon, with individual ethics and morality playing a significant role in how we choose to view and understand sweatshops located both in the West and further afield.

With this in mind, the chapter also delved into the consequences of exporting job roles for a number of different stakeholders, from the perspectives of both host and home countries, before looking at the notion of offshoring service work, which also has a range of complex requirements and implications for workers.

While much of the earlier chapter lent focus to the role of global organizations and workers in discussions of production in the global marketplace, the latter sections of the chapter changed this focus to explore the role of the consumer with the dislocation of production and consumption in mind. The hope, here, was to entice readers such as yourself to consider the approaches taken by global brands, along with the extent to which they are transparent about their practices.

The following chapter explores consumption for the world's poorest and richest consumers using a pyramid model, whereby the poorest consumers exist at the wide base of the pyramid, and the richest exist at the narrow top. With such consumers in mind, the chapter examines the implications of unequal wealth distribution across the globe, connecting the discussion with poverty levels and consumption practices in the global marketplace. Ultimately, the chapter encourages readers to question whether global organizations serving customers at the bottom of the pyramid is a dangerous activity, or whether it is an activity which may prove profitable for all stakeholders involved.

CHAPTER REVIEW QUESTIONS

Kaplinsky and Morris's value chain

- What are the three stages of Kaplinsky and Morris's value chain? Why is it useful for marketers to have an understanding of this model?

Kaplinsky and Morris's value chain and ethics

- Consider the stages of Kaplinsky and Morris's value chain, and its key players of designers, manufacturing workers and marketers. Which stakeholder do you think should be paid the most for their efforts? Why?

- Consider your answer to the question above. How might this answer change or be justified by the ethical theories covered in Chapter 9?

Garment factory worker pay

- Consider the rates of pay awarded to garment factory workers as discussed in the chapter. Do the rates of pay surprise you? If so, how? Why?
- Did you expect the countries named to occupy their positions at the top and bottom levels of pay rates?
- What do these statistics tell us about contemporary global marketing environments?
- What do these statistics tell us about production and consumption?

Worker perspectives

- Consider the quote from Chinese toy factory worker Xiao Fang. Do you agree with her assertion that she is 'one of the luckier workers' (Chamberlain, 2016)? Why, or why not?
- How would you feel about being asked to work with hazardous chemicals during your job role?
- Do you think it is ethical for workers to complete 100 hours of overtime in a month? Would you be willing to do this? Why, or why not?

Sweatshops and choice

- What is meant by the 'nonworseness claim'? To what extent do you agree with this notion?
- Explain your stance in relation to the following assertion from Kates (2023): 'How can it be morally worse to exploit the global poor than not to transact with them at all when exploitation is voluntary and makes them better off?'

Exporting call centre work

- Explain the term 'language trafficking'.
- How would you feel if language trafficking was a requirement at your place of work?
- Why might call centre work be seen as short term by workers at Indian transnational call centres?
- What are the benefits and limitations for Indian's employed in transnational call centres, according to Mirchandani (2004)? Can you think of any other benefits or limitations?

KEY TERMS

Export processing zones: Export processing zones are specific areas in (typically) developing countries, which are often gated and protected by guards. The purpose of export processing zones is to provide enticements, such as in the reduction or removal of potential barriers (often tax breaks and access to cheap labour) to incentivize global businesses to bring their production processes to the area.

Fast fashion: Fast fashion brands have a fast turnaround period, with new designs typically being available for purchase every few weeks.

Offshoring: The process of moving service-based work to another country, typically to take advantage of lower labour costs.

Outsourcing: The process of moving manufacturing and production-based work to another country, typically to take advantage of financial savings via cheaper labour, tax breaks and so on.

Rana Plaza disaster: A 2013 disaster in Bangladesh during which the Rana Plaza commercial building collapsed, killing over 1,000 people and injuring many more.

Tazreen Fashions factory fire: A factory fire in Bangladesh in 2012 which led to more than 100 workers losing their lives.

Ultra-fast fashion: Ultra-fast fashion brands share many of the same characteristics as fast fashion brands. However, ultra-fast fashion brands can provide new items for purchase on a weekly or daily basis, rather than every few weeks.

References

Boohoo (2024) UP.FRONT, www.boohooplc.com/sustainability.htm (archived at https://perma.cc/5A3B-EUSK)

Bracchi, P (2020) 'Anyone saying all their staff are on minimum wage in the garment industry is a fraud:' 'Sweatshop' owner of Boohoo factory confesses he pays workers a shocking £4 an hour, *Mail Online*, www.dailymail.co.uk/news/article-8511651/Sweatshop-owner-Boohoo-factory-confesses-pays-workers-shocking-4-hour.html (archived at https://perma.cc/Q528-BMSG)

Chamberlain, G (2016) The grim truth of Chinese factories producing the West's Christmas toys, *The Guardian*, www.theguardian.com/business/2016/dec/04/the-grim-truth-of-chinese-factories-producing-the-wests-christmas-toys (archived at https://perma.cc/FXC4-U78Z)

Crossan, A and Garsd, J (2017) How a sweatshop raid in an LA suburb changed the American garment industry, The World, www.theworld.org/stories/2017/12/05/el-monte (archived at https://perma.cc/KN34-MTUC)

Dicken, P (2015) *Global Shift: Mapping the changing contours of the world economy* (7th ed), Guilford Press

Doh, J, Bunyaratavej, K and Hahn, E (2009), in Klimek, A (2020) *Offshoring of white collar services: Business and economic perspective*, De Gruyter

Edwards, C (2024) Shein supplier still work 75-hour weeks – report, BBC News, www.bbc.co.uk/news/articles/cg67w73nxqxo (archived at https://perma.cc/32Z9-G6HE)

Fashion Revolution (2022) *Fashion Transparency Index*, https://issuu.com/fashionrevolution/docs/fti_2022 (archived at https://perma.cc/8UJB-4ADY)

Fashion Revolution (2024a) About, www.fashionrevolution.org/about/ (archived at https://perma.cc/XDG2-JAX8)

Fashion Revolution (2024b) What fuels fashion? www.issuu.com/fashionrevolution/docs/full_report_31_july?fr=xKAE9_zU1NQ (archived at https://perma.cc/X78L-8LWF)

Jones, L (2021) Shein: The secretive Chinese brand dressing Gen Z, BBC News, www.bbc.co.uk/news/business-59163278 (archived at https://perma.cc/765M-MMK8)

Jones, S (2020) Fashion Revolution Week: What was the Rana Plaza disaster and why did it happen?, *The Independent*, www.independent.co.uk/life-style/fashion/rana-plaza-factory-disaster-anniversary-what-happened-fashion-a9478126.html (archived at https://perma.cc/3KKW-UMUH)

Kaplinsky, R and Morris, M (2001) *A Handbook For Value Chain Research*, www.researchgate.net/publication/42791981_A_Handbook_for_Value_Chain_Research (archived at https://perma.cc/YVJ4-4HG6)

Kates, M (2023) Sweatshops, exploitation, and the nonworseness claim, *Business Ethics Quarterly*, 33 (4), 682–703

Klein, N (2001) *No Logo*, Flamingo

Lu, S (2018) Wage level for garment workers in the world (updated in 2017), FASH455 Global Apparel & Textile Trade and Sourcing, www.shenglufashion.com/2018/03/04/wage-level-for-garment-workers-in-the-world-updated-in-2017/ (archived at https://perma.cc/4EWL-6J95)

Lu, S (2020) Minimum wage level for garment workers in the world (updated in December 2020), FASH455 Global Apparel & Textile Trade and Sourcing, www.shenglufashion.com/2020/12/04/minimum-wage-level-for-garment-workers-in-the-world-updated-in-december-2020/ (archived at https://perma.cc/BEA6-D7UK)

Martin, D (2024) Boohoo to sell Leicester factory after confirming closure, BBC News, www.bbc.co.uk/news/uk-england-leicestershire-68687701 (archived at https://perma.cc/8HS8-JSR3)

Miller, J (2003) cited in Zwolinski, M (2007) Sweatshops, choice, and exploitation, *Business Ethics Quarterly*, 17 (4), 689–727

Newman, A (2017) Wear and tear series: The women who make our clothes, The World, www.theworld.org/stories/2017/12/04/wear-and-tear-series-women-who-make-our-clothes (archived at https://perma.cc/QJR5-EQXP)

Panorama (2023) Fast fashion: Boohoo breaks promises on ethical overhaul, BBC News, www.bbc.co.uk/news/uk-67218916 (archived at https://perma.cc/E84X-R45R)

Panorama (2024) Boohoo put 'Made in UK' labels of clothes made overseas, BBC News, www.bbc.co.uk/news/uk-67929755 (archived at https://perma.cc/A89E-GY2M)

Papadopoulos, N and Malhotra, S (2007) Export processing zones in development and international marketing: An integrative review and research agenda, *Journal of Macromarketing*, 27 (2), 148–61

Shein (2024a) Shipping info, www.shein.co.uk/Shipping-Info-a-280.html (archived at https://perma.cc/U337-B8ED)

Shein (2024b) About us, www.shein.co.uk/About-Us-a-117.html (archived at https://perma.cc/P9WB-LM2S)

Shein (2024c) Shein: UK Modern Slavery Statement 2024, www.shein.co.uk/SHEIN-Modern-Slavery-Statement-a-1067.html (archived at https://perma.cc/Y8BD-Y4UD)

Shein (2024d) Our impact, www.sheingroup.com/our-impact/ (archived at https://perma.cc/Q6ZJ-9NGJ)

Taylor, P and Bain, P (2004) in Mirchandani, M (2004) Practices of global capital: Caps, cracks and ironies in transnational call centres in India, *Global Networks*, 4 (4), 355–73

Thomas, D, Jones, L and Hooker, L (2024) The rise and rise of fashion giant Shein, BBC News, www.bbc.co.uk/news/articles/cp991n2v0m2o (archived at https://perma.cc/6DH6-7MG4)

11 | Consumption at the top and bottom of the pyramid

LEARNING OBJECTIVES

By the end of this chapter, you should be able to:

- explain the bottom of the pyramid concept, along with how this relates to income and wealth inequalities
- understand the implications of poverty levels for consumers at the bottom of the pyramid
- critically discuss whether the bottom of the pyramid proposition is profitable for all parties, or whether such efforts are a dangerous misconception with regard to the potential for organizational profits and in helping consumers at the bottom of the pyramid in terms of poverty alleviation

Introduction

This chapter explores whether marketing to the bottom of the pyramid (BoP) is an attractive proposition for global organizations, in addition to being a potential route to the alleviation of **poverty**. Beginning with an explanation of the BoP, the chapter uses past and recent poverty levels to provide some context in discussions of which stakeholders are responsible for the eradication of poverty. For instance, the chapter questions whether we should view poverty as an economic, social, political, moral, or marketing and management problem (Karnani, 2007). Levels of consumption across countries are explored, along with the connections between the BoP proposition, global consumers, identity formation and meaning through consumption and the spread of Western influence.

Arguments for targeting the BoP note the geographically clustered nature of the target population, aggregate purchasing power, links to benefits where standardization (Levitt, 1983) has been employed, leading to a win-win situation for all stakeholders. However, we also explore counterarguments which suggest a wide rural geographic dispersion, lack of money for luxuries, and that SMEs are a potentially better fit due to their understanding of the needs of local consumers. This, one might suggest, speaks to marketing to the BoP being seen as a dangerous delusion, rather than a win-win situation.

We also link back to the earlier discussed arguments and theories related to ethics in considering whether the world's poorest consumers have the right to make their own 'mistakes'.

The bottom of the pyramid

As briefly touched upon in Chapter 9, the bottom of the pyramid suggests a 3D pyramid model as representative of the number of consumers who exist in the global marketplace, and the amount of wealth that they possess. Simply put, we see few consumers at the top of the pyramid who hold a high amount of disposable income (as represented by the small point at the top of the pyramid), compared to many consumers at the bottom who have very little disposable income (as represented by the low yet wide base of the pyramid).

Poverty lines

In discussing the bottom of the pyramid, we are talking about consumers who have very little, if any, disposable income. Poverty is certainly not a new problem; however, it is an issue that we might choose to conceptualize and attempt to tackle in a number of different ways. However, poverty does not only relate to monetary concerns and the purchasing power that financial wealth provides. Indeed, poverty can be connected to other significant issues, such as healthcare, food, education, vulnerability to a changing climate and access to infrastructure (World Bank Group, 2024).

While measures and definitions of poverty vary geographically, a common measurement tool for poverty is that of the **national poverty line**. The national poverty line is usually seen as 'a monetary threshold below which a person's minimum basic needs cannot be met, taking into account the country's economic and social circumstances' (World Bank Group, 2024). As you might expect, this threshold varies wildly between different geographical locations, with poorer countries having lower poverty lines than richer countries.

Understanding national poverty lines can be a useful indicator in determining how well countries are doing in comparison to one another, along with providing insights into the standards of living that one might find in a particular country. For instance, the World Bank Group suggests that a poverty line of $2.15 per day would be reflective in some of the world's most poor countries, $3.65 per day for lower-middle income locations and $6.85 for countries with an upper-middle level of income. These figures are typically reflective of the cost of a food shopping basket containing what poor consumers in a particular country would usually eat, with some allowance for spending on non-food items. Much as with the cost of food and other items decreasing and increasing over time, poverty levels will also fluctuate to remain reflective of any changes to the poverty line in a country over time.

International poverty lines

As readers may expect from the discussion so far, poverty levels and lines differ across the globe, resulting in **international poverty lines**.

The contemporary conception of the poverty line has its roots in the 1980s when a group of economists noted that several developing countries suggested a poverty line income of around $370 per year (Alexander, 2012). This amount was supposed to be reflective of the lowest amount of money required for a person to purchase the necessary essential products to survive each month. This thinking was furthered by one of the original economists who realized that dividing the $370 amount by the 365 days of the year would equate to around $1 per day being the benchmark for being able to afford the basic necessities of life in the countries in question.

However, it is also important to remember here that we are not talking about the American dollar but rather a dollar with respect to the currency of each country in question. In other words, a very different amount of money. This required the introduction of a 'specially adjusted dollar' using Purchasing Power Parity, or PPP (Alexander, 2012). This meant that the team of economists explored the price of goods in various emerging economies, and then calculated how much money would be needed in each country to buy a basket of basic goods that costs $1 in the US (calculated referencing national accounts, household surveys and census data (Alexander, 2012).

International poverty lines present a further challenge in efforts to determine poverty lines to allow for international comparison, as the purchasing power of a specific geographical location's currency must also be considered, meaning that multiple data sources are often required.

This can result in an aggregate poverty line being determined, for instance, for the world's poorest countries. The World Bank Group (2024) notes that in 1990 a common extreme poverty line of $1 a day was seen, while the current median poverty line for the poorest countries across the globe sits at $2.15 per day. To provide some further context, the World Bank suggests that 712 million people lived below the $2.15 per day poverty line in 2022, equating to around 9 per cent of the world's population, or around 1 in 11 people (World Vision, 2024).

While the figures discussed in this chapter so far present a somewhat unhappy picture of poverty levels across the globe, it is important to remember that improvements have been seen since the poverty line measure was first introduced.

ACTIVITY

Country comparisons

Let's compare the poverty line in various countries. Choose at least three countries (including your home country). Next, visit www.pip.worldbank.org/home, scroll down to the search box for country profiles and insert your selected countries.

What are the differences between the countries that you selected in terms of their poverty lines? Why might this be the case?

Are there any other significant differences between the information you have found for each country selected?

Where possible, compare your findings with those of another student in your class.

Stakeholder responsibility

As we have seen throughout the chapter so far, poverty is a serious issue for much of the world's population. However, what can we do to solve this problem, and who should be responsible for it?

We can view the problem of poverty in many different ways, as an economic problem, a social problem, a political problem or a moral problem (Karnani, 2007), which suggests that a varied group of stakeholders may hold responsibility for tackling poverty. Traditionally, however, poverty was primarily seen as a problem to be addressed by local governments, the governments of developed countries, international organizations, charitable foundations, non-governmental organizations (NGOs) and the like. Now, however, poverty is also seen as a challenge to be resolved (at least in part) by marketing and management experts.

ACTIVITY

Responsibility

Which stakeholder groups do you think should be responsible for tackling poverty? Why?

As we know from previous discussions in this book, production and consumption inequalities exist across the globe, and consumers at the top and bottom of the pyramid are no exception to these debates. With this in mind, if you were to be the CEO of a global organization, which customers would you target? Those at the top of the pyramid with high levels of disposable income, or those at the bottom of the pyramid with very low levels of disposable income?

When first considering this question, most would likely say that it makes sense to target consumers at the top of the pyramid as they have the most disposable income to spend. However, when we consider the relatively small number of consumers at the top of the pyramid in comparison to the vast number of consumers at the bottom of the pyramid, our considerations become more complex. For instance, The World Bank (2024) reports that low-income people in emerging economies collectively spend over $5 trillion per year (more than the middle and higher consumption segments combined). This includes $2.3 trillion on just food and beverages. Does this change your thoughts as to which customers you would target?

The bottom of the pyramid proposition is an interesting one, as while it may initially seem counterintuitive to target poorer customers, there are certainly some potential benefits that marketers and global organizations should consider.

The bottom of the pyramid might be seen as holding large and relatively untapped purchasing power, due to the high number of consumers and their perceived lack of access to Western goods and brands. Arguments for marketing to the bottom of the pyramid would also suggest that consumers are likely to be geographically clustered, meaning that potential savings would be possible for global organizations who choose to serve these consumers in that advertising and logistics can also be clustered, thus saving money.

We might also suggest here that although individual consumers at the bottom of the pyramid do not have much money, this is not the case if we consider the aggregate purchasing power of such consumers. For example, it may not be possible for an individual bottom of the pyramid consumer to have internet in their home, but it may be possible for a group of BoP consumers to purchase the service together, to allow for a shared access model. Furthermore, we might suggest that if global organizations (along with others) can lead the way with economies of scale, efficient supply chains will enable higher-quality goods to be offered to consumers at the bottom of the pyramid at lower prices. This, we might suggest, can be helpful in efforts to alleviate poverty via the provision of access to goods and services and, from the organization perspective, allows for the potential capture of market share in particular locations.

At this point, we would be remiss if we did not link back to Levitt's (1983) notions of standardization. The majority, if not all, of the potential benefits in marketing to the bottom of the pyramid as discussed in the previous paragraph suggest the requirement of a certain degree of standardization. For global organizations to realistically be able to keep prices low for customers at the bottom of the pyramid, the use of standardization is a helpful tool, in allowing the organization itself to reduce the burden of cost associated with bringing offerings to new markets. This notion is much helped by the argument of urban bottom of the pyramid consumers being geographically clustered, with a standardized approach (as discussed in Chapter 3) often proving a far cheaper approach than that to adaptation to individual markets.

Global consumerism and the bottom of the pyramid

Regardless of whether you initially opted to target customers at the top or bottom of the pyramid, there are a number of considerations that we must also take into account.

To begin, readers may wish to return to the notion of global consumerism, and the increasing desire to purchase and own material goods. This is of course not just a concept that we might assign to those existing at the top of the pyramid, but also to those at the bottom regardless of their level of wealth. Similarly, the previously discussed (see Chapter 5) spread of ideas and offerings from the West to the rest of the world is also a factor here. However, again discussions may have the tendency to become more complex: just because consumers live in varied parts of the world, it does not mean that they will not desire the same products, regardless of whether they can afford them or not.

For a less extreme example, consider your own personal level of wealth and disposable income. Is there a product that you would like to buy but cannot currently afford? Chances are you have probably thought of something that you would like to purchase, and it is this type of thinking that we might transfer, albeit on a perhaps larger scale, to consumers existing at the bottom of the pyramid. Indeed, as we know from Chapter 2, the purchase of offerings can help us to construct our identities and to create meaning in our daily lives. This remains the same regardless of whether consumers are at the top or bottom of the pyramid.

While in theory such considerations are all of relevance to consumers across the entirety of the pyramid, we must however question the extent to which these considerations are likely in practice for BoP consumers. For instance, we might question to what extent the spread of Western offerings can be seen among consumers at the bottom of the pyramid in diverse countries, and how able consumers and customers are to connect with and support groups and movements via their consumption patterns, when taking geographical location into consideration.

For instance, linking back to the inequalities associated with production and consumption on a global scale, we might take the example of Fairtrade products. Customers who support this movement in developed countries will likely have ample opportunities to show their support via the purchases they make. However, this is less likely to be the case for consumers in other geographical locations where consumers primarily exist at the bottom of the pyramid.

ACTIVITY

The poverty clock

A further scale with which we can explore poverty levels across the globe comes in the form of the poverty clock, which provides estimates up to 2030 and captures efforts to reduce poverty across the globe (Data Lab, 2024). Interestingly, the poverty clock allows users to filter results by rural or urban geographical locations, along with other demographics. Visit www.worldpoverty.io to explore poverty in your own, and other, countries.

Lower income groups and the impacts of exposure to television

One might further explore the links between poverty and consumption via the lens of Varman and Belk's (2008) study of subaltern Indian consumers (those perceived as generally holding a low status and amount of wealth due to a number of factors such as caste, age, occupation and so on) and their views on the links between television and consumerism. As a backdrop to this discussion, we might here note Varman and Belk's assertion that in India consumption is often linked to Western values, such as freedom, democracy and modernity, with television as a medium which 'promulgates, perpetuates and legitimizes consumer culture'.

Varman and Belk suggest that contemporary consumption, beginning in the West, 'has now sunk deep roots across the world', with the television being a key medium via which the consumeristic messages of the West might be spread. However, we must also consider how one might define consumerist culture in itself, with Varman and Belk noting negative descriptors such as consumerism as a mechanism for control and harmful to environments, but, more positively, that consumerism has the potential to provide meaning to life, and that it may offer the potential for emancipation for some consumers. This, they suggest, can be achieved via television's efforts to show lifestyles and offerings using a variety of communications elements, such as with 'sounds, words, notes, visuals, gestures, expression[s]' and so on, which ultimately create symbolic representations of consumption in different forms, which people then internalize.

This, we might then suggest, situates television and its programming as a vehicle via which marketers can seek to convince their audiences of a continuous new stream of wants and needs, all of which consumerism might help to fill. Taking a more negative perspective, however, we might also note here the potential for manipulation of consumers via television, efforts to control consumers, and the creation of false wants and needs in consumers via their consumption of television adverts and programmes.

Varman and Belk note their Indian subaltern study participants as residing 'at the fringe of the market mechanism' due to their low participation in markets. However, despite such assertions, the authors do still note that 'the desire to buy objects of consumption has become a far more universal phenomenon even amongst consumers with limited purchasing power'. Thus, the subaltern consumers in the study are no exception to this assertion, despite the potential consequences of their participation.

The study discusses an increase in the number of television channels in the country, along with the rise of advertising spend and a change in the type of media offered via the television to reflect more corporate and advertiser-centric interests, with programmes being 'set in rich, educated, urban-class milieux', the purpose of which appears to be to demonstrate 'an "ideal form" of existence for viewers, one marked by conspicuous consumption'. In other words, if we see individuals portrayed on the television living a happy, glamorous lifestyle, content often due to the products they own, why would we also not aspire to own these products and therefore be happy just like the people on our television screens? Of course, in order to be 'happy', we must then engage in consumption, following examples of the roles 'played by representations of rich people and luxurious settings in television programming in increasing consumer desire'.

Indeed, participants in Varman and Belk's study appeared to be highly influenced by television, with increasing emphasis on promoting and displaying wealth at all levels of society. In actuality, this type of consumption often plays out as competition; if one neighbour purchases a specific item, another neighbour may then feel that they must purchase a bigger, better or more expensive version of the same offering in order to keep up. This links to the notion of goods as symbols of status, and in this case as an important cultural element for the subaltern consumers under discussion.

The Indian subaltern consumers suggested that they must own certain products (for example, televisions, clothes and so on) to be accepted by members of their community, and even by their family. However, due to a lack of funds, being able to afford these items was often difficult, and meant the sacrifice of other items such as food in order to be able to pay for the desired offering, with some participants being very upset that they could not afford to provide items for their children that they had seen advertised on television.

Clear links here to the concept of respect were also seen via the purchases made by individual consumers, or in a lack of respect being given to those who could not afford to purchase specific items. Interestingly, however, the study's participants also suggested links between owning offerings seen on television and their levels of happiness, with individuals blaming the television rather than their own increased desire for material possessions when they were unable to afford the item(s) in question.

Participants also noted a shift in the ways in which communities and the individuals residing in them acted towards each other following the increased focus on television and consumerism. This came in the form of a move away from a collectivist style of culture in which individuals would spend time together and help one another, towards 'an increasing trend towards social isolation and individualism', with television glorifying 'consumption, individualism, and nuclear families in the garb of modernity'.

Despite such arguments, Varman and Belk suggest that the majority of their study's participants believed that it was possible for them to disengage themselves from the television images and think critically about conspicuous consumption with only a few rare cases of participants willing to admit that television was a key component in their imitation of the lifestyles of others (namely, those seen on the television screen). Here then, we might suggest in line with the authors that by increasing material aspirations, media culture (specifically television) contaminates, especially in regions where low income is the reality for many, as it pushes them further towards life-threatening poverty.

ACTIVITY ⬀

Television and consumerism

To what extent does television impact your purchases?

Do you think that your answer would change if you were a part of the subaltern group of consumers discussed in Varman and Belk's study?

To what extent do you agree that, while individuals are critical of consumerist lifestyles, they still often seek to emulate them? Explain the reasons behind your answer.

Spreading a Western conception of life

Varman and Belk's (2008) work explores the perspective of consumers who we might argue exist at the bottom of the pyramid. However, this is only one side of the story. What about the marketers themselves who are largely responsible for making the Western goods via which consumerism might be achieved available to consumers across the globe?

Applbaum's 2000 study helps us to understand such a perspective, via an ethnographic exploration of culture and strategy in relation to marketing managers working in US-based organizations, in consideration of their efforts to market their organization's offerings to people in emerging economies. Here we see once again the distinctions between standardization as a strategic method and a strategy which reflects cultural differences across the globe, with in this case the marketing managers participating in the study often viewing the world as a single market, and thus siding with a standardized approach.

As Applbaum explains, the study's participants operated 'within a consumption-led universalizing paradigm', believing in 'innate universal psychological tendencies that transcend local culture'. Participants also saw Western lifestyles as modern, as equating to progress, and as 'superior', leading to opportunities for marketing managers to create better lives for people through the consumption opportunities that they provide to individuals. Linking again back to notions of standardization and universal appeal, Applbaum notes that business folklore insists that consumers in emerging economies change from 'traditional' to 'Western-modern' lifestyles, from group-oriented to individualist, and from local to global.

Ultimately, the study suggests that consumer education and self-satisfaction are key elements of consideration for the marketing managers in question. As the author notes, material objects allow consumers to become who they want to be and marketing is about drawing people into that desire fulfilment. This leads Applbaum to conclude that marketers' contribution to culture is a vision of identity that transcends geographical boundaries and borders, with consumers achieving any desired identity via their consumption habits, rather than due to their geographical location.

If we assume this statement to be true, for marketing managers themselves then, one might argue that their job is to 'introduce people to the finer things in life, to teach them to be consumers and not just to exchange provisions for money'.

ACTIVITY

The role of marketing managers

To what extent would you agree that the job of marketing managers is to 'introduce people to the finer things in life'?

Do you agree that a consumer can construct any identity that they wish via their consumption practices, regardless of their geographical location? Explain the reasons behind your answer, linking to the bottom of the pyramid and using supporting examples where possible.

Is marketing to the bottom of the pyramid actually worth it?

Well, what do you think? Is marketing to consumers at the bottom of the pyramid worth it for global organizations? Academics Prahalad and Hammond (2002) certainly think so, referring to it as both a noble and lucrative endeavour.

Prahalad and Hammond paint the picture of a bleak future for developing countries, along with an opposing bright view of the future for the same consumers. The future that we end up with, however, is, according to the authors, dependent upon multinational companies investing in the poorest communities, which could improve billions of lives and bring about a more stable world. Despite how this may sound, we are not talking here about global organizations engaging with the bottom of the pyramid market out of charitable concern (which, of course, may still be seen as a byproduct of their engagement), but rather for the organizational benefits of profit generation, operational efficiencies and access to new sources of inspiration and innovation, which may impact multiple areas of an organization's operations, such as with new product development. Equally, Prahalad and Hammond do not claim that global organizations can solve the issue of poverty alone, but rather that they are a part of the jigsaw puzzle, with other stakeholders such as governments also required to play a significant role.

While the authors note that '[e]veryone knows that the world's poor are distressingly plentiful', the article argues that not many of these consumers are targeted by global organizations. Instead, the suggestion is that there are clear reasons as to why organizations may not wish to target consumers at the bottom of the pyramid, such as assumptions that BoP consumers do not have money to spend on anything but the basic necessities of life. The authors also suggest assumptions that other barriers to engagement exist, in the form of elements such as 'corruption, illiteracy, inadequate infrastructure, currency fluctuations, [and] bureaucratic red tape', painting the view that organizations will have a hard road to profitability when engaging with such consumers and markets.

However, Prahalad and Hammond argue that such thinking is outdated, with a huge amount of potential being available at the bottom of the pyramid. For instance, of the assumption that bottom of the pyramid consumers have no money, the authors suggest this is wrong because, while individual incomes may be low, there is significant aggregate buying power in these communities. Further arguments suggest that bottom of the pyramid consumers are only interested in fulfilling their basic needs via their consumption practices, and are not interested in wasting money on other offerings: 'In fact, the poor often do buy "luxury" items.'

In providing an interesting example at the time of writing, Prahalad and Hammond suggest that the majority of households in one shanty town had a television set, a pressure cooker and mixer and a gas stove, as well as 21 per cent with telephones, even though buying a house in the area was not an option for most. In this instance, individuals chose to spend their income on improving their quality of life in the present. This is an interesting proposition, in that it advocates for almost instant gratification, much as many of us are accustomed to in the West, rather than saving money for delayed gratification with bigger or more expensive items.

Regardless, customers at the bottom of the pyramid generally pay more for the items they purchase in comparison to those, for example, in the middle class. This means that if global organizations can establish efficient supply chains and offer realistic prices to customers at the bottom of the pyramid, there is good potential for success. Indeed, perhaps the biggest potential barrier to targeting the bottom of the pyramid relates to access for distribution, rather than the amount of money that potential bottom of the pyramid consumers have to spend on offerings. Prahalad and Hammond argue that if global organizations do provide offerings to consumers at the bottom of the pyramid, it can help to increase standards of living, as well as being a source of profit for the organization itself, and thus 'the results benefit everyone'.

That being said, there is still some emphasis placed by the authors on education and on organizational representatives spending time with consumers at the bottom of the pyramid in efforts to better understand the area and consumers' requirements, which in turn may help the global organization not only to compete on price with its local competitors, but also to hold a better understanding of the wants and needs of local people. 'Moreover, through competition, multinationals are likely to bring to BoP markets a level of accountability for performance and resources that neither international development agencies nor national governments have demonstrated' in the past.

As a result, we might suggest that, from the perspective of Prahalad and Hammond, the bottom of the pyramid has much potential. There are opportunities for global organizations to play a role in solving large societal issues such as poverty, but also in making a profit from the relatively untapped bottom of the pyramid market.

ACTIVITY

Marketing to the bottom of the pyramid

Do you agree with Prahalad and Hammond (2002) that global organizations have a responsibility to help to alleviate poverty via their engagement with the bottom of the pyramid?

If you were the marketing manager of a global organization, would you target consumers at the bottom of the pyramid? Does your answer change if you consider so-called luxury goods, such as televisions, in comparison to traditionally cheap offerings such as shampoo? Explain the thinking behind your answer.

Should global organizations provide consumers at the bottom of the pyramid with opportunities to spend their money, however limited that may be, on offerings other than those associated with basic basket items such as food, clothing and shelter? Why, or why not?

Do you agree with the concept of consumers at the bottom of the pyramid purchasing items (such as televisions) rather than saving for larger purchases such as housing? Would you take the same approach if you were a consumer at the bottom of the pyramid? Why?

How does Prahalad and Hammond's discussion link to the concept of ethics as discussed in Chapter 9?

A critique: Is the bottom of the pyramid proposition actually good for everyone?

While Prahalad and Hammond suggest a largely positive view of marketing to the bottom of the pyramid as increasing standards of living, contributing to the reduction of poverty and offering the potential for organizational profits, there are, of course, some critiques that we might also employ here.

In particular, Karnani (2007) suggests that the bottom of the pyramid proposition is 'too good to be true'. With such concerns in mind, Karnani emphasizes the need to view consumers residing at the bottom of the pyramid as producers rather than consumers, with efforts to purchase from the poor, rather than sell to them, being key. The purpose here is to increase the income of such individuals via additional purchases of the products that they produce, thus helping to alleviate poverty.

Karnani also finds fault with the notion that consumers at the bottom of the pyramid have some, if not much, money which may be used for the purchase of luxury items after fulfilling basic basket needs. Instead, the author proposes that at the bottom of the pyramid, 'the basic needs of survival are met, but just barely'.

Issues are also highlighted with the organizational perspective in efforts to serve consumers at the bottom of the pyramid: the market itself is quite small and unlikely to be profitable for large companies in particular, especially as costs can be high in reaching them (if they are in geographically dispersed areas), meaning that economies of scale are often unlikely, with issues further compounded by poor infrastructure systems, which add additional costs to efforts to serve the bottom of the pyramid.

Furthermore, Karnani notes that organizations seeking to serve consumers at the bottom of the pyramid fail due to mistakes in overestimating 'the purchasing power of poor people and set[ting] prices too high'. One might argue that local organizations would perhaps then be better suited to serving such consumers, due to their familiarity with local markets, needs, wants and desires. In particular, we might suggest such an approach given that, according to Karnani, there are unlikely to be advantages from economies of scale, particularly in relation to the geographically dispersed rural poor.

A particular point of umbrage for Karnani is also apparent in discussions of single servings of products being offered to consumers at the bottom of the pyramid, including 'shampoo, ketchup, tea, coffee, biscuits, and skin cream'. While at first glance offering smaller versions of products for discounted prices might appear to provide a good opportunity for customers at the bottom of the pyramid, it does not, in fact, offer much if anything in terms of monetary savings. Indeed, Karnani discusses such claims of price savings as a 'fallacy'. However, organizations can stand to gain in some respects from, for example, encouraging product trials and sampling of particular brands. Consumers at the bottom of the pyramid also may gain from the option to purchase smaller versions of offerings too – perhaps due to their cash flow taking a smaller hit than if they were to purchase the full-sized version at the full-sized cost.

However, '[t]he only way to increase real affordability is to reduce the price per use. By BoP logic, an easy way to solve the problems of hunger and malnutrition would be to sell food in smaller packages thus making it more affordable to the poor.' This, however, would not change the amount of food actually required by consumers, only the frequency with which they must purchase the smaller quantities provided if they still wish to have access to the products in question. Indeed, such discussions take on perhaps a different light if we apply this type of thinking to arguments around food rather than shampoo.

In cases where consumers at the bottom of the pyramid do purchase luxury offerings, in trial size or otherwise, it is likely that in order to do so, they must divert funds from another purchase. Such actions might be seen, regardless of removing the ability to purchase another offering, as improving the welfare of consumers at the bottom of the pyramid via the increased choice of products available to them. After all, as Karnani notes, lack of income is more constraining than less variety of goods and services in the market.

This brings us to perhaps yet another key debate, linked to ethics, when dealing with the question of whether global organizations should serve consumers at the bottom of the pyramid; should the poor have the right to purchase and consume any offering that they so choose, even if we (the generalized West) might perceive it as being bad for them (for example, consider products like alcohol, tobacco and so on), when it also impacts their ability to purchase offerings that might be deemed good (for example, food, clothing, shelter and so on)? Equally, we might ask whether global organizations should sell such offerings in the first place to consumers at the bottom of the pyramid, where the stakes are potentially very high if income is not spent on the 'correct' products. Here, Karnani argues that both consumers at the bottom of the pyramid and the global organizations serving them should be free to do as they wish, while recognizing the dichotomy between right and self-interest.

Lack of consumer knowledge or marketing deception are two other potential issues raised by Karnani with respect to the purchases made by consumers at the bottom of the pyramid, with the poorest consumers being seen as 'vulnerable by virtue of lack of education (often they are illiterate), lack of information, and economic, cultural, and social deprivations'. Indeed, Karnani's study suggests data showing 'that the poor lack self-control, yield to temptation, and spend to keep up with their neighbours', much as noted by Prahalad and Hammond (2002). Karnani, however, goes further here in stating that consumers at the bottom of the pyramid are no different than people with more money; 'the consequence of bad choices, though, is more severe for them'.

As a result, Karnani notes that imposing a 'price–quality' trade-off on low-income communities is disrespectful of what their preferences might be: it's a myth that low quality equals terrible and dangerous products, so reducing the quality (and price) of certain goods harms people by depriving them of goods they could afford and may want to purchase. Quality should therefore be understood as a relative concept. However, we might still return to questions of responsibility here as, arguably, if we place emphasis on global organizations for the alleviation of poverty via their efforts to serve consumers at the bottom of the pyramid, we reduce the emphasis on the roles and responsibilities of governments in providing for their citizens.

REAL-WORLD EXAMPLE   Whitening creams at the top and bottom of the pyramid

Whitening creams are big business with a long history, predominantly targeting 'women of colour in every region of the world' (CNN, 2024). Used for the purpose of reducing the amount of melanin (pigment) in the skin to make it appear lighter, the creams are manufactured by a number of well-known brands across the globe (including those of the West), and are sold in local shops, markets, online, and even via social media. However, while, for example, in England and Wales whitening products are available via prescription, many of the other whitening product offerings available to consumers are illegal.

This is because many whitening creams have been found to contain banned ingredients which can pose a serious threat to consumer health. This is a particularly serious problem, as some of the illegal products have been found to include ingredients such as hydroquinone, which 'can remove the top layer of skin, increasing a person's risk of skin cancer, liver and kidney damage' (Barr, 2019). Added to this is the risk that many whitening products are being incorrectly labelled, making it even more difficult for consumers to understand which products may potentially be very harmful for their health. That being said, genuine whitening products can be expensive, with the riskier offerings being available at much more affordable prices. In 2018, the BBC sent undercover reporters to visit a number of stores in UK cities, finding that 13 of the 17 stores they visited were selling whitening products containing illegal ingredients (Lakhani and Wicker, 2018).

There are some significant risks not only for consumers in using whitening products, but also for the retailers who sell them, with potential fines of up to £20,000 for those found to be selling the illegal products and a risk of prosecution. But some retailers might argue that these risks are worth it. In 2017, a value of $4.8 billion was placed on the global skin lightening industry. The market was estimated at $8 billion in 2020, with projections suggesting that the market will reach a value of $11.8 billion by 2026 (CNN, 2024).

Why, then, we might ask, do consumers across the globe spend their hard-earned cash on a product that could be potentially seriously harmful to their health? Well, for some, a lack of consumer education as to the dangerousness of ingredients, or the mislabelling of ingredients, may be the key issue. However, there are of course a number of other reasons that consumers may choose to purchase these types of products. For example, CNN (2024) suggests that, historically, paler skin has been linked to wealth and/or status in some regions due to 'manual labourers working out in the sun while the wealthy stayed indoors', with links to colonialism, slavery and globalization also being noted as key points of disparity and potential reasons for the use of skin whitening products.

Indeed, CNN reports: 'Colourism and light-skin privilege have led to disparities in every region of the world, in everything from social treatment to marriageability, education, employment and even, in the US, prison sentencing.'

Questions

- What are the dangers associated with illegal skin whitening products, and why do individuals choose to use them knowing the risks that they pose?
- Discuss the ethical implications of marketing whitening creams to UK consumers.
- Are the ethical implications you have identified for UK consumers the same for consumers at the bottom of the pyramid in developing countries? Why, or why not?
- Should marketers target consumers at the bottom of the pyramid with whitening products when they, as Karnani (2007) suggests, have a lack of education, consumer protection and information?

CHAPTER SUMMARY

In summary, this chapter has explored the concept of the bottom of the pyramid along with varied levels of poverty and their connections with contemporary lifestyles and consumerist practices.

In doing so, we have examined both the potential benefits and limitations of marketing to the bottom of the pyramid, considering multiple perspectives such as global organizations, marketers, customers and consumers. However, questions remain: given that the West has an excess of products, who are we to judge and criticize what others determine worthy of purchase, and equally, is it ethically right for global organizations, marketers and so on to determine what another person should purchase?

While we could raise arguments here that it may seem obvious that the purchase of food over a computer game would be a good move, is this actually our choice to make on behalf of other people? Or are we (the generalized West) doing those other consumers a disservice by reducing their options and therefore their freedom to purchase and live their lives in the ways that they wish?

It is these questions (and others as presented throughout this book) that I leave to you readers, as the marketers of the future, to consider with ethics, sustainability and societal and organizational good in mind...

CHAPTER REVIEW QUESTIONS

- How does the pyramid concept as discussed throughout the chapter relate to global consumerism?

- After reading the chapter, as the CEO of a global organization, would you choose to target customers at the top or bottom of the pyramid? Why?

- Should the poor have the right to make their own mistakes? Explain your answer using supporting examples.

- Do you agree with Prahalad and Hammond's (2002) view of the bottom of the pyramid position as a win-win situation, or do you side with Karnani's (2007) view that the bottom of the pyramid proposition is a dangerous mirage? Explain your viewpoint using illustrative examples.

- Which stakeholders should be responsible for the alleviation of poverty? Why?

- Karnani questions the extent to which the notion of global organizations serving consumers at the bottom of the pyramid hurts those consumers more than it helps them. Explain your viewpoint in relation to this notion.

> ### KEY TERMS
>
> **International poverty lines:** Applied on a global scale, international poverty lines provide a way in which to measure extreme poverty across the globe.
>
> **National poverty lines:** A national poverty line denotes the lowest income threshold that an individual must meet to avoid slipping into poverty in a particular country.
>
> **Poverty:** A lack of financial resources, which often leads to an inability to procure basic offerings such as food, clothing and shelter.
>
> **The Poverty Clock:** An online tool which details the number of individuals living in extreme poverty across the globe.

References

Applbaum, K (2000) Crossing borders: Globalization as myth and charter in American transnational consumer marketing, *American Ethnologist*, 27 (2), 257–82

Alexander, R (2012) Dollar benchmark: The rise of the $1-a-day statistic, BBC News, www.bbc.co.uk/news/magazine-17312819 (archived at https://perma.cc/D275-XUN5)

Lakhani, A and Wicker, E (2018) Skin-whitening creams: The battle against illegal products, BBC News, www.bbc.co.uk/news/uk-45085674 (archived at https://perma.cc/AGW8-PJNT)

CNN (2024) Skin whitening: What is it, what are the risks and who profits?, https://edition.cnn.com/2022/01/25/world/as-equals-skin-whitening-global-market-explainer-intl-cmd/index.html (archived at https://perma.cc/C7XH-AJDT)

Data Lab (2024) The Poverty Clock, www.worldpoverty.io (archived at https://perma.cc/F2LZ-N4Z3)

Barr, S (2019) Skin-lightening creams containing banned ingredients should be avoided 'at all costs', *The Independent*, www.independent.co.uk/life-style/health-and-families/skin-lightening-creams-dangerous-health-scar-ingredients-illegal-banned-a9124071.html (archived at https://perma.cc/39SE-CBZF)

Karnani, A (2007) The mirage of marketing to the bottom of the pyramid: How the private sector can help alleviate poverty, *California Management Review*, 49 (4), 90–111

Levitt, T (1983) The globalization of markets, *Harvard Business Review*, 61 (3), 92–102

Prahalad, C K and Hammond, A (2002) Serving the world's poor, profitably, *Harvard Business Review*, 80 (9), 48–57

The World Bank (2022) Poverty and inequality platform, www.pip.worldbank.org/home

The World Bank (2024) What the data tell us, www.datatopics.worldbank.org/consumption/market

Varman, R and Belk, R W (2008) Weaving a web: Subaltern consumers, rising consumer culture, and television, *Marketing Theory*, 8 (3), 227–52

World Bank Group (2024) Poverty and inequality, www.worldbank.org/en/publication/poverty-prosperity-and-planet (archived at https://perma.cc/LY8R-ZLG5)

World Vision (2024) Global poverty: Facts, FAQs, and how to help, www.worldvision.org/sponsorship-news-stories/global-poverty-facts (archived at https://perma.cc/496M-KP6A)

INDEX

4Ps of marketing *see* marketing mix
24/7 mentality 54, 229–30

acquisitions 27
Adidas 29
advertising 11, 64 *see also* marketing
agents 8
agents of change 202–08
Aikido brands 143
allowances and discounts 6
Alonzo, Carmelita 221
Amazon 49, 52, 56
    lack of recognition of unions 197
    recommendations 180–81
American Express 43
Americanisms 153–54
animations, use in marketing
    communications 108
anti-foundationalism, postmodern
    characteristic 172
Apple 29, 52, 74
artificial intelligence (AI) 49

banking 41
Barbie 75
behavioural segmentation 20
benefit segmentation 21
Benetton 117
Best Buy 42, 50
Bestor, Ted 56, 57
Big Mac Index 151
Black Lives Matter Movement 117
Blends coffee shop 158
Boohoo 206, 232, 233–34
bottom of the pyramid (BoP) concept 241–43
bottom of the pyramid (BoP) marketing
    approach to serving the poorest
      consumers 198
    consumption at the bottom of the
      pyramid 240–57
    critique of the BoP proposition 252–55
    ethical issues 253–55
    evaluation of 250–52
    impacts of exposure to television 246–48
    smaller versions of products 253
    spreading a Western conception of life 248–49
    targeting by organizations 243–45
    vulnerable consumers 254
boycotting 207, 210
brand authenticity and identity 77

brand-based experiences 140–41
brand characteristics 29–30
brand equity 30
brand identity 30
brand myth 134
brands
    associations and credibility with
      consumers 30
    definition of a brand 29
    global context 52–53
    historical examples 29
    role in buyer decision-making 29–30
    see also global brands
brokers 8
Bulgari 53
Bumble (case study) 119
Burger King, Whopper Neutrality advert 115–16
Burgernomics 151
business-to-business (B2B) markets 6, 10, 11
business-to-consumer (B2C) markets 10
business-to-government (B2G) markets 10
buyer decision process
    consumer proposition acquisition process 19
    influence of lifestyle and self-concept 21–22
    influence of reference groups 23
    stimulus response model 18–19

call centres 228–30
Calvin Klein 42, 50
Campbell's Soup 41
Camper Shoes (case study) 138–39
capitalism 53
    subprocess of grobalization 151
case studies
    Bumble 119
    Camper Shoes 138–39
    Christmas marketing 111–14
    cosmetic surgery boom in China 163–64
    Disney theme parks 69–71, 74
    Disney's Celebration town, Florida 140–41
    environmental impacts 199–200
    Fairtrade movement 204
    human implications of the garment
      manufacturing industry 226–27
    Hunter wellington boots in America 96–97
    Inca Kola 183–84
    KFC in Japan 56–57
    Mastercard's 'Priceless campaign' 103–04
    Nike 129–30
    organizational culture 90–94

skin whitening products 254–55
'something' or 'nothing' holiday
        arrangements 160–61
Taylor Swift: 'ethical billionaire' concept
        194–96
Temu and the American Super Bowl 179–80
transparency and ultra-fast fashion 232–34
US Government bans Kinder Eggs 202
Walmart in China 77–79
whitening creams at the top and bottom of the
        pyramid 254–55
cathedrals of consumption 155–56, 161–62
CavinKare Pvt Ltd 71–72
celebrity endorsement 30
Chanel 53
China 52–53, 54, 67, 68, 72, 74, 75
    cosmetic surgery boom (case study) 163–64
    factory working conditions 222
    interpretation of Christmas 112
    lower production costs 128
    responses to offensive advertising 116–18
    translation issues 110
    Walmart in China (case study) 77–79
Christmas marketing (case study) 111–14
chronology (nostalgia for the past), postmodern
        characteristic 172
Citi 36
CNN 140
Coca-Cola 7–8, 36, 65, 136, 141, 143, 183–84
    customer-centric focus 51–52
    history of 41
    translation issues 110
    value of the brand 132–33
codes of conduct, voluntary vs compulsory
        201–02
coffee trade 40
cognitive dissonance 20
Colgate 109
colours
    significance in different cultures 94–95
    source of miscommunications 110
communications see global marketing
        communications; marketing
        communications
competition-based pricing 5
competitive drivers of globalization 48
consequentialist ethics 192
constructive pluralism 193
consumer education, force for change 204–05
consumer proposition acquisition process 19
consumer value 4–5
consumerism, spread of 198–99 see also global
        consumerism
consumers
    agents of change 203–04
    backlash against global brands 136
    challenges to individualism 55

choices as agents of change 205–08
distinction from customers 31–32
market segmentation 20–21
stimulus response model 18–19
patterns of consumption 72–74
tracking and privacy violations 199
vulnerable consumers 199, 254
consumption
    dislocation from production 196–97
    transformation via 207–08
content analysis 26
cost-based pricing 5
cost drivers of globalization 48
country-of-origin effect 95–97, 216
coupons 11
cultural convergence 148–68
    cathedrals of consumption 155–56,
        161–62
    consumption in practice 161–64
    global village concept 149–50
    grobalization 150–64
cultural divergence 170–86
    adaptation and reinterpretation of global
        influences 176–78
    consumer freedom to engage 182–84
    dehumanization of culture 181–83
    increasing cultural diversity 176–78
    individualism 178, 186
    online shopping choices and 178–82
    postmodernism 171–76
    subcultures 177–78
cultural knowledge 88–94
cultural universals 86–87
culture 84–100
    country-of-origin effect 95–97
    definitions 85–86
    global consumer culture 64
    Hofstede's dimensions of culture 106–07
    local versus global decisions 96
    loss of the local 55–57
    misunderstandings and errors 67–68
    organizational 88–94
    patterns of consumption 72–74
    significance of colours 94–95
    sources of 88
    Walmart in China (case study) 77–79
    see also cultural convergence; cultural
        divergence
culture clash, Disney theme parks (case
        study) 69–71, 74
customer-centric focus, development of 50–51
customer service 12–13
Customer Value Triad 16
customers
    agents of change 203–04
    as non-people 159
    distinction from consumers 31–32

customers (*Continued*)
   loyalty and retention 16
   types of 10–11
   understanding their wants and needs 3

data
   analysis 26
   collection 25–26
   types and sources 24
de Quinto, Marcos 51–52
Decent Work and Economic Growth (SDG 2) 2
decline stage of the product lifecycle 28–29
decoding of marketing communications
   104–06, 121
de-differentiation, postmodern characteristic 172
demographic segmentation 21
deontological ethics 192
descriptive ethical realism 193
direct distribution 8, 9
direct marketing 11–12
discounts and allowances 6, 11
Disney
   Celebration town, Florida 140–41
   growth through acquisitions 139–40
Disney theme parks 68, 76
   case study 69–71, 74
Disneyization 156–57
distribution (place), role in the marketing
   mix 7–9, 10
distribution channels 7–9, 10
   channel design 8
   channel intermediaries 8, 10
   horizontal conflict 8
   international channels 9
   vertical conflict 8
Dolce & Gabbana 117

economies of scale 65, 66
education and culture 88
Eisner, Michael 69
Electrolux 109
electronic waste (e-waste) 200
emergency products 3–4
Emin, Tracey 126
emotional marketing messaging 107–09
emotional value of brands 133–34
encoding of marketing communications
   104–06, 121
environmental awareness 43–44
environmental concerns 54
environmental impacts 199–200
ethical concerns 196–202
   agents of change 202–08
   consumer tracking and privacy violations 199
   dislocation of production and
      consumption 196–97

environmental impacts 199–200
exploitation of labour forces 197
false and/or misleading claims 201
greenwashing 200–01
serving the poorest consumers first 198
spread of consumerism and cultural
   homogenization 198–99
sweatshops and choice 222–27
voluntary vs compulsory codes of
   conduct 201–02
vulnerable consumers 199
ethical consumerism 207–08
ethical realism 193
ethical theories 192–93
   potential pitfalls 193–96
ethics 189–211
   bottom of the pyramid (BoP) marketing
      253–55
   brand interactions everywhere 190–91
   distinction from morality 191
   relevance to marketing activities 190–91
ethics of ethics 193–96
exchange 2–3
exhibitions 11
explicit communication 9
export processing zones 217–21
   contractors and subcontractors 218–19
   extreme implications 219–21
   poor working conditions, hours and pay
      219–21
   processes and consequences 218
extended marketing mix 12–13
   people 12–13
   physical evidence 12, 13
   process 12, 13
external data 24

Facebook 52
Fairtrade International products 37, 73, 245–46
Fairtrade movement (case study) 204
family and culture 88
Fashion Revolution 231–32
fast fashion 54, 237
   environmental impacts (case study) 199–200
   ultra-fast fashion 232–34, 237
fear, use in marketing communications 108, 109
financial markets, integration of 43
focus groups 25
Ford 109
   Model T 49–50, 65
foreign direct investment (FDI) 48, 59, 217
fragmentation, postmodern characteristic 172

garment worker wages 220
geographic segmentation 20
geographical pricing 6

Germany, responses to offensive advertising 116, 118
global brands 124–45
    Aikido brands 143
    beyond branding 139–41
    brand-based experiences 140–41
    brand interactions everywhere 190–91
    components of the value chain 127–31
    consumer backlash 136
    cross-promotion 140
    definition and importance of branding 126
    downside of the value shift 130–31
    emotional value of brands 133–34
    existence in our minds 131–33
    global myth 136–37
    growth opportunities 139–40
    how brands work 131–35
    importance of brand perceptions 132–33
    infidel brands 141–43
    key dimensions in consumer choice 135–39
    mergers and acquisitions (M&A) 139–40
    negative aspects 141–43
    quality signal 136
    shift away from production focus 128–30
    social responsibility 136–39
    symbolism of brands 134–35
    value of brands 125–26
    value shift towards marketing and
        branding 129–31
    see also brands
global business 36
global consciousness 44–45
global consumerism 37, 63–64
    and increased production 53–55
    consumers at the bottom of the pyramid
        245–48
global marketing communications 102–21
    causes of offence 116–19
    Christmas marketing (case study) 111–14
    emotional messaging 107–09
    encoding and decoding 104–06, 121
    Hofstede's dimensions of culture 106–07
    language translation issues 109–10
    message appeals 107–09
    miscommunications 109–14
    standardization versus adaptation 120
    standardized approach 103–06
    use of colour 110
    use of humour 108, 114–116
global markets 42
global myth of brands 136–37
global thinking 41
global village concept 149–50
globalization 150
    1960s to the present day 41–42
    aspects of 36–38
    before the 18th century 40

debate over the existence of 45–46
    definitions 38
    drivers of 47–49
    history of 40–45
    KFC in Japan (case study) 56–57
    meaning of 38–39
    mid-19th to mid-20th centuries 40–41
    potential downsides 53–57
    Shrinking World concept 46–47, 49
    time–space compression 46–47
glocalization 150
    advantages 75–76
    at subnational level 77, 81
    different levels of 77
    disadvantages and challenges 76–77
    think globally and act locally 74–77
    Walmart in China (case study) 77–79
goods-based offerings 15–16
governments
    agents of change 202
    drivers of globalization 48
Great Pacific Garbage Patch 200
Green Giant 109–10, 126
greenwashing 138, 145, 200–01
grobalization
    Americanisms 153–54
    Big Mac Index 151
    capitalism 151
    consumerism and 155–56
    definition 150–51
    Disneyization and 156–57
    McDonaldization 151–53
    'something' and 'nothing' consequences
        157–61, 168
    subprocesses 151–54
growth stage of the product lifecycle 28–29

Heinz 41
Hirst, Damien 125–26
Hochschild's feeling rules 133–34
Hofstede's dimensions of culture 106–07
homogenization 175, 182, 198
HP 36
Huawei 52
humour in advertising 108, 114–116
Hunter wellington boots in America (case
    study) 96–97
hybrid offerings (product and service) 13
hyperconsumption 161
hyper-reality, postmodern characteristic 172

identity construction
    consumption habits related to 174
    individualism 178, 186
Ikea 116
implicit communication 9
impulse products 3–4

in-person surveys 26
Inca Kola 52
    case study 183–84
India 71–72, 74, 75
    call centres 228–30
    impact of television exposure of lower income
        groups 246–48
    yoga 177
individualism 178, 186
    challenges to 55
Industrial Revolution 49, 128
infidel brands 141–43
innovation 27
intangibility of services 14
integrated marketing communications 32
internal data 24
international distribution channels 9
international poverty lines 242–43
internet cookies 180, 186
introduction stage of the product lifecycle 28–29
involvement 8, 20, 32
Islam, infidel brands 141–43

Japan 70, 73, 74, 75
    KFC in Japan (case study) 56–57
Jenner, Kendall 117

Kaplinsky and Morris's value chain 127–31,
        215–17
KFC 76
    humorous advertising 116
    in China 67
    in Japan (case study) 56–57
    translation issues 110
Kinder Eggs, ban by the US Government (case
        study) 202
Klein, Naomi 126, 129, 217–21
knowing–doing gap 206, 211

L'Oreal 72
Laing, Hector 129
language
    culture and 88
    translation issues 109–10
language trafficking 229
Levitt's theory of standardization 64–66
lifestyle, influence on purchasing decisions 21–22
lifestyle branding 140–41
Likert scale 26, 32
lip balm 178
local business success stories 71–72
local companies, understanding of their
        customers 67
local culture and businesses, loss of 55–57
local preferences, patterns of consumption 72–74
local shops and high streets, decline of 155
local versus global, meeting consumer needs 96
localization 68

importance of local differences 68–72
logos 30, 52
    No Logo (Klein, 2000) 126, 129, 217–21
Lucas, Sarah 126

machine learning 49
management, five management philosophies
        16–18
manufacturing see production
market drivers of globalization 47–48
market-penetration pricing 6
market segmentation 20–21
marketing
    definition 2–3
    development of a customer-centric focus
        50–51
    global context 52–53
    implications of the global context 53–57
    rise of importance for business 49–52
    understanding customer wants and needs 3
marketing communications 9–12
    integrated marketing communications 32
    tools 9
    see also global marketing communications
marketing concept, marketing management
        orientation 18
marketing management orientations 16–18
    marketing concept 18
    product concept 17
    production concept 17
    selling concept 17
    societal concept 17–18
marketing mix 3–12, 50
    extended for services 12–13
    place 7–9, 10
    price 4–7
    product 3–4
    promotion 9–12
marketing research, definition 23
marketing research process 23–26
    data analysis 26
    data collection 25–26
    data types and sources 24
    qualitative research 25, 26
    quantitative research 25, 26
    sampling process 25
    survey methods 25–26
Mastercard, 'Priceless' campaign 42, 66, 74
    case study 103–04
Mathlouthi, Tawfik 143
Mattel 75
maturity stage of the product lifecycle 28–29
McDonald's 52, 75, 76, 117, 136, 141, 142
    key concepts of the business 151–53
McDonaldization 151–53, 156
Mecca Cola 143
mental health, challenge of the 24/7 mentality 54
Mercedes-Benz 110

merchandizing 156
mergers and acquisitions (M&A) 139–40
Metro Trains Melbourne, 'Dumb Ways to Die'
    campaign 115
Microsoft 36, 72
mobile phones 43
modern slavery 226–27
morality, distinction from ethics 191
Motorola 43
multinational corporations 65
music, role in marketing appeals 108

national poverty lines 241–42
nationality and culture 88
Nestlé 141
Netflix 140, 181–82
new product development 27
niche markets 10
Nike 52, 221
    marketing and branding focus (case
        study) 129–30
No Logo (Klein, 2000) 126,
    129, 217–21
No Poverty (SDG 1) 2
Nokia 36
non-media advertising 11
non-people 159, 160, 161
non-places 159, 160
non-services 159, 160, 161
non-things 159, 160
normative ethical realism 193
'nothing' offerings 157–61, 168

offensive advertising 116–19
offshoring
    manufacturing operations 129–31
    relevance to global consumption 230–34
    services 227–30
Okawara, Takeshi 56
Olympic Games 41
online shopping choices 178–82
online surveys 26
Orange 110
organizational culture 88–94
organizations
    agents of change 202
    false and/or misleading claims 201
    focus within the value chain 215–17
    voluntary vs compulsory codes of
        conduct 201–02
outsourcing
    export processing zones 217–21
    exporting jobs 221–27
    production (manufacturing) 54, 128, 215–21
    relevance to global consumption 230–34
ozone layer, action over depletion 44

Parker Pens 109
pastiche, postmodern characteristic 172

Peace, Justice and Strong Institutions (SDG 16) 2
people (staff and customer service), role in the
    extended marketing mix 12–13
Pepsi 67
    controversial advertisement 117
    miscommunications 110
personal selling 11
phone surveys 26
physical evidence (of a service), role in the
    extended marketing mix 12, 13
place, role in the marketing mix 7–9, 10
plastic waste, environmental impacts 200
pluralism, postmodern characteristic 172
Porter, Michael 127
postal surveys 25
postmodern characteristics 172
postmodern consumers 172–84
    consumer freedom to engage 182–84
    sources of identity and consumption
        habits 174
    symbolic value of offerings 175–76, 187
postmodernism 171–76
    definitions 171
    links with consumption and marketing 172
    postmodern consumer arising from 172–84
poverty
    definition 257
    marketing to low-income people 243–45
    stakeholders' responsibility for tackling
        243–45
    see also bottom of the pyramid (BoP)
poverty clock 246
poverty lines 241–43
price, role in the marketing mix 4–7
price ceiling 5
price cuts 6–7
price floor 5
pricing
    relation to promotion 5–6
    strategies 5–7
primary data 24
process (service delivery), role in the marketing
    mix 12, 13
Procter & Gamble 72
product concept, marketing management
    orientation 17
product lifecycle 11, 28–29
product safety 67
production
    and the global marketplace 214–37
    dislocation from consumption 196–97
    export processing zones 217–21
    exporting jobs 221–27
    outsourcing 215–17
    relevance to global consumption 230–34
    sweatshops, choice and ethics 222–27
    value chain and organizational focus 215–17
production concept, marketing management
    orientation 17

products
definition 3
hybrid offerings 13
role in the marketing mix 3–4
types of 3–4
promotion
relation to pricing 5–6
role in the marketing mix 9–12
promotional mix 10–11
promotional pricing 6
promotional tools 11–12
prospects 29, 33
psychographic segmentation 20
psychological pricing 6
public relations (PR) 12
publicity 12
Purchasing Power Parity (PPP) 242
PureGym 162
pyramid model of consumers by incomes 198, 241–43

Quaker Oats 126
qualitative research 25, 26
quantitative research 25, 26
quota sampling 25

Ralph Lauren 42, 50
Rana Plaza factory disaster (2013) 226
random sampling 25
real-world examples see case studies
recommendation algorithms/engines 55, 59, 180–82, 186
reference groups, influence on purchasing decisions 23
relationship marketing 16
religion 40
culture and 88
infidel brands 141–43
McDonaldization 153
research and development 27
Responsible Production and Consumption (SDG 12) 2
retailers 8
risk mitigation strategy 76, 81
Robertson, Roland 74
Rokka, Joonas 57

sales promotions 11
sampling process 25
Samsung 36
Schweppes 109
secondary data 24
self-concept, influence on purchasing decisions 21–22
self-services 15
self-symbolism of brands 135

selling concept, marketing management orientation 17
service-based offerings 15–16
services
definition of a service 13
distinction from goods 14–15
extended marketing mix 12–13
hybrid offerings 13
inseparability of production and consumption 14
intangibility 14
key characteristics 14–15
matching supply and demand 15
people (staff and customer service) 12–13
perishability 15
physical evidence (of a service) 12, 13
process (service delivery) 12, 13
variability 14–15
Shein 232–33
shock, use in marketing communications 108 ,109
Shrinking World concept 46–47, 49, 149
skimming strategies for pricing 5–6
skin whitening products, global market for (case study) 254–55
social class and culture 88
social responsibility, global brands 136–39
social symbolism of brands 135
societal concept, marketing management orientation 17–18
something–nothing continuum 160
'something' offerings 157–61, 168
South Africa, Christmas market 111–14
sponsorship 12
Spotify Wrapped campaign 116
spy pixels 180, 187
stakeholders, responsibility for tackling poverty 243–45
standardization
advantages 66–67
disadvantages 67–68
Disney theme parks (case study) 69–71, 74
Ford Model T 49–50, 65
global marketing communications 103–06
Levitt's theory of 64–66
marketing to the bottom of the pyramid 244–45
over-standardization 68
staple products 3–4
Starbucks 158
statistical analysis 26
stimulus response model 18–19
stratified sampling 25
subnational level glocalization 77, 81
substitute offerings 4, 5, 17, 19, 27, 28, 30, 33
Sugarhill Brighton 206

supermarkets 8
supply chains and logistics 42
survey methods 25–26
Sustainable Development Goals (SDGs) 2, 54
sweatshops 37, 131
    choice and ethics 222–27
Swift, Taylor (billionaire ethics case study)
        194–96
symbolic value of offerings 175–76, 187
symbolism of brands 134–35

taste testing 132–33
Tazreen Fashions factory fire (2012) 226
technology
    drivers of globalization 49
    electronic communications 42–43
    enabling globalization 36
teleological ethics 192
television, impacts of exposure on lower income
        groups 246–48
Temu and the American Super Bowl (case
        study) 179–80
Tencent QQ 52, 72
The Hidden Persuaders (Packard, 1957) 205
The North Face 42, 50
Time Warner 140
time–space compression 46–47, 59
trade, global developments 36
trade promotions 11
transformation via consumption 207–08
transport, global links 36
travel, package holidays 41
triple bottom line approach 203, 205–06, 211
Turner Broadcasting 140
Twenty-First Century Fox Inc. 139–40

ultra-fast fashion 237
    case study 232–34

unionization of workers 197
United Biscuits 129

value 4–5
    Customer Value Triad 16
    of brands 125–26
value chain 127–31
    components of 127–31
    Kaplinsky and Morris 127–31,
        215–17
    organizational profit focus 215–17
Van Cleef & Arpels 53
Volkswagen 52
Volvo 29
vouchers 11

Walmart 42, 50
    in China (case study) 77–79
Warner Bros 140
wealth inequality 45
Westernization 45, 53–54, 66–67
    Christmas marketing (case study)
        111–14
    grobalization 150–64
    infidel brands 141–43
    spreading a Western conception of life 248–49
Which? 204–05
wholesalers 8
workers
    call centres 228–30
    conditions in Chinese factories 222
    conditions in export processing zones 217–21
    exploitation of 197
World Wide Web 43

X (formerly Twitter) 52

yoga 177

Looking for another book?

Explore our award-winning
books from global business
experts in Marketing and Sales

Scan the code to browse

www.koganpage.com/marketing

More from Kogan Page

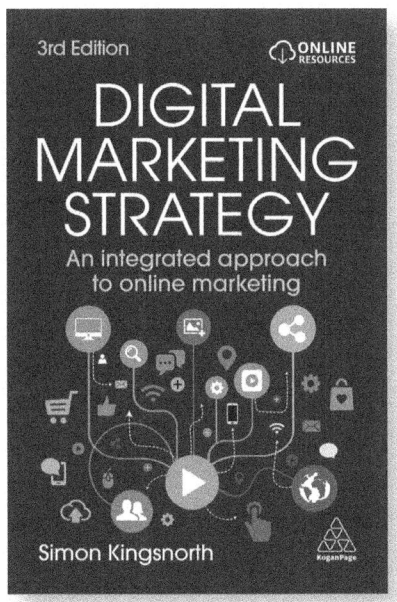

ISBN: 9781398605978

ISBN: 9781398611719

ISBN: 9781398608870

ISBN: 9781398609006